THE SEPOY REVOLT

THE SEPOY REVOLT

A CRITICAL NARRATIVE.

BY

LIEUT.-GENERAL McLEOD INNES, V.C.

GYAN

Published by

Gyan Publishing House
5, Ansari Road
Daryaganj, New Delhi-110002
Phone: 011-47034999, 9811692060
E-mail: books@gyanbooks.com

Distribution Network
gyanbooks.com
India, USA, Canada, UK, Australia

ISBN: 978-93-6208-392-0 (PB)
First Published, 1897

2nd Impression 2024

Printed at: Gyan Press, Delhi.

THE SEPOY REVOLT
Author: MCLEOD INNES

THE SEPOY REVOLT

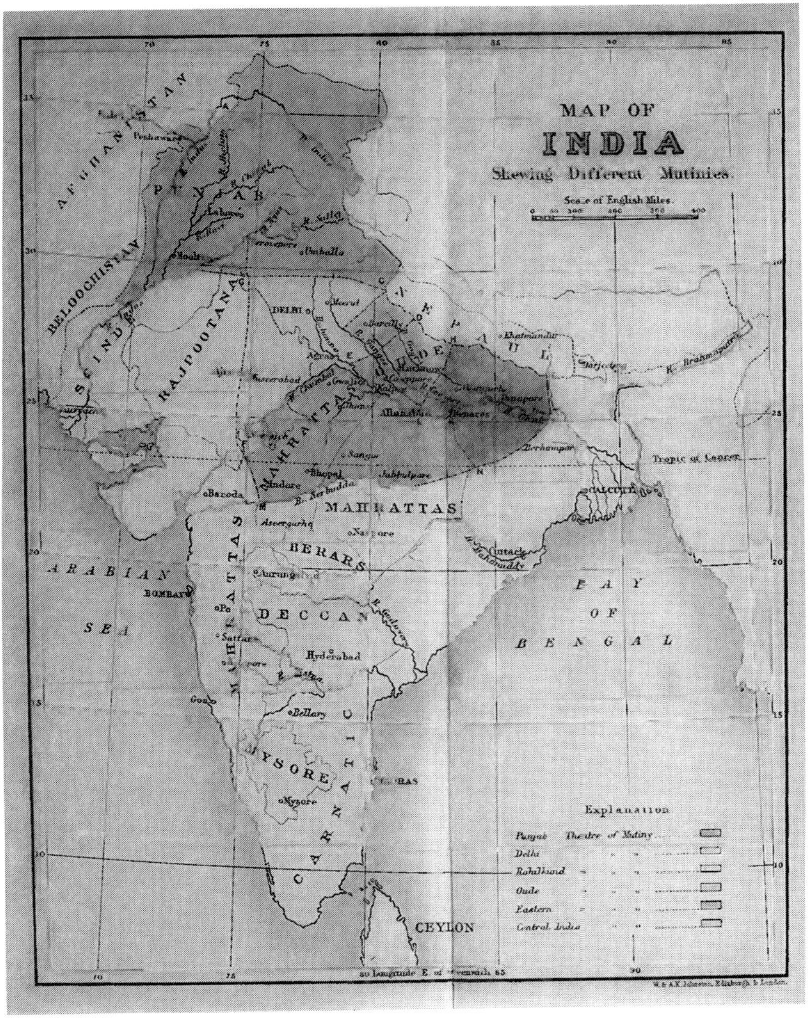
MAP OF
INDIA
Shewing Different Mutinies.
Scale of English Miles.
AFGHANISTAN
BELOOCHISTAN
PUNJAB
SCINDE
RAJPOOTANA
DELHI
NEPAUL
OUDE
MAHRATTA
MAHRATTAS
BERARS
DECCAN
MYSORE
CARNATIC
CEYLON
ARABIAN SEA
BAY OF BENGAL
Tropic of Cancer
Peshawar
Lahore
Umballa
Meerut
Agra
Cawnpore
Benares
Allahabad
Dinapore
Bhopal
Indore
Jubbulpore
Baroda
Nagpore
BOMBAY
Hyderabad
Bellary
Mysore
Goa
CALCUTTA
Cuttack
Darjeeling
R. Brahmaputra
R. Nerbudda
Explanation
Punjab Theatre of Mutiny
Delhi
Rohilkund
Oude
Eastern
Central India

THE SEPOY REVOLT

A CRITICAL NARRATIVE.

BY

LIEUT.-GENERAL McLEOD INNES, V.C.

AUTHOR OF "LUCKNOW AND OUDE IN THE MUTINY."

LONDON:
A. D. INNES & CO.,
BEDFORD STREET.
1897.

PREFACE.

THE outline of this narrative has been given in the introduction to my previous volume, " Lucknow and Oude in the Mutiny."

The object of that work was to give a detailed account primarily of the siege of Lucknow, and the operations connected therewith, as to which I could speak with precise personal knowledge. The comments on it, however, led me to believe that a volume dealing with the Revolt generally, on a similar method but with less technical detail, would be found acceptable; and might serve to elucidate various points as to which some degree of misunderstanding is prevalent.

J. J. M. I.

CONTENTS.

BOOK I.

ORIGIN OF THE REVOLT

CHAPTER I.

CHAPTER II.

CHAPTER III.

CHAPTER IV.

THE ANNEXATION OF OUDE

CHAPTER V.

HENRY LAWRENCE IN OUDE

CHAPTER VI.

THE GROWTH OF THE ACTIVE DISAFFECTION

BOOK II.

THE DEVELOPMENT OF THE REVOLT

CHAPTER I.

THE SITUATION DEVELOPED BY THE OUTBREAK

CHAPTER II.

MEASURES TO RESTRICT THE AREA OF THE REVOLT

CHAPTER III.

PREPARATIONS IN OUDE

CHAPTER IV.

Preparations in the Punjab and of General Anson

CHAPTER V.

Five Groups of Mutineers, and Five Theatres of War

CHAPTER VI.

Operations against Delhi in June

CHAPTER VII.

Oude and Lucknow in June

CHAPTER VIII.

THE EASTERN AND SOUTHERN DISTRICTS AND ELSEWHERE

CHAPTER IX.

SOME SPECIAL FEATURES OF THE MUTINIES AND THE REVOLT

BOOK III.

THE VITAL STRUGGLE

CHAPTER I.

THE STAGES AND THEATRES OF THE CAMPAIGN

CHAPTER II.

THE PUNJAB

CHAPTER III.

The Siege of Delhi

CHAPTER IV.

The First Defence of the Lucknow Residency

CHAPTER V.

Havelock's Campaign for the Succour of Lucknow

CHAPTER VI.

EASTERN AND SOUTHERN THEATRES IN THE FIRST STAGE OF THE CAMPAIGN

PAGE

BOOK IV.

THE DECISIVE CONTEST

CHAPTER I.

INTRODUCTORY—AND THE PUNJAB AND DELHI THEATRES

CHAPTER II.

THE OUDE THEATRE—SECOND DEFENCE OF THE RESIDENCY, AND ITS RELIEF BY SIR COLIN CAMPBELL

CHAPTER III.

Operations preliminary to the Attack on Lucknow City

CHAPTER IV.

The Siege and Capture of the City of Lucknow

CHAPTER V.

The Eastern and Southern Theatres

BOOK V.

THE SUPPRESSION OF THE REVOLT

CHAPTER I.

GENERAL, AND IN OUDE

CHAPTER II.

THE OUDE THEATRE—HOT-WEATHER CAMPAIGN

CHAPTER III.

The Rohilkund Campaign

CHAPTER IV.

Final Winter Campaign in Oude

CHAPTER V.

The Eastern Theatre

CHAPTER VI.

THE SOUTHERN THEATRE

BOOK VI.

SUMMARY AND COMMENTS

CHAPTER I.

SUMMARY

CHAPTER II.

REMARKS AND COMMENTS

LIST OF MAPS.

BOOK I.

ORIGIN OF THE REVOLT.

THE SEPOY REVOLT.

BOOK I.

ORIGIN OF THE REVOLT.

CHAPTER I.

ITS SUDDENNESS—CHRONIC LATENT DISCONTENT—ITS SOURCES.

FOR a hundred years—from 1757 to 1857—the rule of the British had been steadily advancing and extending over India; but, until the very close of that period, the people of England practically knew but little about it. It was only during the last fifteen years that steam communication had begun. Public knowledge about the events of the century had been concentrated on the more important wars, and their heroes—Clive, Warren Hastings, the Wellesleys, Bhurtpore, Afghanistan, Scinde, Gwalior, and the Punjab. Of the people and government of India, Englishmen knew and seemed to care very little. Their chief ideas respecting their countrymen there were connected with bad livers and the shaking of the pagoda tree. The natives were looked on as mere black savages, who now and then, from their enormous numbers, gave our soldiers some trouble. There was an idea that the Queen and Parliament had but little to say to our rule, and that it lay in the hands of a set of old fogies, merchants of the East India Company, whose chief aim was to make money out of the country, whose chief merit lay in the patronage at their command, and whose real fitness to rule could be gauged by the absence of any material improvement in their vast dominions. But during the last ten years there seemed to have been an awakening. British prowess had been vindicated, as usual, if not more than usually; but besides this a definite and exceptional stage had been reached in the extension of British rule. The whole of Hindostan between the sea and the Himalayas had been brought within a ring fence under the sway of England, and great and wide-ranging steps had been taken towards the moral improvement and material development of the country.

In 1857, at the end of that period, England was resting and recovering from the losses and sorrows of the Crimea. There were no public events stirring of greater moment than the expeditions against Persia and China. People were beginning to look forward with a complacent glow of national pride to the centenary of Plassey. The latest hero of the day was Lord Dalhousie, who had returned home in shattered health, but covered with honour, on completing the British Empire of India. The Press was full of eulogies of his brilliant career and his beneficent and successful administration, as painted in his own lucid exposition of it, in which the picture drawn showed a soundly organized government, a prosperous and progressive country, and a happily ruled people.

The rumour, therefore, which then reached England of the outbreak of the Mutiny in Bengal was as a thundercrash from a cloudless sky—a bolt from the blue. Not only was the outbreak wholly unexpected, but the ferocity and race-hatred which characterized it were so utterly at variance with the state of feeling which was supposed to have been created and to prevail in the native community, that fears arose of the fabric so suddenly run up by Lord Dalhousie being seriously rotten; and a bitter reaction ensued in the public regard towards the statesman, whom they were now as ready to condemn as they had before been to idolize.

But in this there was some injustice. The account that Lord Dalhousie had given of his administration was true and precise. What he had done he had described correctly both in fact and tone. But he had disregarded many grave elements of good government, and what he had thus failed to do or to care for had likewise been omitted in his report. It is with the critics of those days that the fault rests for the failure to notice that while the most intense care had been taken of the moral and material needs of the country, there was not a line to indicate that any regard had been paid to the feelings, wishes, and thoughts of the native community, to the over-growth and indiscipline of the native troops, to the weakness of the British army, or to the defects in the military arrangements for the security of the State; all of these points forming, as will be seen, the most important factors in bringing about the great convulsion we are dealing with.

The actual Mutiny broke out in May, 1857, consequent directly on the excitement and ill-feeling engendered in the Bengal army by the well-known cartridge incident. Any such military outbreak would naturally cause much civil disturbance and find numerous supporters outside the army; but the wide range and the virulence of the general commotion that ensued were exceptional, and the rising was marked by a variety of phases and by singular episodes, for which the disaffection of the troops and the cartridge incident did not, of themselves, adequately account. A reasonable explanation of them, however, is readily found on turning to antecedent events and circumstances, and to the state of public feeling prevalent among various sections of the community. Investigation in those directions provides us with facts, and points to conclusions and probabilities which seem to indicate obviously and amply the several influences that led to the origin of the outbreak, swayed and chequered its development, and also served materially to affect the progress and shape the course of the contest that ensued.

First to be noted is the *chronic* state of public feeling, that is, its general state when not affected by any gravely exceptional excitement or agitation.

Up to 1856, the year before the outbreak, there had been for a whole century a continuous aggressive advance of the British power till it completed the ring fence of the Empire by the annexation of Oude. During all that time it had either been engaged in actual conflict or had been forming dominant relations with the several races of the country, and had reduced them, one after another, to subjection; some provinces being brought under its direct administration, and others being left as feudatory or vassal states under their native rulers. At the start, the old Moghul Empire, of which the capital was Delhi, had been in a hopeless state of decay, leading to all the horrors of internecine war; and some of the native principalities had gladly turned for safety to the shelter of English protection and supremacy. But the great mass of the people had been brought under our rule by conquest or by forcible annexation. With ruling dynasties thus set aside, reduced, or crushed, with great races humiliated, and bitterness and misery spread broadcast by the loss of power, place, and property, it would be an outrage on common sense to doubt that we had created a host of enemies. Moreover, there had been no rest, no time to reduce their numbers or their irritation. The benefits of civilized rule, of the *Pax Britannica*, were felt only skin-deep, and the old fierce instincts, the outcome of centuries of strife and oppression, were still in the ascendant. The memory of injuries was still keen and vivid, the newer cases helping to recall the old ones to mind, and to reopen sores that might otherwise have been getting healed; so that, briefly, the mood and temper which prevailed were those of a conquered people who had wrongs and humiliations to remember, and were chafing at having to endure the sway of aliens in race and creed. There existed, in fact, under the best circumstances, a mass of constant disaffection, and whole hosts of malcontents.

Of these, the most powerful and dangerous were the Mussulmans. The entire Mahomedan population were, as a body, rebels at heart, and resented the Christian supremacy, if only on religious grounds and from fanatical pride. And the Moghuls of Delhi and the upper provinces had, in addition, a natural longing to revive their old predominance, and restore their old Empire.

Next may be mentioned the Mahrattas, a warlike and unscrupulous Hindoo race, who, though now split up into rival states, had been most powerful as a confederacy, and felt that, but for the British, they would have been the masters of India.

Another extensive body of malcontents consisted of those who were direct sufferers from British conquest or annexation, or from the action of British Land Policy.

And a fourth group, specially dangerous from their spirit and energy, was formed by those who fretted at the closing of those outlets for ambition, and the loss of those opportunities for aggrandizement through political intrigue or military prowess, that had been current of old.

Such a mass of disaffection, however latent or suppressed, was obviously a standing menace to the tranquillity of the country, constituting a solid basis, and providing a powerful agency, for the rousing of evil passions and the promotion of seditious enterprise—a sure factor in any movement or question involving the peace or security of the State, and a danger to be reckoned with in any cases of innovations or of measures that might be at variance with the traditional habits or prejudices of the people.

Under these conditions, it is sufficiently obvious that in the event of any undue temptation arising, any general cause increasing discontent, this underlying disaffection would be liable to be awakened into activity; with its agents ready to seize every opportunity to intensify and exaggerate every source of irritation, but especially those involving a cleavage between the British and the native races.

Next we have to observe permanent sources of friction; conditions, that is, not in themselves irritating, but affording opportunities for irritation through any failure of care and tact.

There is a prevalent tendency to speak as if the "people of India" could not be regarded as one people at all, because they embrace many and various races and creeds, aspirations and interests. In relation to certain specific aspects of political life, the theory is true enough; but in relation to a European dominion, it is entirely misleading. As against the British, they are emphatically one people in the very important sense that despite their variations they all share characteristics, interests, traditions and modes of thought which tend to unite them against any Western race. However much they differ among themselves, their differences from us are greater, their points of contact with each other far more numerous. They belong to the soil, while the British are aliens, *feringhees*. They are dark-skinned, *kala admi*, while the British are fair. Their creeds are not ours. Their social habits and usages, their traditional rights and points of honour to which they cling passionately, and their modes of thought, are Oriental and not European. They are subjects, and practically barred from rule, while the British are rulers, and virtually autocratic. If the English, even apparently though not actually, ignore or slight—much more if they treat with insult, or outrage—these points of difference, it is folly to suppose that the several races will not tend to combine and act as one people in hostility to us.

If this antagonism of East and West were disregarded—if essential prejudices of the Oriental mind were overlooked—the chronic but usually latent ill feeling was certain to be roused into activity; whether such disregard might be due to the pressure of inevitable circumstances, or to inconsiderate miscalculation, or to mere heedless perversity. But to find impressive and conclusive examples of it, there is no need to go further back than the administration of Lord Dalhousie, which terminated in 1856. These form the next subject of our inquiry.

CHAPTER II.

CAUSES OF DISAFFECTION BECOMING ACTIVE.

FOUR measures, or groups of measures, occurred in the time of Lord Dalhousie, and one for which his successor Lord Canning's government was responsible, which may be set down as calculated directly to arouse distrust and antipathy—to stir the chronic but latent discontent into the active disaffection which culminated in the mutiny of 1857.

In the course of the seven years during which Lord Dalhousie was Governor-General, the boundaries of the British dominion were immensely extended, so as to include the whole country from the sea to the mountains—by conquest, as in the case of the Punjab; by suppression of an allied government, as with Oude; or by absorption of feudatory states, such as Jhansi, which, though already included within the British dominion and recognizing its suzerainty, had hitherto been left under the sway of their dynastic chiefs, but were now removed from native rule, and brought under direct British administration. These annexations in the aggregate implied a type of policy which very seriously affected the native mind: impressing it with the idea that British greed was insatiable—that the limit of British rapacity had not yet been attained.* This was the first great cause of the growth of disaffection.

In the second place, apart from the general suspicion thus engendered, most of these annexations were attended by their own particular crop of grievances. The conquests might indeed be recognized as the necessary result of direct provocation. Of the suppression of Oude, we shall speak separately. But the absorptions of feudatory states were far more numerous; and in every case involved the removal of some friendly and loyal dynasty, and the inclusion of the principality and its revenues under direct British administration. All were owing to one feature, the lapse of the dynasty concerned, caused by the failure of direct heirs to it. Direct or natural hereditary succession was always restricted to a very small circle, and was constantly liable to become extinct; and in such cases the custom was to adopt an heir, subject to the approval and recognition of the paramount power. Of those that occurred in Lord Dalhousie's time, there was one only—that of the Mahratta State of Nagpore of which the Bonslah Rajah was the chief—in which the state lapsed fairly

* This policy was specially Lord Dalhousie's own. He promulgated it by stating his "strong and deliberate opinion that in the exercise of a sound and wise policy the British Government is bound not to put aside or neglect such rightful opportunities of acquiring territory or revenue as may from time to time present themselves."

to the Crown; because there was no lawful claimant to the direct succession, and the Rajah would not adopt any heir. In all the other cases, the British Government declined to sanction the proposed adoption, and then absorbed the principality, in virtue of the default of a dynastic heir to it; whereas adoptions had formerly been occasionally rejected, but, as a rule, had been accepted by the paramount power, and the custom had been a most cherished one, for obvious reasons.

The rejection of a proposed adoption, formerly the exception, now became the practice; some fifteen or sixteen principalities, including the Mahratta States of Sattara and Jhansi, were thus absorbed under British rule, while the dynastic families were deprived of their ruling power and status. This startling increase in one direction alone of British aggression (and the case of Jhansi in particular) attracted serious attention, created a most uneasy feeling, and was universally regarded as significant of annexation being, under similar circumstances, the settled measure for the future. This caused grave anxiety and irritation throughout the feudatory states, and especially affected the goodwill of the great Princes of Rajpootana, hitherto markedly loyal and contented.*

* The evil of this violation of the sentiments and practice of the people was afterwards fully recognized, and in 1862 the Government gave formal engagements to the several ruling chiefs that, on failure of natural heirs, the adoption of successors, according to native law and the customs of their race, would be recognized and confirmed.

Thirdly, following on the annexations, and resulting directly from them, was the most momentous matter of all. As territory extended, the *native* army was proportionately increased, but without any corresponding augmentation being made of the *British* troops. The consequence was that the sepoy force attained to overwhelming preponderance over the British, their infantry in Bengal being at one time in the proportion of twenty to one. This destroyed the equilibrium of the military organization, and thereby endangered its stability and the security of the State.

The risk thus involved was enhanced by the fact—well known—that the Bengal sepoys had been showing signs of laxity in tone and discipline. Besides one positive mutiny, a group of regiments in the Punjab had been checked in a tendency to combination about an alleged grievance. And, worst of all, there had been successful resistance to orders when troops had been required to proceed on service which entailed a sea voyage. Further, the danger of the temptation which their overwhelming strength held out to a force in which such a tone prevailed, was increased by the absence of any effort, on the part of the Government, either to conceal or to counteract by improved military arrangements the weakness of the British troops. For these were mainly massed in the Punjab, leaving huge stretches of country and positions of the first importance, such as Allahabad and Delhi, absolutely denuded of their presence; while only three regiments garrisoned the nine hundred miles between Calcutta and Meerut.

Further, it was after the annexation of Burmah and the Punjab, and after this great increase of the native army, that the Crimean War broke out. The British garrison of India was then reduced and weakened in order to increase our army before Sevastopol; and this loan, so to speak, of troops was never replaced. The British contingent in India remained short of its proper cavalry force alone by two regiments, and Lord Dalhousie's earnest appeals to England for three more regiments were practically disregarded.

That the native army was fully aware of its own preponderating strength, and of the weakness of the British element, there can be no doubt whatever; still, in spite of the consequent temptation that the situation must have offered, and of the defects in its discipline, no sign was ever then given by the sepoy army of any improper attitude or feeling *towards the State*—a fact which was specially singular, when the measures and action are considered that were then being taken by the malcontent party.

The preponderance, then, of the native army, owing to its increase consequent on the great extent of Lord Dalhousie's annexations, was the third cause of the growth of disaffection—not, of course, in the sense of creating ill feeling, but from the temptations, encouragement, and opportunities, which it held out to the disaffected.

In these several matters, the action of Lord Dalhousie was very similar to that of the proprietor of a newly acquired mansion, who insists on expanding and heightening it into a palatial edifice, without considering whether he is not thereby disturbing its foundations.

The *fourth* cause lay in the results of Lord Dalhousie's own strong personality. Able, energetic, and bold, and withal devotedly bent on fulfilling his duty to the country, he conferred lasting benefits upon it. But he was essentially an autocrat, exceptionally imperious, self-willed, and self-sufficient. So he set aside all obstructing considerations—among them the prejudices, feelings, habits, traditions, and modes of thought of the native community—and would brook no advice. Formerly, local rulers and other responsible authorities were expected to convey information, and to tender suggestions, advice, and opinions freely and frankly, and also to act upon their own judgment in minor matters and in cases of urgency. These were the traditional principles of administration by which the empire had been built up. But Lord Dalhousie practically changed all this. Instead of acting promptly and resolutely on their own judgment, officers had to wait for orders; advice or suggestion, except from a favoured few, was apt to be regarded as unparalleled presumption; so that independent thought and promptitude of action were checked, public and official spirit was greatly deadened, and many valuable sources of observation and information naturally became closed or useless. This was the worst feature of all, for the seething disaffection that prevailed, the sedition that was being spread, and the certainty eventually felt from infallible signs by the monetary classes of an imminent outbreak, seemed to remain unknown to the Government.

The two most prominent cases of Lord Dalhousie's autocratic action were those of Sir Charles Napier and Sir Henry Lawrence. The former was removed from the command of the army, and replaced by Sir William Gomm; the latter was removed from the administration of the Punjab, and replaced by his brother John.

In the specific dispute with Sir Charles Napier, the latter was, without doubt, in the wrong, but he was the ablest soldier in the British army; and it may be reasonably urged that it was more important in the public interests that such a man, however troublesome, should be at the head of the military administration than that Lord Dalhousie should be relieved from annoyance, and have in that post some one on whom he could depend to leave matters alone which he did not himself initiate, or specially care for. The Duke of Wellington had certainly insisted on the necessity of agreement between the Governor-General and the Commander-in-Chief; but in so doing he can hardly have meant that the latter should be made a mere cypher, with the consequent loss of any adequate, vigorous, and independent professional control of the military needs of the country, and the inevitable muddle that therefore ensued.

In the case of Sir Henry Lawrence, who had counted the good-will of the people as the first matter to be secured in the rule of a newly conquered province, Lord Dalhousie held those views to be more suited for a political post in a native state, than for the civil administration of a British province, and preferred to him his brother John, who had more orthodox ideas in regard to financial economy. The consequent change in the policy and tone of the rule of the Punjab could not fail to check and damp the hearty good-will that had pervaded the province, and to tend to bring it down to the dead level of the public feeling in the older provinces.

In these four ways, then, the administration of Lord Dalhousie was responsible for creating or fostering disaffection—by the general extension of dominion ; by the refusal to recognize adoption ; by the resulting enlargement of the sepoy force, incidentally accompanied by the reduction of the British force ; by the introduction of an autocratic system which reversed the traditions of administration, slighted many of its essential elements, and greatly increased the difficulties of his successor.

The *fifth* cause of increased ill feeling—and a very grave one, especially with respect to the coming mutiny—was the measure which that successor, Lord Canning, himself carried out during his first year, called the General Service Enlistment Act. This made an entire revolution in the future terms of service of the sepoy army, as they would have to be prepared to cross the Blackwater (as they called the ocean), despite caste or religious obligations. Would Brahmins and Rajpoots enlist under such terms, or would they give up military service as their career? This apparent attack on caste privileges seemed to fit in but too well with the sinister rumours which had, by this time, begun to spread respecting the aggressive intentions of Government against the creeds of the country. The matter became an all-absorbing and agitating topic in the regimental lines, and was the first actual and tangible strain on the loyalty of the men and their sense of their relations to the State.

But this measure, it must be understood, was not one of Lord Dalhousie's, but of Lord Canning's.

The annexation of Oude has not been treated among these causes of increased disaffection, since its case was so peculiar, especially in regard to the fluctuations of the feelings of its people, and it occurred at so late a period, that it will be best dealt with by itself further on.

CHAPTER III.

NEUTRAL, OR COUNTERVAILING INFLUENCES.

THESE, then, were the more prominent of the chronic conditions and the active causes producing and fostering the seditious spirit which culminated in the Mutiny.

That the recent annexations *by conquest* are not to be included among them, except as pointing vaguely to a policy of "grab," needs some explanation.

These annexations had been three in number. Out of the three, that of part of Sikkim, near Nepaul, was insignificant. That of Lower Burmah was important in its way; but, as far as concerned India proper, the only appreciable effect of it was the military drain of garrisoning it. But the third, that of the Punjab, actually resulted in a great acquisition of strength to the British power. Although, like other acquisitions of territory, it may have been reckoned an additional proof of British greed, and did necessarily affect the position and numbers of troops, it proved in the event to have been singularly fortunate.

After the death of their great monarch, Ranjit Singh, and the disastrous events at Cabul in 1842, the Sikh nation had fallen virtually under the domination of a curiously democratic army, which was vehemently hostile to the British. In 1845 that army invaded British territory. Within three months, during which four pitched battles had been fought with a stubborn valour on the part of the "Khalsa" unparalleled in our Indian wars, we dictated terms of peace to the Lahore Government. An honest attempt was made to bolster up an independent nation; but in two years a revolt broke out—nominally against the Government, really against British influence. In six months the revolt developed into a general rising of the Sikhs. In six months more the Sikh army had been shattered, and the Punjab was annexed. In those two wars of 1845–46 and 1848–49 our stubborn enemy had learned to honour British military prowess; in the years that followed they learned that their conquerors could be both just and generous. From bitter enemies they were converted into loyal friends; and the men of the conquered province did yeoman's service when the sepoys of the Ganges basin turned against British rule. Primarily, at least, this was owing to the fact that Sir Henry Lawrence was placed at the head of the administration of the province immediately after its conquest; and, through a carefully selected staff, most of whom he imbued with his own spirit, carried out such a liberal policy, and showed such a genial demeanour to the proud and warlike race who were smarting under the sense of defeat, that he turned them from enemies into friends, and won their confidence for their English rulers. This good-will had its foundations laid deep; and, though somewhat affected by the colder and harder rule that replaced Sir Henry's on his transfer to another post, it lasted, under the staff which he left behind him, till the time of trial came and put it successfully to the test in 1857, when it helped to save the Empire.

Hence the acquisitions by conquest had no sinister effect, except as forming part of the expansion of the Empire, and as leading to a great increase in the native garrison of the country, and to the consequent mischief.

The causes that might and did increase the chronic, but usually latent, ill-feeling among the natives have now been described, as well as those cases that might have been expected to increase it, and did not do so; and before proceeding to show how those causes operated, and how, step by step, the disaffection grew till it culminated in the outbreak, it becomes necessary to refer to those political and social elements that checked and tended to keep that disaffection latent, and militated against any attack on British rule.

The essence of those favourable elements was that any tendency to give vent to this ill-feeling in serious action against the British was restrained by the universal sense that our presence constituted the only safeguard against a recurrence of the internecine wars of old, with all their attendant horrors, of which the memories and traditions were still in force; whilst also each of the great races—Rajpoot or Mahratta, Mahomedan or Sikh or Jat—felt that the British rule was preferable to that of any of its native rivals, by whom it might possibly be overcome in a contest for the supremacy.

For a clear understanding of this point, a brief reference to the previous history of India seems advisable. During the three centuries after the year 1300 there had occurred a series of Moghul (or Toorki) invasions of the country, leading to the establishment of the Moghul Empire of India, which then lasted up to the middle of the eighteenth century. The older kingdoms and races of the country had been successively attacked and destroyed, and the wars and conquests had been carried on with ruthless ferocity and barbarity, and without regard to life, honour, or property. There were bright gleams under such a reign as Akbar's; but, on the whole, the memory and traditions of the wrongs and horrors of that period remained ever fresh in the minds of the people. Matters grew still worse with the decay of the Moghul Empire, the rise of the Mahrattas, the ravages of their hordes, and the intestine commotions between the various races and states—the Punjab, the North-West, Rajpootana, Oude, Bengal, Malwa, Central India, the Deccan, the Carnatic, Mysore, and so forth.

In all these wars and commotions the country had been a prey to devastation and to utter disregard of life and rights and honour. Forcible conversion to Mahomedanism was everywhere rife; but it had not been so successful elsewhere as in the northern provinces, owing to the resolute adherence of Hindoo and Buddhist to their own creeds.

But in the British course of conquest—beginning with Bengal and Madras, and extending through Southern India to Bombay and the Mahratta states, advancing through Oude and Rohilkund to Delhi and Rajpootana, and eventually enclosing Scinde and the Punjab—there had been no such ruthless features. The wars, so far as the English were concerned, had been conducted on civilized lines and with due regard to private rights.

Hence the public feeling in regard to the British conquest and rule was entirely free from that sense of unspeakable hatred and dread which attached to the memories of the old internecine wars of the native states and races.

Under this counteracting influence the chronic disaffection had usually remained latent and suppressed, and rarely ruffled the otherwise placid state of public feeling.

Further, it is to be noted that the uneasiness was confined in the main, though not exclusively, to the Ganges provinces. While the position of the Punjab was, as we have seen, entirely exceptional, the Presidencies of Madras and Bombay were not subject to quite the same conditions as that of Bengal. Hitherto they had been practically more independent of the control of the Supreme Government than they have since become. They were therefore less influenced by Lord Dalhousie's autocratic system, and the native states in them were less directly affected by his measures. Their armies, too, were not at one with the old Hindostanee army of Bengal. Under a sounder discipline, they bore more general resemblance to the frontier and special troops of Upper India, and were largely imbued with the spirit of jealousy and rivalry, instead of unison, in their attitude to the Bengal sepoys. The Hindus of the Ganges belonged to different races from those of the south. The Mussulman conquerors, who had established their dynasties in the Deccan, were not akin to the Moghul invaders, against whom they had fought long and stubbornly. Stress has been laid on the importance of remembering the tendency of the Indian peoples to unite as against the British; but it need not be denied in consequence that they have a tendency to divide as against each other.

To this it has to be added that at the commencement of Lord Canning's Governor-Generalship, the general feeling outside of the Ganges provinces was improving, rather than growing worse. If the Punjab had lost Henry Lawrence, Rajpootana had gained him; its princes felt his magic influence at once, becoming, under his benign and sympathetic guidance, less anxious as to their own future and the aims of the paramount Power. Moreover, some other great native states, notably those of Gwalior and Hyderabad, where the turbulent character of the people might have been expected to render them dangerous, were wisely and firmly handled by loyal and able ministers—Nuwab Salar Jung and Rajah Dinkur Rao—well supported by Colonel Davidson and Major Macpherson, the British representatives at their courts.

CHAPTER IV.

THE ANNEXATION OF OUDE.

WE will now turn to the story of the annexation of Oude, and the part which that province played in connection with the origination of the Mutiny and revolt.

It was the last of Lord Dalhousie's annexations, and it was a case of the *suppression of the native rule.* It was carried out just as he was on the point of handing over the reins of Government to Lord Canning. There had been much anxiety, for several reasons, as to whether it could be effected peaceably, and there was, therefore, much satisfaction when it was carried out without any *émeute.* But the province became the chief theatre of the war of the Mutiny, and this fact, combined with the peculiarity of the circumstances of the annexation and the subsequent events there, makes it expedient to give a brief account of them and of the province.

The map shows where Oude lies, with Lucknow, its capital, near its centre. Its chief feature was that it was the fatherland of the bulk of the sepoy army; and that during the hundred years of the rise of

British power, it had been allowed to remain under the sway of its native dynasty, though all the surrounding provinces had been absorbed under British administration. The cause of this exception was that from the first years of the rise of the British power, in the time of Lord Clive, the rulers of Oude had remained true and loyal allies of the English. The eventual dethronement of the Nuwab, and the absorption of his province in 1856, resulted, not from any disloyalty to the British, but from his misgovernment being so gross, so persistent, so hopeless, and inflicting such terrible wrong on the people as well as being in direct violation of his treaty obligations, that his rule could not be allowed to continue.

The misrule lay, not, as Oriental story might lead one to expect, in any personal ferocity, barbarity, or violent crime on the part of the Nuwab and his predecessors, but in their abstention from the duties of government, and their delegation of its functions and powers—uncontrolled and unchecked—to worthless favourites and unscrupulous bidders for office; with the inevitable results from the union, under such circumstances, of insatiable greed with entire absence of restraint.

Now, the ruling race and a large proportion of the inhabitants of the towns were Mahomedans of Moghul descent; but the country peasantry and their chiefs were, almost universally, Rajpoots—a race of fine physique, who formed the nursery of the bulk of the sepoy army. They were the warrior caste of the Hindoo community, divided into clans, and with feudal organization and tendencies; with a strong traditional sense of honour, but not naturally ferocious and bloodthirsty like the tribes on the Afghan frontiers. If let alone, they formed an excellent, orderly body of cultivators, but they were not a race that would submit tamely to the extortion of the Court Officials to whom the revenue had been farmed out, with license to extort—with the support of the troops, and by any means, however violent and murderous—the utmost they could manage, without regard to assessments, engagements, or rights of any kind.

The Rajpoot clansmen, under their chiefs (generally known as *Talookdârs*), forcibly opposed the Oude officials, or "*amils*"; and hence rebellion, as this opposition was called, became chronic through the province. Had the several clans combined and made common cause against their oppressors, the amils, they could have kept them at bay, and laughed at them. But they would not do this, owing to their mutual jealousies and quarrels, the outcome of an extreme type of feudal organization; and each clan, or sept, abided in its forts the onslaught of the enemy. There were some 1600 of these forts scattered about in the province, many of them armed with artillery, all surrounded with almost impervious bamboo-thicket fences, and situated in jungles difficult to penetrate.

And so it came about that ever since the beginning of the present century the whole province of Oude was the scene of chronic warfare between the amils, or farmers of the Government revenue, on the one hand, and the Rajpoot chiefs, or talookdars, and their clansmen on the other. The barbarities and miseries that resulted could not be overstated. The more powerful clans held their own, but they did not prosper as they might have done; while the weaker ones were ruined. Hundreds of miles of country lay devastated, and the province was infested with gangs of brigands and robbers; while those estates which were not depopulated, but from which the owners had been driven, usually became the property of the amils who had ousted them.

There were two marked and important results from this state of matters. One was that it was strongly recognized that the general welfare of a clan—in fact, its actual safety—lay in a concentrated organization in which all were to hold and work together, in which there was an identity of interests throughout all classes, and in which it was of moment that their chief and representative should be a territorial magnate, a man of power and position. With the better clans, the men were devoted to their chief; the chief was the veritable father of the clan: its welfare was his care, and his will was law. It will be seen presently in what a surprising manner this told on the Mutiny.

Another result of the misrule was to create a favourable feeling towards the English. In the contests of the Rajpoots with the amils, and their quarrels with the Lucknow court and its emissaries, they ever found sympathy and friendly advice and help from the few English officers scattered about; and they always knew that the Resident at Lucknow—as the British Minister there was called—was the truest friend they had, ready to interpose, whenever possible, to relieve suffering and secure redress for wrongs.

This feeling, moreover, was supplemented and strengthened by the fact that in every village there were men who were living on British pensions, and considered themselves identified with British rule, and sharers in its prosperity and renown. At the same time, though the talookdars were imbued as strongly as their followers with this goodwill towards the English personally, they did not feel the same liking towards the policy in force with the British administration. They heard strange rumours of that policy, and of the action of the law courts; of the families of position, and the natural leaders of the people, falling rapidly into decay, and being dispossessed of their estates—partly from the dead set made against them by the doctrinaire school, then in the ascendant, and partly by the intricate working of the law courts, and the chicanery and trickery of the usurer class, who had become all-powerful. The Oude men felt that they would be helpless against such foes; whereas, under the existing *régime*, they might hold their own, though with the chance of much risk and suffering.

Such, then, were the characteristics and the results of the misrule that had prevailed in Oude for the last century, and that seemed to be on the increase.

The weaker clans and landholders had been crushed and ruined, and their positions and estates had been usurped by the amils, who had become more powerful than ever, and were pressing more strongly against those stouter clans and chiefs who had heretofore kept them at bay.

The Oude Durbar continued provokingly deaf and callous to the remonstrances of the British Government. The Nuwabs believed, in their hearts, that these remonstrances were a mere farce, and that so long as they remained loyal and faithful to British interests, shortcomings in other respects were of no moment.

The position was becoming intolerable; and the British Government could no longer avoid facing the fact that, by its protection and support of the Oude rule, it was sharing in the responsibility for the shameful state of matters in the province. In 1854, therefore, when, happily, General Outram, who was noted for his generous sympathy with all classes of the native community, with princes as well as with peasants, was the British Resident at Lucknow, he was instructed to investigate the subject and report on it fully. This he accordingly did, and there could be but one tenor to the report. The misrule was so outrageous, so dangerous, so unjust to the people, so flagrant a violation of treaty engagements; it entailed so serious a responsibility on the British Government, by whose protection only it was rendered possible, that it could not be allowed to continue.

The Government of India forwarded Outram's report to Her Majesty's Government, and urged the necessity for removing the administration of Oude from the rule of its Nuwabs, suggesting various alternative measures, and dwelling at the same time on the generous treatment which the unswerving loyalty of the dynasty merited at the hands of the British. The decision in England was for absolute annexation, and the orders and detailed instructions reached Lord Dalhousie on the 2nd January, 1856.

Meanwhile, during the latter half of 1855, events had been taking place in Oude which confirmed the necessity for the change contemplated, and also affected the state of public feeling. The city of Fyzabad had always been notorious as a centre of religious fanaticism and strife. And now a *moulvie*, named Ameer Ali, had started a story that the Hunnooman Gurhee, the great Hindoo temple there, had been built on the site of a Mahomedan mosque. Having then collected a band of followers, he had attacked the temple, but had been repulsed by the Hindoos, who had flocked in to its defence. The story was groundless, and was proved to be so by reference to the archives at Delhi; still the Nuwab by his attitude encouraged the moulvie, and a religious war would have ensued had not General Outram stepped in and insisted on the maintenance of law and order. The moulvie, however, continued his threatening attitude towards the temple, and eventually, trusting to the secret support of the Nuwab, advanced to its attack, but was met by troops commanded by English officers, with the result that he was himself killed and his followers dispersed.

This episode destroyed any latent reluctance that there might otherwise have been to remove the Nuwab from the rulership of the province; but it had also two other notable results. One was that the Hindoos of Oude, including the Rajpoot chiefs, knowing the part played in the crisis by the English Resident, became especially well disposed towards the British. The other was that Rajah Maun Singh, hitherto one of the most detested of the amils, having come forward with his followers to the defence of the Hunnooman Gurhee, and posed as the champion of Hindooism, lost much of his unpopularity, and acquired the respect of the Rajpoots to such a degree as to enable him to act during the Mutiny as the representative and leader of the country community.

Such, then, was the state of affairs when, on the 2nd January, 1856, Lord Dalhousie received the orders from England for the annexation of Oude. The preparation of the detailed instructions and arrangements for carrying those orders into effect occupied the greater part of the rest of the month. But at length Outram received these instructions, and was directed to depose the Nuwab and assume the administration of the province.

On the 4th February, 1856, General Outram carried out his orders. He announced formally to the Nuwab that Oude and its revenues were to be brought under British administration, while the Nuwab would retain his sovereign rank and title, and sundry privileges and estates, with an annual income of £150,000. The letter from Lord Dalhousie, which he received at the same time, gave the reasons for this decision of the English Government—that the Nuwab had forfeited the position secured to him under the existing treaty by his persistent violation of its most important stipulation, that he should establish and maintain a good government; that his misrule had brought widespread misery on his subjects, and become a standing reproach, in which the British Government was involved, owing to its relations with the Nuwab; that this state of matters would not be tolerated any longer, and the forfeiture of his position must therefore be enforced, and the treaty annulled and replaced by a fresh treaty. The loyalty of the Nuwab and his dynasty was recognized, and his status and provision for the future were settled on the terms proposed.

The Nuwab, however, would have nought to say to the treaty. He was the servant, he said, of the English Government, while treaties were valid only between equals. But he protested against his deposition, inasmuch as he had ever been faithful and loyal, the only obligation he recognized as real and binding. And he would go to the Governor-General, and, if need be, to the Queen of England, to plead his cause in person.

Three days of grace were given him for consideration, but he remained unyielding, and so General Outram assumed the administration of the province, and issued his proclamation. The Nuwab, true to his attitude, discharged his troops and officials from their allegiance to himself, and enjoined on them implicit obedience and deference to the British rule.

The assumption of the administration by General Outram was effected with perfect tranquillity. This was due, no doubt, in a measure, as regards Lucknow itself, to the bearing and injunctions of the Nuwab; in the country it was owing largely to the prevalent feeling of good-will towards the English; and everywhere it was materially influenced by the terms and tenor of the proclamation, of which a copy, with a separate letter, was sent to every chief and person of position. Among the sepoys there was excitement, but no stronger feeling.

Under the proclamation, and the attendant measures which were immediately adopted, careful attention seemed to be paid to the welfare of every class, and to befriending the lot of those who were likely to suffer most from the change. Suitable provision was promised for the collateral members of the royal family, consideration and employment for those who had lost office and position. The Nuwab's troops and retainers were to be recruited into the local forces and police, or to be pensioned. All classes were assured of protection and justice and the full enjoyment of their rights. The land revenue was to be organized on a fair and clear basis, while its first settlement was to be for three years, on a moderate assessment, and to be made direct with those in actual possession, leaving proprietary rights an open question for future decision.

At this juncture, then, there was general satisfaction and contentment, at any rate among the Hindoo community of the province, though the Mussulmans, not only of Oude, but of all Upper India, were embittered and angered by the suppression of one of the few Mahomedan reigning houses which had been left in power.

But immediately after Oude was annexed Lord Dalhousie left, and was succeeded by Lord Canning, and on his taking up the rule the first result was the withdrawal of that personal sway which Lord Dalhousie had inaugurated. The natural effect was that real, vigorous control on the part of the Supreme Government seemed to cease altogether, and administrative discipline was greatly weakened. Hence, though the old tone among the higher officials was not restored, strong-willed subordinates, feeling the relaxation, became inclined to kick over the traces, ignore orders, and disregard authority.

The most serious instance of this that occurred was in Oude; and it occurred very soon, and was attended with very mischievous results. Lord Dalhousie had, in his proclamation of the annexation, made certain promises which protected the interests of the talookdars, of the royal family, and of the dependents of the deposed king; and consequently, as already described, contentment at first prevailed. But at the end of April, 1856, Sir James Outram, who had carried out the annexation so quietly and successfully, had been forced by ill health to resign the rule of the province. While he was there, his conciliatory and generous measures had produced a most beneficial effect; but, even during his time, a tendency had been shown by the revenue officers, in a degree which attracted the attention and drew down the disapproval of the Governor-General, to depart from the terms of the proclamation in respect of the land revenue arrangements, and to violate the promises that the assessment should be moderate, and that the settlement should be made direct with the persons in actual possession.

After Sir James Outram's departure the state of feeling grew rapidly worse. Except in the matter of employing the Nuwab's sepoys and retainers in the new local regiments and police, there seemed to be an entire cessation and disregard of the beneficent and conciliatory arrangements which had been promised, and in a measure started. As described in Lord Stanley's despatch of October 13, 1858, the members and stipendiaries of the royal family were treated with discourtesy, and even reduced to great straits from their allowances being withheld, while the ex-officials and men of influence were studiously kept out of the employment and position which they had been led to expect. All these combined to form the nucleus of a powerful malcontent party. Though thousands of the soldiery had been brought into British service, other thousands had been discharged without the means of subsistence; and, in Oude, to discharge a sepoy so was to create a bandit.

On the top of this came the General Service Enlistment Act, which, with its effect on the army, as already described, also filled with dismay or grave anxiety the sepoys' homes in Oude, and the hearts of their kinsmen and of the clansmen generally; who had habitually looked to the army as the great field for the employment of their sons, but who now felt that henceforward the British service would be very materially changed, as if from a militia to a general service army. So the jungles came to be more and more infested with groups of dacoits or brigands.

Moreover, most serious of all, the irritation among the Rajpoot community, chiefs and peasants alike, grew apace, owing to the increasing violation, already touched on, of the promises respecting the land revenue. Besides the matter of unduly high assessments, the bias shown in deciding on the parties to be dealt with as being in actual possession gave the most serious offence. For the officers usually treated with the villagers themselves, and ignored the talookdars or chiefs. Now, it was well known that by whatever process they had obtained the position, the chiefs were generally the parties holding actual possession at the time of annexation, while their followers and the peasantry were only their tenants; and it was also universally recognized that it was by means of this very position and these relations that the talookdars had acquired that power and station which had cemented the clan organization, and enabled it to resist successfully the oppression of the Durbar amils and troops. As a natural result, the clansmen were apt to feel that any diminution of the territorial or other wealth of their chief involved a lowering of his status and power, and injured the welfare of the community in general. When, therefore, by the action of the English revenue officers, such rajahs as those of Dharoopore, Amythee, and Dera, such chiefs as Beni Madho and other heads of the great Byswara clan, were mulcted of half their estates, not only were those magnates angered and embittered, but their clansmen sympathized, and joined in the resentment.

Thus it was that after the middle of 1856 the whole of Oude was in a state of bitter disaffection, which increased as the year advanced.

CHAPTER V.

HENRY LAWRENCE IN OUDE.

OUR narrative has now reached 1857; and the events of the first months of that year have now to be related. The exigencies of the case require us to devote attention first, and separately, to Oude; but it becomes necessary in consequence to enumerate the contemporary events elsewhere, which will be detailed in a subsequent chapter, but must be alluded to in the course of the Oude narrative. These are: the cartridge incident, which occurred in January; the mutinies at Barrackpore and Berhampore, in February and March; the outbreak of incendiarism at Umballa, in the north, in March; and the Meerut mutiny on the 10th May.

Throughout the closing months of 1856 matters in Oude were growing steadily worse. By the beginning of 1857 the feeling had become virulent, and early in the year there arose a new moulvie, or fanatic leader, called variously Ahmed-oolla Shah or Sikundur Shah, who openly raised the standard of revolt at Fyzabad, and proclaimed a *jehad*, or religious war, against the British. At the same time brigandage was steadily growing in extent and in audacity, till a crisis was reached, when a gang, led by a notorious desperado named Fuzl Ali, resisted and killed Mr. Boileau, the officer in command of a party which had been sent against them.

But at this juncture—none too soon—a most fortunate change was made in the government of Oude, for Sir Henry Lawrence now came over from Rajpootana to assume charge of it. Considering the exceptional part which, as will be seen later on, he, personally, and the province, through the results of his measures, played in the impending struggle, a short notice of his character and views will be useful.

No one could be named who so thoroughly gauged and understood the disaffection that was at work, or who was so competent to deal with it where it was exceptionally prominent and threatening, as was the case in Oude.

How he realized the gravity of the crisis was obvious from his conversations whilst on his way from Rajpootana to Lucknow, from the measures he took immediately on arrival, and from his letters to Lord Canning and others. How such a crisis ought to be met he had shown in his writings, and especially in an article penned in 1843, which will be presently noticed. His special fitness to deal with the local irritation was marked by his previous success under the equally difficult circumstances in the Punjab, and by the widespread character which he had thereby gained as a beneficent ruler and a staunch friend of all classes of the people. This reputation, preceding his move to Oude, caused his arrival there to have an immediate effect on the excitement in the province.

Lawrence's knowledge of the state of public feeling, and his insight into the causes that affected it, were unique, both from his natural sagacity and instincts, and also from the varied opportunities which he had enjoyed and used. These had brought him into close contact with all classes of the country population, and also with the chiefs and peoples of native states, and of the old feudal races. In the one case he had been impressed with the grave injustice with which the upper classes—who were held to be effete, but were still the natural leaders of the people—were being treated, in the interests, as was assumed, of the peasantry; and, in the other, he had seen the dangerous feeling resulting from the prospect of the possible extinction of the native dynasties by the attitude of Government in minimizing the practice of the adoption of heirs. Adding to these the Mahomedans and other embittered classes, he felt that the grave disaffection of so many large and influential sections of the community tended towards a general combination against the State.

As to the native army, he had long been outspoken about its treatment and want of discipline, its dangerous growth and preponderating strength; and now he was appalled at the animosity roused in it by the General Service Act, and by the blunders of the cartridge business.

He had written of it in 1843, that the true basis of the British power lay in the army being well paid, well disciplined, and thoroughly reliant, from experience, on the good faith, wisdom, and energy of the Government and its leaders. And he had shown the danger that would arise if, quick-sighted as they were, they came to detect any shortcomings in our good faith or spirit, or otherwise to lose confidence in the British.

He had pointed out that constant success had made us careless and blind to the dangers to which we were liable ; that it was necessary to be always on our guard as to the sufficiency of our military means, and the efficacy of our military arrangements and organization ; and that, above all, timely energy and resolute action might surmount grave and formidable dangers, while want of military spirit or soldierly bearing would tend to cause catastrophe under even trifling difficulties.

It was under the influence of these convictions and this spirit that Sir Henry Lawrence acted on his arrival at Lucknow, imbued as he was with a profound sense of an impending rising of the troops, and of a possible combination of the whole native community against the State.

He assumed charge of the province about the 24th March, and took immediate steps, first for the enforcement of law and order ; next for the reduction of the local discontent and disaffection ; and third for inquiries and preparations to meet the coming crisis.

A brigand chief, Fuzl Ali, had, as we have seen,

repulsed and slain the English officer who tried to capture him. So Sir Henry attacked and killed Fuzl Ali, and dispersed his followers. The Fyzabad moulvie was ostentatiously preaching sedition, and proclaiming a *jehad* (religious war). He was therefore forthwith seized and imprisoned.

To deal with the local discontent, the pensions and allowances so long withheld were immediately paid up, and all discourtesy and harshness were peremptorily stopped. Increased employment was given to the old officials and soldiery; and last, but not least, the wrongs of the chiefs and talookdars were dealt with. They, or their representatives, were met in durbars or at private interviews, at which Sir Henry announced that the terms of the proclamation of February, 1856, should be strictly adhered to; that those at that time in actual possession of estates and property should remain in possession for the three years originally notified; and that all classes, chiefs as well as peasants, should have justice secured to them, and be protected and assured in the enjoyment of their rights. As Sir Henry's character and antecedents were known throughout the province to be in accord with these avowals, an immediate change resulted. The Rajpoot leaders were not only appeased, but all sense of irritation and anxiety seemed to disappear; the country population settled down into contentment and tranquillity; brigandage ceased; and the revenues flowed freely and fully into the district treasuries.

Having thus cleared the ground in respect of local

difficulties and opposition, he began his preparations for dealing with the crisis which he felt to be imminent. He was not yet in military command of the province — Brigadier Handscombe commanded the district, and Brigadier Gray was in special command of the Oude local force — but he procured an improved distribution of the force at Lucknow itself; and having decided in his own mind on the old Sikh * fort of Mutchi Bhown as the best local place of refuge in case of an *émeute*, he directed that it should be quietly cleared out, cleaned, and put in repair; dealing with it, not, however, as a military business, but as part of the customary winter repairs of public buildings. The Mutchi Bhown was a massive but dilapidated structure on a high site, and had long been used merely as a storehouse, being no longer thought suitable for any other purpose. Sir Henry examined the city and suburbs and surrounding country in respect of their resources and capabilities for defence. He instituted inquiries into the defensive positions in other parts of the province. He summoned in the more intelligent officers from the outlying stations for consultation. He inquired keenly into the character and capacity of the officers of all ranks in the province, being, alas! often told in reply, not of their intelligence, energy, resolution, and influence, but of their carefulness and punctuality in office routine. To get this knowledge at first hand as much as possible, he joined in rackets and at other games, exercised wide hospitality, and gave a large

* Gubbins's "Mutinies in Oude."

al fresco entertainment to the 32nd and other British troops. He saw as much as he could of the native nobles and gentry of Lucknow, and also had long and valuable conversations with various native officers. These conversations fully confirmed his impressions of the unpleasant ideas these men had gradually formed, of their dissatisfaction with their position under the British Government, and of the active disloyalty to which they might be roused.

As yet the ill feeling in the troops had been shown only by the isolated mutiny of two regiments in Bengal, and by incendiary fires at Umballa, where there was a large camp of exercise. But nothing else overt had occurred anywhere when, on the 1st and 2nd May, a local regiment, the 7th Oude Infantry, stationed in one of the suburbs of Lucknow, refused to obey their officers in regard to using their cartridges, for reasons set forth in the ensuing chapter. Sir Henry next day surrounded the regiment, paraded and disarmed it, imprisoned, tried, and punished the ringleaders, and at the same time promoted and rewarded those who had behaved with prominent loyalty.

That Sir Henry read correctly the signs of the times there can be no question. His prognostications and views regarding the character, insight, and conduct of the native army; his declared opinions of the state of public feeling; his statements to his friends in ordinary conversation; his actual measures of precaution and anticipation on reaching Lucknow; —all these prove his foresight, and, at any rate, he took practical preliminary steps for defence, which no one else did.

No strong or startling warnings from him to the Governor-General seem to have come to light. But a certain Calcutta set was so entirely in the ascendant as to drown all outside or gratuitous advice. And the well-known information that existed there through the mercantile communications with the upper provinces had been disregarded.

In fact, by no person, except Sir Henry Lawrence, had the certainty been realized, that a crisis of the utmost gravity was impending. Most assuredly, by no one else had any plans been formed, or practical steps taken to prepare for it—not by the Government of India; not by the Commander-in-Chief; not by the Lieutenant-Governors of Bengal, or of the North-western provinces; not even by him whose vigour and courage were shortly to make him the most prominent actor in the coming drama—Sir John Lawrence. For when the storm burst, on the 10th May, he was on the move for his summer residence in the Murree Hills, in the north of the Punjab.

Meanwhile, even on the very days of the outbreak, the country generally seemed to the ordinary public to be fairly tranquil, and people were moving about the districts and travelling to the hill stations and elsewhere freely, and without serious anxiety. The English community was not yet alarmed, so much as vexed and, at the worst, anxious at the unusual feeling that had been evoked, and angry at the blunder, now to be related, that had evoked it. There was no idea prevalent of any grave racial animosity having been aroused, or of any mutiny or revolt against the State being imminent.

In thus dealing with affairs in Oude we have gone in advance of the events elsewhere preceding the outbreak, and to these we must now turn.

CHAPTER VI.

THE GROWTH OF THE ACTIVE DISAFFECTION.

WE have as yet described the *causes* that tended to increase disaffection, and the counteracting elements that tended to repress it; and we have shown the developments that followed on the annexation of Oude. We will now deal with the more immediate circumstances which kindled the train thus laid.

It has been shown that there existed a huge body of malcontents; and that, though the disaffection was generally latent or suppressed, there were always at hand active and enthusiastic agents ready to take advantage of opportunities to rouse ill-feeling and promote sedition.

These agents of discontent found their first important opportunity in the disloyal feeling awakened in the feudatory states, as a consequence of the persistent annexations on the lapse of natural heirs. This chance they immediately seized, both to disseminate sedition in those states, and also to intrigue with the army. They scattered abroad among the chiefs, the native community of the country in general, and the sepoys, the seeds of the belief that the British greed was insatiable, had become barefaced, and must be stopped; that the great native potentates were now being threatened with extermination, and would all rise in revolt; and that the sepoy army was in such preponderating strength that it was master of the situation, and could be counted on to strike in and free the country from the rule of the alien.

The army did not at first respond at all; but the sedition in native communities spread, and especially among the chiefs and in the native states.

Then, in the last year of Lord Dalhousie's rule (1855), the Crimean War was in full progress, and the tales that were current of the losses and privations of the British troops led to the dissemination, by the sedition-mongers, of reports that the British army was being annihilated, and could not be recruited, and that the vaunted British power was a myth.

Further, the great material improvements, especially railways and telegraphs, introduced by Lord Dalhousie, were developing; and, at this stage, instead of their benefits being patent to the native community, they were regarded as mysterious and magical inventions of the British—ideas on to which were soon grafted sinister suspicions of the aims of the English rulers, who meant, it was said, to ride rough-shod over the rights, the castes, and the religions of the country. These last suggestions, however, were not broached till close on the termination of Lord Dalhousie's rule.

In 1856 these seditious rumours were still being

sedulously spread. The Mahomedans were roused by the suppression in Oude of one of their few remaining dynasties. Then the General Service Act was seized on to inflame the Oude Rajpoots (already excited by the violation of the terms of the proclamation) and still more the sepoy army, which now felt the first strain on its loyalty, and began to listen to the whispers of sedition. A further incentive to revolt lay in the promulgation of an alleged prophecy that the British rule was destined to last for one hundred years only, and should end, therefore, in 1857.

With popular feeling at this pitch of uneasiness there occurred, in January, 1857, what is known as the cartridge incident. The musket with which the native troops had been heretofore armed was about to be discarded and replaced by a rifle. This rifle required cartridges of a new kind; and these were accordingly being made up in the Government factories near Calcutta. The utmost care had heretofore been customary in avoiding objectionable ingredients; but in the present case the contractor had managed, without detection by the authorities, to introduce as one of the lubricants, cow's fat, which would have involved contamination to a Hindoo; though perhaps no lard or any other material that would have contaminated Mussulmans had been used.

One day, however, in January a factory workman was having a squabble with a sepoy, and taunted him with the impending loss of all caste throughout the army, as the cartridges they were about to handle contained both hog's lard and cow's fat. As the story was partly correct, and, therefore, could not be *absolutely* denied, it was believed and adopted in full, and circulated swiftly through the army. And thus a chance spark, but a very fiery one, fell upon combustible material, and caught at once.

This incident, then, occurred in January, 1857, and the outbreak of the Mutiny on the 10th May following. Three important matters were going on in this interval of four months: (1) The spread of the mutinous spark and its isolated explosions; (2) the war with Persia; and (3) the subsidence of the disaffection in Oude under Sir Henry Lawrence's influence, which has been already dealt with.

The flame of the spirit of irritation and anxiety in the native soldiery, which consummated in mutiny, naturally began near Calcutta, where the cartridge incident had occurred. A sort of Alsatia had been created there by the followers of the dethroned Nuwab of Oude, and intrigues now became rife. But a very sensible and resolute officer, Major Cavanagh, was the town major of the fort there—Fort William—and by moving some British troops into it, and taking other precautionary measures, he checkmated the local intrigues and kept all quiet in Calcutta itself.

But in the neighbouring military station of Barrackpore intense excitement prevailed; and incendiary fires began forthwith, which prevailed for some time. Of the four native infantry regiments stationed there, one—the 34th—was specially disaffected, and some of its companies, which were sent on detachment to the next station north of it—Berhampore—spread such evil reports there as to excite its garrison, the 19th, into riotous and mutinous conduct, and to tempt the Nuwab of Moorshedabad (the descendant of Meer Jaffier) to revolt. But both these dangers were tided over; and the 19th Native Infantry were sent down to Barrackpore to be disbanded. Before the 19th arrived there, however, the 34th, which had incited them, had itself mutinied; and both these regiments, the 19th and the 34th, were disbanded before the end of April, the 84th Foot having been previously brought over from Burmah to Barrackpore to strengthen the situation.

Meanwhile, the cartridge scare had taken a strong grip of the troops in the far north, especially at Umballa on the borders, where there was a camp of exercise going on and a large body of sepoys had been collected. Incendiary fires blazed out there in March, and though it was close to the headquarters of the army, the Commander-in-Chief seemed unable to realize or tackle the situation.

Then, in Lucknow, in Oude, on the 3rd May, one of the new local regiments, as already narrated, mutinously refused to use the cartridges. Sir Henry Lawrence, however, at once surrounded and disarmed the regiment, and suppressed the military revolt for the time. This was an absolutely isolated case, and the other troops in Lucknow were not implicated in it.

A week later occurred the actual outbreak at Meerut on the 10th May.

Meanwhile—that is, while this ill feeling was growing so seriously and attracting attention everywhere—the Government and the Commander-in-Chief had taken no effective measures whatever to cope with the crisis beyond summoning the 84th from Burmah to Barrackpore; though Major Cavanagh had made Fort William safe by throwing into it a party of the 53rd Foot. Allahabad and Delhi, the two chief fortresses, arsenals, and strategical positions of the North-Western Provinces, were still without the protection of British garrisons; and no steps, such as the collection of supplies and carriage, had been taken anywhere for the prompt movement or mobilization of British troops.

During this period the war with Persia had begun, and been going on, successfully as regards the British army, but with an unquestionable accession of irritation to the Mahomedans of Northern India. With this feeling, and the spread of the cartridge agitation, their intrigues became more and more virulent, and culminated in the Meerut and Delhi outbreaks of the 10th and 11th May.

Of those outbreaks the incidents are so well known that they hardly need to be given here. Some cavalry troopers at Meerut, forty miles from Delhi, had been imprisoned for insubordination. On the 10th May their comrades, roused by the taunts of the bazar, riotously broke into the jail, liberated the prisoners, and being then joined by the rest of the sepoys, went off in a body for Delhi. The ruffians of the bazar rose at the same time, and murder and violence ensued. But General Hewett, who commanded, was—like all the generals of those days—an aged man, much beyond the limit now laid down for superannuation ; and the British garrison of Meerut remained passive throughout, neither attacking nor pursuing the mutineers, who, next day, reached Delhi, and were welcomed by the sepoys there and by the city population. Then the palace of the puppet emperor was forcibly entered, and *the restoration of the Moghul rule was proclaimed.*

The secret correspondence by which the conspiracy was fostered was ascertained to have been at first mainly Mahomedan, very cautiously worded, and written in cipher. Later, when it spread amongst the sepoys, it was more diffuse, and easier of detection, being in ordinary language, with the allusions crudely veiled. The inference to be drawn from the general course of events, and especially from the Delhi proclamation, is thereby corroborated ; namely, that the lead in the rebellion lay with the Moghul faction, and that the cartridge incident was used by them that they might make a catspaw of the sepoy army.

BOOK II.

THE DEVELOPMENT OF THE REVOLT.

BOOK II.

THE DEVELOPMENT OF THE REVOLT.

CHAPTER I.

THE SITUATION DEVELOPED BY THE OUTBREAK.

THUS far we have traced the origin of the rising and the Mutiny. First of all a chronic state of disaffection, generally latent, but roused into life by the irritation produced by the policy latterly in force respecting the adoption question; then the Mahomedans, always looking forward to the recovery of their rule, further excited by the knowledge of the ill feeling thus brought about in the native states, and afterwards again exasperated by the suppression of the Mahomedan dynasty of Oude and the war with Persia; then the ill feeling roused among the talookdars of Oude; the sedition awakened by all these causes being coloured by allegations of sinister designs on the part of the British against the native religions; attempts to tamper with the native army, hitherto futile, gradually becoming easier with its preponderating growth; lax discipline, facilitated by the General Service Enlistment Act, and made successful through the cartridge incident; and finally, the combined move of mutiny at Meerut and Delhi, and the proclamation of the restoration of the Moghul Empire. On the other hand, the entire absence, except in Oude, of any effort to take measures to avert or meet the impending crisis.

Doubtless, it would be unreasonable to blame the Government for failure to foresee that Delhi would be the site for the unfurling of the flag of rebellion, and to take special precautions against that particular movement. But Delhi was unquestionably one, if not the chief, of the three or four most important political and strategical centres in Upper India—in the heart of the area of active disaffection—as shown by its ebullitions. And it seems impossible to excuse the inaction implied in failing to occupy it and the other centres and strongholds with British troops, and to arrange for transport and mobilization in their neighbourhood.

We have now to deal with the development of the rising, much of which, indeed, will throw a clear light on the origin.

The first broad and important fact after the actual outbreak is that, except in the smaller military stations in close vicinity to Meerut and Delhi, no further mutinies occurred for three weeks; that is, until the end of May. The next is that no native states or their princes at once declared against the English. The third is that there was forthwith a cessation of the *Pax Britannica*, and an entire disorganization of the civil administration in the upper provinces, *i.e.* the plains watered by the Ganges and the Jumna, down to Bengal proper; the criminal classes and the predatory tribes there at once showing their teeth, and making life and property unsafe. The fourth is that by the end of June the Mutiny developed fully into insurrection, and sporadic conflicts merged into actual warfare.

This halt of three weeks in the spread of the Mutiny proved that the Meerut outbreak was not, especially in respect of the army, a specific and prearranged part of any programme or matured plan; and that if it had been suggested in connection with any larger scheme, it had been precipitated by some undue cause, and the scheme itself disconcerted and more or less upset. No one came forward to guide the revolt, or even to assume the lead at Delhi.

The army, in fact, was not yet prepared for the rising. Its chiefs had not settled their plans, however busy they may have been in arranging them. With the Moghul party, on the other hand, the selection of Delhi as the seat and centre of the rebellion was obviously a fundamental point to be ensured, regardless of any other considerations; and this had doubtless been pressed on all parties as the first step to be taken in the revolt. It certainly was not taken haphazard or on the spur of the moment; it had probably been agreed on universally, and, except for the precipitation, was a masterly move. The strength and political importance of Delhi made its seizure a challenge which forced the hand of the English, and fixed the vital struggle at the site where the only large body of English troops in India could be most easily dealt with. Here they would be hemmed in and cut off from their resources, and ought soon to disappear, from sheer absence of means for replacing the losses which would befall them in fighting and from other causes. The insurgents, on the other hand, might easily count on an ever-increasing accession of numbers, and the eventual concentration of a gigantic army.

On the other hand, the steps taken at Delhi, in placing the old emperor on the throne and proclaiming the restoration of the Moghul rule, point to the precipitancy and aggressiveness of the Moghul element; and this was, in fact, so obvious and glaring that it was at once recognized by the other native races; or rather, the eyes of their princes were opened to the actual circumstances of the case, which checked forthwith and altogether their recent tendency to act in concert against the British.

The disorganization of the civil rule of those provinces was natural and inevitable. The native officials, and especially the subordinates and the police, were more or less infected with the local sedition; the predatory tribes were glad to seize an opportunity for disorder; and the ordinary population had not yet thrown off their old feelings towards their natural leaders, who were, one and all, disaffected under the grievance of the land policy, at that time in the ascendant there without check.

At the same time, the fact that the rising should

not spread at once and rapidly was singular, in the face of the weakness of character, of conduct, and of military strength, evinced by the British in their immediate dealing with the Meerut outbreak itself; even though a bright contrast to the action there had been shown at Delhi in the heroism of Lieutenant Willoughby and his staff in defending and eventually blowing up the great arsenal and magazine.

Before proceeding to further events and proceedings, the actual position in certain important points may be first described.

As to the high and responsible authorities: In Calcutta, the capital of India and of Bengal, was Lord Canning, the Governor-General, with his Council; there, too, was the Lieutenant-Governor of Bengal, Mr. Halliday, whose rule extended northwards up to near Benares; in the North-Western Provinces, the seat of the outbreak, Mr. Colvin was the Lieutenant-Governor, at his capital, Agra; in Oude, Sir Henry Lawrence was the Chief Commissioner, at Lucknow; in the Punjab the reins of government were held by Sir John Lawrence, but he was not, on the outbreak, at his capital, Lahore, the chief authority there being, at the time, held by Mr. Montgomery; Scinde, on the Bombay frontier of the Punjab, was ruled by Bartle Frere; Lord Elphinstone was the Governor of Bombay; and Lord Harris of Madras; the Commander-in-Chief, Sir G. Anson, Gomm's successor, was at Simla, on the hills overhanging Umballa.

Next, as to the different classes of men of whom

the troops were composed, and the characteristics of the races of the several provinces—on the variety and peculiarities of which largely depended the tendency for the Mutiny to spread, and the consequent anxieties of the Government :—

Throughout the Bengal Presidency, exclusive of the Punjab, the native army consisted chiefly of Hindostanees—either Brahmins, Rajpoots, or Mahomedans. Two or three regiments of Sikhs were mixed up with them in the plains, and some regiments of Ghoorkas were stationed on the Himalayas on the border. In the Punjab, in addition, there were several regiments, comparatively recently raised, of Puthans, Sikhs, and Punjabee Mussulmans, who, like the Ghoorkas, had no sympathies with the Hindostanees. Nor had the people of the province any such sympathies; on the contrary, they had a strong dislike to them. For while the British, recognizing and admiring their gallantry, had become on friendly terms with them, the Hindostanee sepoys had never ceased to irritate them by their swaggering demeanour and arrogant lording as over a conquered race. The Madras troops, the local troops in Scinde, and a large part of the Bombay troops, were composed of local races naturally antagonistic to the Hindostanees, as also were many local regiments in Rajpootana and Central India. But a considerable proportion of the men in Bombay were Hindostanees, who, however, were out of touch with their Bengal brethren, and were kept under much stricter military discipline.

Finally, the military position :—

As to external attacks, it was to a small degree necessary to watch the Nepaul frontier. We had no troops there. But the Nepaulese, though steady in defence, were not powerful for aggression, and Jung Bahadur was believed to be true to impressions created by his visit to England.

The Afghan frontier was a matter of serious moment. The most powerful body of British troops lay there, but they were now needed for the internal defence of the country; and well, therefore, was it that Lord Dalhousie had entered into a treaty of alliance and friendship with Dost Mahomed, the great Ameer of Cabul, our notable enemy in the old Afghan War, and that the Dost now showed his intention to abide by that alliance, which, while it lasted, would keep our frontier secure. The treaty had been entered upon in March, 1855, at the suggestion of Herbert Edwardes, and in opposition to the views of Sir John Lawrence; and had been ratified at a personal conference between Sir John and the Dost, in January, 1857.

As to internal arrangements, no precautionary measures had been taken, either to have the troops ready to move in case of a rising, or to improve their location. The great forts of Allahabad and Delhi were still unprotected by British soldiers. One additional regiment, the 84th, had been brought up from Burmah in connection with the suppression of the mutinies of the 19th and 34th Native Infantry. There were British troops in the forts at Calcutta and Agra; two other British regiments were at Dinapore and Lucknow; and there was a comparatively strong British army in the Punjab and on its borders.

CHAPTER II.

MEASURES TO RESTRICT THE AREA OF THE REVOLT.

EXCEPT the few incidents already described, nothing overt was done by the disaffected or the mutineers for three weeks after the Meerut outbreak, except in the Punjab; and there their action was, as will be seen, not so much aggressive as in defensive opposition to the vigorous measures of the Punjab authorities.

But after the three weeks the mutinies spread rapidly, and this halt naturally divides the narrative of the development at the first week in June.

Let us describe first what, under these circumstances, was done to limit and curtail the area of the rising.

On hearing of the outbreak, the Calcutta authorities acted vigorously. They summoned troops from Burmah and Madras, and forwarded all whom they could spare to Benares and Allahabad. They sent for assistance to Ceylon and the Mauritius. They hurried back the army which had been employed in the Persian war, and also took steps to stop and direct to India the expeditionary force which had already started for China. Aid and reinforcements from England were, of course, urgently applied for, and General Anson, the Commander-in-Chief, was pressed to operate at once against the enemy at Delhi. At the same time the commanding guidance, which would have come into force under Lord Dalhousie, was wholly wanting. Not merely was every local chief left entirely to his own devices, or want of device, but no specific orders were given on matters of imperial necessity, such as the security of Dinapore, Allahabad, Cawnpore, or Agra.

Except about Calcutta itself, Dinapore was the only station in the lower provinces (*i.e.* south of Benares) where there was a British regiment, the 10th Foot; and this was not employed to disarm the native troops, though there was a large and fanatical population in the adjacent city of Patna. From this inaction, as will be seen, serious and prolonged evil resulted.

The Madras Government took immediate action, at once sending off the Madras Fusiliers to Calcutta, and keeping a vigilant watch over their own districts, with the result that no rising or mutiny occurred in them.

Similarly, the Bombay Government took prompt steps to suppress any rising, or any concert with the mutineers and the disaffected of Upper India; and on the return of the troops of the Persian Expeditionary force, which began in May, they sent them on at once, beginning with the 64th Foot, to Calcutta, organizing arrangements also for the despatch of a column of British and other troops northwards to the Nerbudda.

In Scinde, where the Beloochee tribes which formed the population had no sympathy with the people of the upper provinces of Hindostan, Bartle Frere at once despatched a British regiment towards Mooltan in the Punjab to strengthen Sir John Lawrence's position.

In the middle of India, south of the Nerbudda, the country remained comparatively quiet. North of it, however, and between it and the Jumna, where there were no British troops at all, but numerous native states and large numbers of native troops, more or less of kin to the Hindostanee sepoys and in touch with them, the contagion of disaffection caught hold at once; and was fostered by the population, which consisted of Bondeelas and other predatory tribes analogous to the Goojurs and others of the upper provinces which had already thrown off the restraints of civil rule. Colonel Durand kept many of the native rulers true to the Government, but they were powerless to aid him, and he had no means ready at hand anywhere to coerce the rebels.

In Rajpootana, on the west of the Jumna, Sir George Lawrence, who had there succeeded his brother Sir Henry, on the one hand influenced the great Rajpoot princes to remain passive, disaffected though they had been on the Adoption Question; and, on the other, with a view to checkmating the Hindostanee regiments that mainly garrisoned the province, he seized the chief position of Ajmere with its arsenal; throwing into it the Mhairwarra battalion, a regiment raised from the local aboriginal tribes, who had no religious or racial sympathies with the sepoys. He thus averted all serious rising in Rajpootana, and, it may be at once said, never ceased to exercise the control and administration of the province.

These remarks indicate in what manner the tendency to outbreak, both military and civil, was checked and confined to the upper provinces, within a circle stretching from lower Bengal, round by Madras, the states south of the Nerbudda, and Bombay, up to Scinde, on the southern confines of the Punjab.

We have now to show the steps taken in direct contact with the actual rising, in the North-Western Provinces and Bengal, in Oude, in the Punjab, and by the Commander-in-Chief.

In the North-Western Provinces, exclusive of Delhi, already held by the rebels, there were two most important fortified strategical positions, Allahabad and Agra. They were, both of them, large arsenals. The former was a fortress of the European type; the latter of the native type. At Agra a British regiment was stationed, and the Lieutenant-Governor of the province, Mr. John Colvin, used it to disarm the native regiments of the garrison; so that practically he made Agra secure against any force that might venture to attack it. This was not done, however, till the 31st May, when the spread of the Mutiny began. Allahabad, on the other hand, a much more important position, situated at the junction of the Ganges and the Jumna, was entirely devoid of British troops, though there was a regiment of Sikhs (Brasyer's) in the fort itself. Yet no steps whatever were taken, either before the outbreak or during the lull that followed it, to secure or even strengthen our hold on that position, though Sir James Outram had brought the danger there very strongly to notice as early as 1856.

Here may be suitably noted the assistance sent direct to these upper provinces from Calcutta itself. From the first Lord Canning made the most strenuous exertions to forward troops to help and protect those provinces. The most immediate and urgent military need was to prevent Allahabad from falling into the power of any hostile party, and to secure it instead as the basis and key of our own operations up-country. This was a specific step of incalculable importance to the whole conduct of the war; and it was really the primary and immediate objective of the British advance from Calcutta; to be effected, if possible, before any general spread should begin of the Mutiny, which was as yet confined to the Delhi districts. Yet positive orders to carry out this step—the securing of the Allahabad fort by occupying it with British troops—do not seem to have ever been given. Probably the necessity for the measure was thought to be self-evident. However, as soon as the Government heard of the Meerut rising, they immediately began to send up-country whatever troops they had to spare, and to follow them up with others as fast as they arrived. At first these troops were forwarded only by the road route (which was the quickest), being conveyed either in horsed vehicles or by the Government bullock-train—an organized train of waggons drawn by relays of bullocks, which were picketed at regular stages all along the trunk road. Afterwards they were also despatched on steamers by the river route. Those sent on at first were in detachments. The 84th led the way; then came the Madras Fusiliers, on their arrival from Madras; and after them the 64th and 78th, on their rejoining from the Persian expeditionary force. A detachment of 150 men of the 10th was also sent forward from Dinapore to Benares.

For three precious weeks the native army in these lower provinces, as well as elsewhere, delayed in following the example set at Meerut and Delhi; and during these three weeks there was a constant but thin stream of these detachments of British troops flowing northwards from Calcutta without let or hindrance. As they reached Benares they were sent on to Allahabad; as they reached Allahabad they were not retained there, but were sent on to Cawnpore; and even the party of the 84th that reached Cawnpore was sent on by General Wheeler to Lucknow. So long as the sepoys refrained from breaking out, so long did the local authorities shut their eyes to the need of securing the fortress of Allahabad; the dominant influence being, apparently, a chivalrous desire to aid those who seemed to be in the greatest need. Hence, at the end of May, when the Mutiny began to spread, Allahabad was still held by only native troops.

Between Allahabad and Agra was Cawnpore, of which the strategical importance lay in its being at the site of the passage of the Ganges, on the way to Lucknow, the capital of Oude. Besides a large brigade of native troops, its garrison contained only a small detachment of the British regiment, the 32nd, which was stationed at Lucknow. The only defensible post in it was the old Magazine on the river. This Sir Hugh Wheeler, who commanded there, had been exhorted to fortify and hold, and to secure the boats there under its command; but he objected on the ground that the native garrison would lie between it and Allahabad, and be able to intercept and attack any British troops coming up thence to their assistance. The Ganges also was said at first to be very low; and Sir Hugh was afraid that the supply of water at the Magazine would be insufficient. Also he refused, in his heart, to believe that the native troops would really, as a body, rise against the Government, whatever the misconduct of the men who had come under the influence of Delhi. So during May he took no precautions beyond selecting one of the barracks and putting a few days' supplies into it, as a place of refuge for the families in case of any temporary *émeute* or trouble.

At the same time there are good reasons for assuming that the letters he had received from Calcutta had led him to expect that there would soon be a daily flow of British troops, if only in driblets, from Calcutta to Cawnpore; that on the arrival of the first 50 men he was confirmed in this impression; and so, thinking that others would follow immediately, he sent on those 50 at once to Lucknow. He is said to have expected 200 more men in a few days, and had planned that in a week or so he would be able to send off his families, with a sufficient escort of the new arrivals, over to Allahabad. But those other troops, which he had so expected, never arrived, and he fell between two stools—disappointed of reinforcement on the one hand, and without any secure position on the other.

CHAPTER III.

PREPARATIONS IN OUDE.

WHEN we turn to Oude and Lucknow, a perfectly different spirit is found to be guiding the conduct of affairs. It has been already shown that Sir Henry Lawrence had apprehended the approach of a crisis, had begun to prepare the Mutchi Bhown for a place of refuge some time before the outbreak, and had disarmed a mutinous regiment. On the 13th and 14th May, he received fairly correct intelligence of the outbreak at Meerut and Delhi, and of the immediate cessation of the *Pax Britannica* all over the upper provinces.

So he proceeded to place trusted troops and guns in the Mutchi Bhown, and to divide his English force between the cantonments of Lucknow—known as Murriaon, where the sepoys were mostly stationed—and the Residency position, where he directed the English families to assemble, and which he proceeded to fortify. The early morning of May 17th accordingly saw Sir Henry holding these three positions—the basis of the plans which he had already formed, and was now about to carry out, for defence against any contingency that might arise. What that contingency might be it was impossible to say, but he certainly dreaded the worst; for, although, except round the immediate centre at Delhi, there was no sign of the Mutiny itself spreading, nor of the rising being joined by any of the native states or chiefs, or by any other classes except the predatory castes of the north-west, he knew it was unchecked and had full scope to sweep onwards and rage as it might list, as neither the Government nor the military authorities had taken a single step to meet it.

Nothing is more remarkable than the singular exactitude with which Sir Henry had forecast the Delhi catastrophe in his article written in 1843, which has been already alluded to. After commenting on the habitual carelessness of the Government, and its disregard of ordinary military precautions and preparedness, he had shown how possible it consequently was that a hostile party might seize Delhi, and, if it was not speedily dealt with, what grave consequences might ensue. "Let this happen," he said, on June 2nd, "and does any sane man doubt that twenty-four hours would swell the hundreds of rebels into thousands, and in a week every ploughshare in the Delhi states would be turned into a sword? And when a sufficient force had been mustered, which would not be effected within a month, should we not then have a more difficult game to play than Clive had at Plassey, or Wellington at Assaye? We should then be literally striking for our existence at the most inclement season of the year, with the prestige of our name tarnished." Going on then to suggest that Meerut and Umballa and Agra might say that they had no troops to spare from their own necessities, or that they had no carriage, "should we not then," he said, "have to strike anew for our Indian Empire?"

With such convictions and forebodings working on his mind for fourteen years, and latterly confirmed and intensified by what he saw of the growing disaffection, of the increasing imprudence of Government, and of its haughty disregard of precautions, it can be readily imagined what his view of the position was when he heard of the catastrophe at Delhi. He knew that the British troops could not move against it for some weeks; that all that the Government could now do was to summon and collect such forces as they could manage to spare from elsewhere, and send them on eventually up-country from Calcutta; and that the whole of the north-west was in a state of anarchy. But he trusted that his old friends—"his children"—of the Punjab would remain loyal, although he was not without misgivings as to the possible effects of the harder rule of his brother John. He hoped also that the Rajpootana states would keep quiet under the guidance of his brother George. But it is doubtful whether he realized until after another month how the self-assertion of the Moghul party, and the proclamation of the restoration of the Delhi empire, had disconcerted the leaders of the Mutiny and of other disaffected communities, and had upset their plans and unity of action, especially choking off the Mahratta and Rajpoot states from participation in the rising.

Now, however, the time had come to take definite action ; but what that action should be was not at all so simple a matter to decide in regard to Lucknow as it was in regard to Delhi. Should Sir Henry hold on to Lucknow and Oude, or were there some other positions to which the families might be removed, and on which the British and loyal troops should concentrate? One thing is certain; he never received any orders or suggestions as to the step he should take. And, left to himself, he decided on Lucknow. He doubtless held that neither Cawnpore nor any other place that was at all accessible would be more secure for the families, as the only defensible position at Cawnpore—the Magazine—was, he knew, being deliberately set aside; while any attempt to move the British regiment from Lucknow would certainly be the signal for the revolt of the city, and of the sepoy troops in the province and at Cawnpore; so that concentration there, with the Ganges intervening, would have been impracticable. He unquestionably regarded it as an imperative necessity to avoid doing anything that could be construed as losing heart or yielding to the crisis, or as at variance with that bold and resolute attitude and that assertion of British supremacy which were indispensable to our success in coping with the danger. The British colours must never be hauled down ; they must be nailed to the mast.

And so he resolved to hold on to the Residency at Lucknow, and to defend it to the last, supported in his hope of success by the knowledge that he had already minimized, if not removed, the disaffection of the upper classes, and of the talookdars and Rajpoot country population.

Now, the city of Lucknow is more than five miles long and two broad, and the River Goomtee runs eastward through its length. The Residency position, which he resolved to hold *permanently*, consisted of the grounds of the Residency, *i.e.* Resident's palace, with various other houses and offices attached to it, or in its immediate neighbourhood. It lay on the south bank of the river, near the Iron Bridge, and was only a tiny spot of some thirty-four acres in the midst of the large city. Besides the prestige attaching to it, it possessed important advantages for purposes of defence. It was a healthy site, well supplied with water, and with means of shelter and accommodation, and stood high, commanding the river and the ground adjacent to it, and being nowhere itself commanded by sites on which artillery batteries could be erected.

With this position chosen for the site of the entrenchments for the eventual defence against any attack in force, he selected also two other sites for *temporary* use during the construction of the entrenchment. One was the old small Sikh fort, called the Mutchi Bhown, about three-quarters of a mile higher up the river, which he had already been clearing out to serve as a place of refuge, and which lay beside the Stone Bridge, as it was called. So that Sir Henry thus secured the command of both the bridges which spanned the Goomtee. And the third position which he occupied was the south, or city, end of the cantonments of Murriaon, the military station two miles off on the north, where he could watch the native troops, and prevent any concert or joint action on their part with the city, one of the largest and most turbulent in India. It would also serve to keep the country open, and get in supplies.

Sir Henry's action, then, on hearing of the Meerut outbreak, was to hold on to Lucknow and prepare the Residency position in it for defence against a powerful force equipped with artillery, occupying also two other posts *temporarily*—(1) the Mutchi Bhown, which was to serve as a place of refuge if needed, and to dominate the city and keep it quiet while the Residency entrenchments were being constructed, but not to be itself prepared for a siege; and (2) the city end of the cantonments; whence he could watch and deal with the native troops, cutting them off from the city itself, and also keeping open the country roads so as to get in supplies, until an attack in force should become imminent.

He had a quarter of a million sterling stored in the Residency, and he knew well what a magnet that treasure would be to any hostile troops. He felt sure that as the Mutiny spread a very large body of the enemy would elect to operate against Lucknow, but he trusted to be able to fortify and prepare the Residency position to meet their attack successfully. The risk was very great that he might not have time enough. The most strenuous efforts were necessary, and, above all, a resolute front; and if, by God's help, he succeeded, a powerful enemy might be detained there, who would otherwise be helping to swell the force against us in the vital struggle at Delhi—an all-important feature in the strategical possibilities of the situation.

The step that was most immediately urgent in part of the measures that had been resolved on was the strengthening of the Mutchi Bhown, so as to make it secure as a place of refuge, impregnable against an ordinary *émeute*, and sufficiently armed to dominate the city and over-awe the ill-disposed. This work was effected in six days. On the 23rd May the Mutchi Bhown was held by a company of the 32nd Foot, and six companies of Sikhs and selected native troops, and was armed with 15 heavy guns and mortars, 14 field-guns, and an array of some 200 native wall-pieces along the upper parapets.

So Sir Henry breathed more freely, and, feeling secure against the city, proceeded vigorously with the Residency entrenchments and the collection of supplies.

A week later, the bulk of the sepoys in the cantonments rose in mutiny, and were thereupon driven off and pursued into the country. But the 13th Native Infantry, a regiment of Sikh cavalry, the native artillery, and some men of the other sepoy regiments, did not join in the rising, and were retained in the garrison.

One important feature of Sir Henry's policy was that it was essential to keep with us a certain proportion of native troops. These, of course, must be selected men; and, in order to be sure of retaining the best, he abstained, purposely and resolutely, in spite of much opposition, from disarming or coercing any troops that had not mutinied; for this would have alienated the friendly sepoys, and driven them into the ranks of the enemy; and he further summoned in from the districts two bodies of pensioners, one of infantry and one of artillery, who remained faithful, and did good service. The numbers, however, both of sepoys and of pensioners, was deliberately and carefully restricted; otherwise the native garrison would have been much larger.

Another of his measures was to send over assistance to Wheeler at Cawnpore, and to detach troops along the various roads so as to keep the country open. The party to Cawnpore consisted of a company of the 32nd, two guns under Lieutenant Ashe, and Gall's cavalry.

Such, then, was the action taken in Oude in the first three weeks after the Meerut outbreak, and, admirably as he was assisted by some of his Staff, the whole initiation, guidance, and pressing on of the operations rested with Sir Henry Lawrence.

By the end of May he had secured the control of the city, turned the Mutchi Bhown into a sure place of refuge, defeated and driven off the local mutineers, retained the support of a valuable body of native troops, and was preparing vigorously for defence against an army by constructing the Residency entrenchments and laying in supplies.

CHAPTER IV.

PREPARATIONS IN THE PUNJAB AND OF GENERAL ANSON.

IN the Punjab, to which we now turn, equal vigour was shown, but the circumstances were much more favourable. There were ten British infantry regiments in the province, besides some cavalry and a powerful body of artillery. There was a large local and frontier force, headed by that splendid corps, the Guides. The population was made up of Sikhs, Punjabees, and Mooltanee Mussulmans, Puthans, Dogras, and the like, who had no sympathies with the Hindostanee sepoys or the Delhi Moghuls. The sepoy army in the Punjab was certainly large, but not at all in the preponderating strength that it was elsewhere; and, lastly, there was a body of officers, both civil and military, in high places throughout the province, exceptionally fitted to cope with this crisis; having been selected, on the annexation, and found efficient, to rule such a race as the Sikhs, and to deal with the wild tribes of the frontier.

The matters at first needing immediate attention were—

1. The guidance of the chiefs between the Sutlej and Delhi.

2. The security of Lahore and Umritsir, the capitals, and of Ferozepore and Phillour, the arsenals of the province.

3. The security of the Peshawur frontier.

The chiefs between the Sutlej and the Delhi were the Rajahs of Puttiala, Jheend, and Nabha, and the Nuwab of Kurnaul; who, through the judicious action of Mr. Barnes and Mr. Forsyth, the officers specially in touch with them, were all led to cast in their lot heartily with the British, to mobilize their troops and followers, and with them to command and keep open the road towards Delhi.

At Lahore there was a British regiment, the 81st. The officer in command was General Corbett, and the chief civil officer was Mr. Montgomery. On hearing of the crisis, on the 12th May, Mr. Montgomery at once summoned the leading officers to council, among them being Major J. D. Macpherson, the military secretary, and Captain Richard Lawrence, the head of the police—the fourth of the Lawrence brothers then in India. The latter, with Macpherson's energetic support, suggested that the sepoys should be disarmed; and this proposal, with the alternative of only securing the ammunition, was laid by Mr. Montgomery and Major Macpherson before the General at Meeanmeer. By the evening, General Corbett, under the force of Macpherson's arguments, decided on disarming—going the whole hog, as he called it. Complete arrangements having been made during the night, the sepoys in the military station, Meeanmeer, were disarmed next morning, as also those in the Fort of Lahore; and, further, a detachment of the 81st, which had been sent forward to Umritsir, arrived there during the day, and entered and secured its Fort of Govindgurh. These vigorous measures started the tone of action for the Punjab, though John Lawrence disapproved the disarmament.

At Ferozepore, Brigadier Innes heard of the Delhi outbreak on the 12th, and also that the sepoys had received news of it, and meant to seize the arsenal. He had three native regiments and one English, the 61st. He placed half the 61st in the arsenal and fort, to secure it—a matter of vital importance, imperial rather than local—and ordered a parade at which he meant to disarm the sepoys. In marching towards the parade, one of the native regiments broke off in mutiny, and made for the arsenal; but they found themselves forestalled, were attacked, and driven off and dispersed. The other native infantry regiment did not mutiny, but was disarmed, and thus was the all-important Ferozepore arsenal saved and secured at the same time as Lahore, by the brigadier's action.

At Phillour, the arsenal on the Sutlej, lay the 3rd Native Infantry, and twenty-four miles off was Jullundur, where a British regiment, the 8th, formed part of the garrison. General Anson had at once sent off an express to despatch some of the 8th to Phillour. This was effected, and the arsenal secured before the morning of the 13th; but the artillery officer in charge, Lieutenant Griffiths, had already, during the previous day and night, been taking steps and organizing arrangements to repel an attack and facilitate the defence.

Thus all these first measures, prompt, vigorous, and effectual, had been initiated and carried out by the local authorities, except at Phillour, where they were due to the action of the Commander-in-Chief; and, as will presently be seen, the same was the case on the Peshawur frontier. Sir John Lawrence, the ruler of the province, was at Rawal Pindi, on his way to his summer residence, and was wholly taken by surprise at the news of the outbreak, so that for some few days he took no initial steps of his own.

At and about Peshawur was a group of men of exceptional vigour and capacity—Herbert Edwardes, John Nicholson, Neville Chamberlain, and Sydney Cotton, the brigadier. Edwardes, who took the initiative, was the chief civil and political officer on that frontier, with Nicholson as his assistant; Chamberlain commanded the frontier force; Cotton commanded the garrison of Peshawur.

The Delhi news arrived on the 12th, and Edwardes immediately held a council of the principal officers. The native force was large and scattered, and consisted of very diverse elements. For this reason, probably, the question of disarming was not even mooted for another fortnight, but one strongly suspected regiment—the 64th—was sent out into the district at the foot of the Afghan hills, and three specific proposals were formulated and sent on to Sir John Lawrence at

Rawal Pindi: (1) to form a movable column to secure the important positions, support the loyal, and deal with all local mutinies; (2) to raise local levies of Mooltanees, Derajat men, and others held to be well affected; and (3) to have General Reed, the senior officer in the Punjab, appointed to the supreme command in it. By this last step unity of action was likely to be ensured on a satisfactory basis, as General Reed was in accord with the members of the Peshawur Council. Edwardes also felt that the great measure which he had initiated with Lord Dalhousie, and had carried out—the treaty with the Ameer Dost Mahomed—was bearing good fruit, and the frontier tribes were giving no trouble. He hoped that this would continue, with the influence of the two Lumsdens, the British agents to the Ameer; and even that, perchance, those very frontier tribes might give valuable recruits to the new levies which he was bent on raising.

John Lawrence replied on the 14th May. He was aghast at the outbreak, and could not understand it. He referred about General Reed to the Commander-in-Chief, and quickly received his assent. He agreed to the formation of the movable column, with Neville Chamberlain to command; but he would not accede to the raising of the levies, as the emergency did not seem to him sufficient to warrant it.

The Guide Corps, being under Chamberlain's orders, was at once utilized in advance of sanction for the formation of the movable column. It seized Nowshera on the night of the 13th, the Fort of Attock on the 14th, and reached Rawul Pindee on the 16th May. Meanwhile, the sepoys were moved about, so as to diminish their collection in force, and two of the regiments having mutinied at Nowshera and Hotee Murdan respectively, the sepoys at Peshawur were disarmed on the 22nd May; all except the 21st Native Infantry, which, from the perfect confidence placed in it, was exempted from the humiliation.

By this time—that is, by ten days after the outbreak—the movable column had already been formed and started, and levies were beginning to be raised from the frontier and other tribes, John Lawrence having at length given his consent. The regiments that had mutinied were pursued and destroyed, partly by these troops and levies, and partly by the border tribes.

Meanwhile, two other points of importance had been secured by the action of the local officers—the Fort of Mooltan by Colonel Crawford Chamberlain's judicious use of the 1st Irregular Cavalry, and the Fort of Kangra by throwing into it the Shere Dil Regiment of military police.

Thus did the Punjab meet the crisis up to the date when the mutinies began to spread. Still, some mishaps occurred; one was the failure at Jullundur to check and defeat the mutineers there, who were permitted to move off to Loodianah and thence to Delhi, unimpeded save by the efforts of the police and of detachments of Sikh regiments. Another was that as the comparatively unimportant districts lying between the Punjab and the deserts on the south—Hansi, Hissar, and Sirsa—remained unguarded, the troops there rose in mutiny, and the English officers and families were killed either by them or by the local predatory tribes.

By the end of May Sir John Lawrence, fully alive to the emergency, was furthering the vigorous measures already taken, and was concentrating all his energy and daring on the steps needed for the recovery of Delhi ; in all of which one man, but rarely mentioned—Major J. D. Macpherson, his military secretary—was not only the practical worker, but also largely took the initiative, ceaselessly pressing the needful measures on Sir John.

It remains to describe the measures of General Anson, the Commander-in-Chief, and his Staff. His immediate steps were: (1) to send off expresses to secure the arsenals at Ferozepore and Phillour, which was successfully accomplished; (2) to order down the British regiments in the neighbouring hills to Umballa, and move some on to Kurnaul, halfway to Delhi, as soon as carriage for the tents and food was procurable (they began to reach Kurnaul on the 19th May); and (3) to send down the Sirmoor battalion of Ghoorkas, and the Sappers from Roorkee, to Meerut, to increase the force there, so as to enable a brigade from it to take the field in good strength. Unfortunately, on the Sappers reaching Meerut, a *contretemps* occurred which caused a panic and a mutiny in that regiment.

Still, with all these efforts there was grave delay in getting forward any large body of men; this, however, was due in no degree at all to supineness or want of energy in the Commander-in-Chief, but wholly to the scandalous system for carriage, supplies, and storage of equipment, devised for times of peace, with which the army authorities had been hampered by the Government on the ground of economy, and which he had been powerless to oppose or remedy. The army had to employ contractors for everything, and under the circumstances, contractors were for the time almost worthless.

But the civil officers were under no such restraint. Their subordinates had full power to invade the villages and impress carriage and supplies freely; and the obvious logical position was that, with this power, the duty also and the responsibility lay with them of procuring the carriage and food needed, and assigning them to the proper army departments for distribution to the troops. Nor did the civil officers fail. They worked grandly. But from the absolute suddenness of the outbreak and the want of all preparation, delay at the start was inevitable. For that delay the fashion was to lay blame on General Anson and the army departments, the most prominent supporter of this charge being Sir John Lawrence; who, besides ignoring the system in force and its practical bearing, seemed to assume, from some legends of the exploits of British troops of old, that they could march and fight in the summer heats without tents, supplies, or ammunition, and could storm fortifications without breaching them.

Such blame as can attach to General Anson in this matter does not lie in any inaction after the outbreak, but in his not earlier—say in April—realizing the gravity of the coming storm, and insisting on the needful precautionary measures for the improved distribution of the troops, the provision of carriage, and similar preparations. But in this failure to foresee the crisis, he erred in common with perhaps every man of high position in India, except Sir Henry Lawrence.

As it was, by the 25th May he had collected at Umballa, and started the advance of, the force that was to attack Delhi. He had also sent orders, through Lieutenant Hodson, to Meerut, for a brigade to march thence to join his own force on the way to Delhi; and having preceded the Umballa troops, he had reached Kurnaul, only to be at once attacked by cholera, and succumb to the attack.

He was succeeded by General Barnard, who, on taking over the command, awaited the arrival or approach of the troops from Umballa and from Meerut.

The Meerut brigade, in accordance with General Anson's orders, marched out on the direct road to Delhi, and having there occupied the site at Ghazee-ood-deen Nuggur, which commanded the passage of the Hindun, found itself challenged by the Delhi mutineers. Thence ensued the first combat of the war, on the 31st May, as will be described later on.

And now, on the 30th and 31st May, and the succeeding days in June, the general spread of the

Mutiny began. The only mutiny that had broken out earlier, except in the Delhi neighbourhood, had been at Nusseerabad, on the remote confines of Rajpootana, where the 15th and 30th Native Infantry facing the Bombay Cavalry that affected to charge them, shot down the officers who led the charge. These two regiments held a unique position throughout the war. They remained together as a distinct brigade, retained their discipline under their native officers, and behaved and fought to the end as if commanded by British officers.

Hence, in the three weeks' lull in the spread of the mutinies after the Meerut and Delhi outbreak, the only mutinies that had occurred outside the Punjab proper had been in its southern districts bordering the desert, in the near neighbourhood of Delhi, and at the remote station of Nusseerabad. General Anson had died on the 25th May, having by that time placed his advanced troops at Kurnaul, collected the whole force available against Delhi, either at Umballa or at Meerut, and ordered their advance and junction near Kurnaul for the onward movement towards Delhi. In the Punjab the places of importance had all been secured. The native troops had been disarmed at Lahore, Ferozepore, and Peshawur, and a movable column had been formed, headed by the Guides, and commanded by Nicholson, to suppress any further attempt at mutiny, and then to support the force at Delhi. At Agra, also, in the upper provinces, the sepoys were disarmed on the 31st May. In Oude arrangements had been carried out to control Lucknow, and to prepare the Residency position for a siege. From Cawnpore to Calcutta nothing had been done to make the country or stations safe. In Calcutta troops had been summoned from every available quarter, and had been sent on in small detachments towards Benares, and up to Cawnpore and Lucknow; but neither the stations on the way nor Allahabad itself had been secured. The Madras and Bombay Governments were keeping a watchful eye over their territories, and sending on troops, including those returning from Persia, to Calcutta; and Frere, in Scinde, had sent on an English regiment to Mooltan.

In regard to the detailed measures adopted in dealing with the crisis, there is none about which there have been more divergent opinions than about the disarming of the sepoys. But it seems obvious that no one general rule could apply to all cases. Where there were British troops present, disarming, more or less immediate, was generally advisable; but an exception was clearly necessary where, as in such a case as Lucknow, it was essential to retain the services of picked bodies of sepoys. Delay was occasionally useful, as at Peshawur; but actual omission or grave delay usually proved mischievous, as at Dinapore and Jullundur.

CHAPTER V.

FIVE GROUPS OF MUTINEERS, AND FIVE THEATRES OF WAR.

AT the end of May, then, the lull in the action of the mutineers ceased, and the spread of the Mutiny began and progressed rapidly.

Oude and Rohilkund, the nearest districts to Delhi, were the first to start, and practically on the same day. The dates were—

In Rohilkund: Bareilly and Shahjehanpore, on the 31st May.

In Oude: Lucknow on the 30th May, followed on the 3rd June by Seetapore, and some days later by Fyzabad and Durriabad, Sultanpore, and Salone, and, lastly, by Secrora, Gonda, and Baraitch.

The signal given at Lucknow was followed in three or four days in the stations lying outside the east and south of Oude—Azimgurh, on the 3rd June; Benares on the 4th; Cawnpore and Jaunpore on the 5th; and Allahabad on the 6th.

Neemuch, away on the far west, followed, on the 3rd June, the example that had been set by Nusseerabad on the 28th May.

The other stations that mutinied in June were: Jhansi on the 5th, Nowgong on the 10th, and Gwalior on the 14th—all in the native states south of Agra—and Futtehgurh, on the south-west corner of Oude, which did not rise till the 18th June.

The places where the troops deferred their mutinies till later months were Dinapore and Segowlie, to the east of Benares; Indore, Saugor, and Jubbulpore, far to the south.

With this spread of the mutiny in June, the struggle became fully developed, and branched off into well-defined courses. The features of these mutinies will now be described; then the counter steps of the British; and then the position and prospects at the end of June.

In Rohilkund, where there were no English troops to check the rising of the sepoys, they had a free hand. The Rohilla race, descendants of the fierce and fanatic Afghans, and traditionally at feud with the English, sided with the mutineers, and the outbreak was accompanied by murderous attacks on the English community. (The Rohilkund mutineers all set their faces towards Delhi.)

In Oude the most important of the mutinies was at Lucknow itself, in its military cantonment of Murriaon. On the night of the 30th two native infantry regiments and the 7th Cavalry broke out, and kept up a desultory fire in the direction of the 32nd Regiment. The intervention of that regiment there, and the loyal conduct of the police in the city, averted any junction of the mutineers with the city rabble; and during the night Harding's Sikh Cavalry attacked bodies of the mutineers whenever it had a chance. Next morning, the 32nd, the Sikh Cavalry, and the volunteers attacked the mutineers, and drove them off, putting them to flight, and taking some prisoners. The families had all been removed from Murriaon into the Residency position, so there was no maltreatment of the ordinary British community. The mutineers, on being expelled, moved off, at first towards Seetapore, afterwards turning towards Futtehgurh.

Partly in consequence of the move of the Lucknow mutineers in its direction, and partly owing to its lying between Lucknow and Shahjehanpore, which had already mutinied, Seetapore was the next station to rise. The mutiny there was marked by murderous attacks on the families as well as on the officers.

The other stations in Oude did not break out till the troops in the neighbouring districts outside the province had mutinied and begun to march into Oude. Thus, Fyzabad rose on the 8th, on the approach of the mutineers from Azimgurh and Benares. The officers and residents were not maltreated on the outbreak, being, indeed, helped in their attempts to escape, though they did not all meet with complete success. Durriabad rose the same day; but its officers and families were unmolested, and were escorted safely into Lucknow by a faithful detachment of Sikh Cavalry.

At Sultanpore the troops mutinied on the 9th, and attacked some of the officers, but allowed others to escape.

At Salone the mutiny occurred on the same day, but no harm was done to the officers and residents, who were at once sheltered by Rajah Hunwunt Singh.

The risings at Secrora, Gonda, and Baraitch, all, occurred on the 10th or 11th, and were unattended by any attacks on their officers. One officer, Bonham, of the Artillery, held on there for another day; but he could not induce his battery to remain loyal, and so he departed for Lucknow, to which some of his men escorted him.

In the districts on the east and south of Oude, Azimgurh was the first to break out, the direct incentive being the lust of treasure—£70,000, which had fallen into the power of the troops. But they did not molest the officers or residents, who escaped into Benares or Ghazeepore. This was on the 3rd of June.

Next day came the mutiny at Benares, which, however, bore more resemblance to the cases in the Punjab than to those in the lower provinces; for, besides the Hindostanee troops at Benares, there was a regiment of Sikh infantry, as well as small bodies of British infantry, newly arrived, of the 10th Foot from Dinapore, and of the Madras Fusiliers, under Colonel Neill, from Calcutta. Other troops—some of the 84th, for instance—had preceded them, but had been sent onwards to Allahabad, Cawnpore, and Lucknow. On Neill's arrival, and on hearing of the outbreak at Azimgurh, a parade was formed of the whole force ; but on a movement being made to disarm the sepoys, they broke into mutiny, and were unexpectedly joined by the Sikh regiment. The British troops, however, and the artillery, succeeded in defeating and driving off the mutineers and saving the station.

On the 5th the sepoys mutinied at Cawnpore ; but they did not *then* molest the officers or residents, starting off instead towards Delhi ; the Nana Sahib, however, induced them to halt and return, and begin, on the 8th, the attack on the Cawnpore garrison.

At Allahabad the garrison consisted of two regiments—one, the 6th Native Infantry, in the cantonment ; the other, an Irregular Regiment of Sikhs, under Captain Brasyer, in the fortress. The sepoy regiment had quite recently received the thanks of Government for its effusive loyalty and demands to be led against Delhi ; now, however, on the 6th June, it rose in virulent mutiny, attacking and murdering its officers and such residents as had not taken shelter in the fort, which it then endeavoured to seize. But the Sikhs, under Brasyer's stern influence, remained loyal, refused admittance to the sepoys, and, supported by a few English volunteers and pensioners, held the fortress for the State.

Meanwhile, at Benares, after the mutiny on the 4th, Colonel Neill had assumed command, and despatched some of his regiment onward, under Lieutenant

Arnold, to Allahabad. This party arrived and reinforced Brasyer on the 7th; on the 11th, Neill himself came up with the rest of his regiment, attacked and drove off the mutineers across the river into Oude, and so *secured Allahabad.*

This was the first point of primary importance scored in the war, though it never attracted a tithe of the public attention that was due to it. This was owing partly to its having been effected without much fighting, and partly to the more sensational events that were taking place at Delhi, Cawnpore, and Lucknow.

But of the paramount importance of the operation there can be no serious question, nor of the gravity of the crisis. The loss of the fortress was desperately imminent, and, if lost, what the consequences would have been are beyond conjecture. It is enough for practical purposes to point out that by securing it our virtual base of operations was transferred from Calcutta to an impregnable position five hundred miles ahead. It is of interest to note that this turning-point of the war was coincident in date (June 12th) with the decision at Delhi to give up the thought of immediate assault, and to undertake the prolonged siege from the Ridge.

With this all-important success at Allahabad the name of Brasyer must ever be associated; for, on the crisis of June 5th, and until supports arrived, the saving of the Fort would have been hopeless except for his personal weight with the Sikh soldiery, and his resolute and undaunted bearing. On the other hand, in the bold and rapid movement of the handful of men that sufficed for the support needed for that purpose, and in the advance generally during that critical period, Neill was the moving spirit, the leading personality, and chief actor.

The next mutiny to which we turn is that at Neemuch, in the far west—in the corner, it may be said, connecting Rajpootana, the Central Indian States, and Bombay. The troops rose on the 3rd June. The officers and residents were, most of them, unmolested, and took refuge in the old Fort there, whence they eventually moved out towards Oodeypore, finding shelter with the Rajpootana chiefs. The earlier mutiny, in the extreme west, at Nusseerabad, has been already described (p. 93).

We now come to the mutinies at the three stations south of Agra—Jhansi, Nowgong, and Gwalior. Jhansi was a very special case. An intensely bitter feeling prevailed there against the English. The state had been absorbed under their rule on the failure of direct heirs to the Dynasty, and the widow of the late Rajah had become a sworn foe to the British. After some incendiarism, the outbreak occurred on the 5th June. The residents and some of the officers were in the Fort, the rest in the cantonments. The latter were all killed, and then the Fort was attacked. It was bravely defended, and held till provisions failed; when promises of safety were given by the Ranee. In reliance on these promises the Fort was evacuated. But they proved absolutely false and treacherous, and the whole of the occupants, when once clear of the Fort, were ruthlessly murdered.

At Nowgong the troops belonged to the regiments at Jhansi, but there was not the same evil influence predominant. They mutinied on the 10th, but the officers and families were allowed to leave in safety, escorted by some faithful sepoys, to the shelter of the Ranee of Chutterpore.

At Gwalior the sepoys of the British contingent, after various threatenings and fluctuations, rose on the 14th. Shelter and assistance had from the first, and repeatedly, been offered by the Maharajah to the families, and he had shown his intention of holding by the British. But when the mutiny actually broke out in the cantonments of Morar, the officers and families were still there. Such of them as escaped came to his palace, were received with all kindness, and sent on in his vehicles and otherwise, under the escort of the Rajah's bodyguard, towards Agra, till near the Chumbul, whence they were protected into Agra itself by friendly Thakoors and the Rajah of Dholepore.

The last of the mutinies of June was at Futteh-gurh, in the south-west corner of Oude. The garrison, the 10th Native Infantry, remained loyal till the arrival of the 41st Native Infantry, which had mutinied at Seetapore. On this, on the 18th, the 10th advised their officers to retire into the Fort, saying they could no longer obey them, but would not molest them.

The results of these several mutinies up to the end of June were as follows :—

Early in June the mutineers that had joined at Delhi were those from Meerut and Delhi itself, and from the neighbouring stations of Allygurh, Hansi, and Hissar.

Then, later on in June—

1. The Rohilkund mutineers joined at Delhi.

2. All the Oude mutineers, including those of Futtehgurh, were still in Oude.

3. Those from Azimgurh and Benares came into Oude.

4. The Allahabad mutineers dispersed to their homes.

5. The Nusseerabad and Neemuch mutineers marched for Delhi, but were still *en route*.

6. The Cawnpore mutineers were at Cawnpore.

7. The Nowgong and Gwalior mutineers were remaining on the south of the Jumna, but the Jhansi men went to Delhi.

Hence, besides those who, as above mentioned, had belonged to the nearer districts, there were at Delhi, or concentrating on it, after the siege began, the parties from Rohilkund, from Jhansi, and from Nusseerabad and Neemuch; besides those mutineers who had escaped from Umballa, Ferozepore, Jullundur, and other places in the Punjab. And here obviously was to be the scene of the vital struggle.

There were in or about Oude all the Oude

mutineers and those belonging to Azimgurh, Benares, Cawnpore, and Futtehgurh, with contests going on, or imminent, at Cawnpore, or Futtehgurh, and Lucknow.

The mutineers south of Agra were remaining in those districts, but there were no British forces to oppose them, and there were no contests imminent, either there or to the east of Oude.

Hence, at present, the struggle seemed likely to be confined to Delhi and to Oude, the Punjab having been successfully held in check, while the sepoys to the south of Agra and to the east of Benares had not yet given signs of joining in any contest, if in the outbreak at all.

This was obviously a most fortunate matter. It was all-important that, the enemy having selected Delhi as the gage of battle, and our only large body of troops and our chief resources being in that direction, the strength of the rebel force there should be as small as possible; for, as the sequel will show, though we succeeded there in the end, we only barely succeeded, though we were opposed by only one-fifth of the mutineer army, instead of by the whole of it.

CHAPTER VI.

OPERATIONS AGAINST DELHI IN JUNE.

THE concluding remarks of the last chapter somewhat anticipate events, for they show the position developed by the end of June, when all the mutinies had taken place.

The counter-steps, meanwhile, of the English troops and authorities have now to be described. These were in four principal groups—the Punjab, Delhi, Oude (including Cawnpore), and the reinforcements from Calcutta. We deal with the Punjab before Delhi, because it acted as the base for Delhi.

In the Punjab, then, Sir John Lawrence was agreeing to, if not himself initiating, vigorous measures. He was fortunate in the men of energy and resolution and clear insight whom he had round him—Edwardes at Peshawur, Macpherson at Lahore, and Chamberlain—and he had rather to repress their ardour, to check and postpone the steps they proposed, than to press them forward himself; nor would he as yet raise any Sikh levies, nor denude the Punjab of troops to the extent that those officers were already urging. Still, the Guides were well on their way on their record march to join the force that was to operate against Delhi. The movable column had started under John Nicholson, and was disarming the native troops at the several stations on the road down to Jullundur and Loodianah; Edwardes at Peshawur was raising tribal levies; and some few chiefs were bringing forward small bodies of their clansmen for service. Then wherever reliable native troops could be substituted for English troops, the latter were sent on to join the force for Delhi. And lastly, the Cashmere Rajah organized a contingent of his Dogras to aid in the operations against Delhi, so that by the end of June the efforts of the Punjab had raised our force there to 6500 men.

But, meanwhile, one of the most astonishing proposals ever mooted in such a crisis had been laid before the Governor-General by Sir John Lawrence. Having hitherto distrusted Dost Mahomed, and opposed the treaty being entered into with him, he was now so nervous about the military operations against Delhi that he thought it necessary to provide against the chance of their failure; and his proposal for this contingency was to abandon Peshawur and the Trans-Indus—to invite Dost Mahomed, as a friend, to Peshawur, and give it to him—to withdraw our own troops to Rawal Pindee—and to make the Indus our future border! He sent forward this proposal to Lord Canning on the 12th June; unaccompanied, however, by the strong remonstrances and counter-arguments which he had received about it from all the principal political officers of the Punjab. Fortunately, Lord Canning took no notice of it at the time, and eventually negatived it.

We now turn to the development of the operations at Delhi. The Umballa force had reached Kurnaul about the 1st June. A small brigade under Wilson from Meerut was already at Ghazee - ood - deen - Nuggur, where the road to Delhi crosses the Hindun river, and had the day before, as already mentioned, had a smart action with a body of mutineers from Delhi. These had fought well, crossing bayonets with the 60th Rifles, but had been routed by a flank attack. They returned to the contest next day, when they were thoroughly defeated; after which the Meerut force marched to unite with the Umballa column, and, crossing the Jumna at Bhagput, joined it, on the 7th June, at Alipore, ten miles from Delhi. Hodson having reconnoitred and reported on the enemy's position, the whole force advanced next morning to attack them where they were entrenched at Badli Serai, four miles in front of Delhi.

The troops available for the attack, excluding those who had to be detached or otherwise employed, numbered 3000 men and 22 guns. The enemy were about 8000 strong in disciplined troops alone, including, as they did, the mutineers of Meerut, Delhi, Allygurh, Muttra, Hansi, Sirsa, and Hissar; also the Sappers from Roorkee, and the 45th from Ferozepore.

The British attack was a direct one, supported by a cavalry movement against the enemy's left rear. It was met by a heavy artillery fire, which caused serious loss; but a charge of the 75th carried the enemy's position, driving them out of it with the loss of several guns. The sepoys, however, took up a second position on the famous Ridge; and to attack them there General Barnard moved on both their flanks and then on their front. Again the enemy were defeated, and this time driven into Delhi, from the walls of which, however, a heavy cannonade was kept up; so that it was not found practicable at first to occupy the Ridge by any force stronger than a line of pickets. A third effort was made by the enemy in the evening, but without effect.

During the next four days the enemy made daily attacks on the British position, greatly impeding the endeavours to strengthen it; and, as it had become clear that the force was quite unequal to attempt a siege, plans were formed for an attack by *coup de main* for the morning of the 13th. But these plans were frustrated by a mistake respecting the pickets; so they were abandoned, and the force settled down to hold the Ridge until sufficient reinforcements should arrive to admit of siege operations. The advisability of the proposed *coup de main* has been the subject of much controversy; but audacity was nine points of the game, and the seizure of a coign of vantage is generally a gain, even though not immediately followed up by further success.

Meanwhile, and to the end of the month, accessions to each force continued arriving. On the 9th the Guides joined the English camp, and additional troops from the Punjab brought its numbers up, at the end of June, to 6500 men. The enemy were joined on the 11th by a regiment from Rhotuk (in the neighbourhood), on the 17th by the Nusseerabad brigade, on the 21st by mutineers from Jullundur and Phillour in the Punjab, and on the 1st July by the Rohilkund force. So that the preponderance of the sepoy army in Delhi over their besiegers increased greatly during the month. But in spite of this, the British managed to repel all attacks, to destroy the batteries which the enemy tried to construct against their flank, and to erect defensive batteries on their own flank and rear, as well as some in advance. The enemy made attacks almost daily, the most serious one being that undertaken on the 19th under the leading of the newly arrived Nusseerabad brigade.

CHAPTER VII.

OUDE AND LUCKNOW IN JUNE.

IN Oude (including Cawnpore and Futtehgurh), as already described, the Futtehgurh Fort had been occupied by the English officers and residents on the 18th June, on the arrival of the mutineers from Seetapore. And at Cawnpore the mutineers had first started for Delhi, but having been recalled by the Nana Sahib, had returned on the 8th June, when the English concentrated in some of the barracks.

Now the Futtehgurh garrison held the Fort till the 3rd July—only 33 fighting men to start with. These were gradually reduced by the fire of the enemy and by the losses entailed by mining and sickness, and at length they secretly evacuated the dilapidated Fort, starting in boats down the river; but most of them perished, a few only escaping through the kindness of Oude villagers.

The story of Cawnpore is too well known. The inmates of the entrenched barracks held out, despite a ceaseless fire and poverty of food, from the 8th until the 26th June, when the General accepted the treacherous offers of the Nana Sahib, and evacuated the position next day, only to meet with murder and massacre.

In Lucknow, Sir Henry Lawrence, after driving off the mutineers, continued to use the Mutchi Bhown to overawe the city and keep it quiet and also to serve as an *entrepôt;* and at the same time pressed on vigorously the construction and arming of the entrenchments at the Residency position, the collection and storage of ammunition and supplies, and all the other requirements for a prolonged siege. Communications were kept up with the talookdars and the country people, and grain and supplies of every kind came pouring in; refugees were escorted into the Residency by friendly parties—chiefs, villagers, or sepoys—from Seetapore, Secrora, Gonda, Durriabad, and elsewhere; the gatherings of the sepoys were watched, as also the advance of the troops from Calcutta up country; and Sir Henry was beginning to hope, from the supineness of the enemy, that the impending siege might not be so serious as he had anticipated, when he received intelligence of the surrender of Cawnpore. He well knew that then all the inaction of the enemy would be at an end.

He had been kept informed of their gradual concentration beyond Nuwabgunge on the north-east. On the 28th he heard of their beginning to stir, and next day of their being at Nuwabgunge, and intending to send on their advanced guard to Chinhut. So he prepared to meet and check them as they approached, and to concentrate for the subsequent defence in the Residency position. Nearly all was ready. The defences, which had progressed equably all round, were at an advanced stage. All the supplies and live stock had been stored and collected into the sheds and yards. The artillery was mostly massed there, though there was still a good deal of powder and ammunition in the Mutchi Bhown, and guns for its defence. The troops in Murriaon were withdrawn thence on the evening of the 29th June, and divided between the Mutchi Bhown and the Residency position, and portions of both the garrisons were told off for a reconnaissance in force for the following morning. The two parties united formed a force about 700 strong—half British, half native. They crossed the river by the Iron Bridge, and advanced on the Fyzabad road as far as the Kokrail bridge, where they were halted under Brigadier Inglis, Sir Henry Lawrence being ahead reconnoitring. Rations had been sent out with them to be issued during the halt, but they never received them, and were consequently suffering both from want of food and from the intense heat, when sent for by Sir Henry to advance to the front. The enemy approached presently, at a later hour than had been expected, and with their whole force instead of only the advanced guard. But they were in reality in no heart for the contest, for, though elated by the fall of Cawnpore, they had been intimidated by the vigour shown by Sir Henry at Lucknow. The position he had chosen for the fight was good—swampy ground in front, with villages on the flanks which we were to hold, the artillery being on or close to the road itself; the advanced guard in Ishmaelgunge on the left; and the 32nd in support behind it. Our native troops duly seized and held the village on the right, and afterwards, with the help of the cavalry, kept the enemy at bay there.

This was the dangerous flank, as the communications with the Residency lay on this side, and so it was here that the chief precautions had been taken. The artillery had wholly silenced the enemy's guns and actually made their force disappear for a time. But on the left a belt of groves curled round from Chinhut to the close neighbourhood of Ishmaelgunge. Apparently no pickets had been placed in those groves to guard against the approach of troops from that direction. So, while the advanced guard was occupying Ishmaelgunge and the 32nd were in line behind it, the enemy collected in the groves, dashed in mass on Ishmaelgunge, and, driving out the advanced guard, seized it at once, and began a vigorous fusilade on the 32nd, on the artillery on the road, and on our forces on its right.

With this the contest was virtually over. When the retreat had begun some of the native artillery joined the enemy; and the native cavalry, though they did not desert, yielded ground and gave way. But our native infantry remained staunch, and, supported by the volunteer cavalry, held the retreat. The enemy followed up, but could not cross the river at the Iron Bridge, which was under the command of our guns. Before the day was over, however, they had crossed lower down, and had closely invested the Residency, but not the Mutchi Bhown.

Orders had not as yet been given actually to evacuate the Mutchi Bhown. But these were semaphored the next day, the 1st July; so on that night its garrison, having laid a train which blew up its magazine, marched out with all its guns, save three which had to be left at the further outpost, and reached the Residency; unmolested by the enemy, though the intervening ground had been occupied by them the whole day. This evacuation of the Mutchi Bhown and concentration in the Residency was admirably conducted by Colonel Palmer. And thus the outbreak in Oude and its neighbourhood developed into the defence of the Residency position against the whole force of the insurgents there.

CHAPTER VIII.

THE EASTERN AND SOUTHERN DISTRICTS AND ELSEWHERE.

To turn to the measures in Calcutta for assistance to the upper provinces. As troops arrived from Burmah, Madras, and Ceylon, and then from the Persian Expeditionary Force, they were sent on up country as rapidly as it was held that they could be spared from the neighbourhood of the capital. There were two routes, one by the Ganges, the other by direct road, the two converging at Benares, and then going on side by side to Allahabad and Cawnpore. The river route passed by Patna and the military station near it—Dinapore—where was quartered the only British regiment, the 10th, between Calcutta and Cawnpore. The troops were all sent up in detachments; the 84th led the way, and then the Madras Fusiliers, and the 64th and 78th. There were other regiments in Calcutta; but they were needed there, though a wing of the 37th was held ready to start. These troops were thus sent forward, but no specific orders were given to utilize them to secure the Allahabad Fort, or to disarm the native troops at Dinapore. Captain Brasyer, it has been shown, did seize the Allahabad Fort, and hold it till reinforced by Colonel Neill; and now General Havelock, on his return from Persia, was sent on there to conduct this campaign. Neill had as yet found his force too weak to advance towards Cawnpore, till further troops should join him; but, on the 30th June, the day on which Havelock arrived to take up the command, he sent forward an advanced party under Captain Renaud.

Meanwhile, at Barrackpore, near Calcutta, the native troops had been disarmed.

At Patna, a large city near Dinapore, filled with a fanatic and turbulent Mahomedan population, Mr. Taylor, the principal civil officer, had seized the leading men, whom he knew to be hatching conspiracy, and had staved off any rising for the time. His chief support in this effort lay in a very magnificent newly raised body of Sikh police, known as Rattray's Sikhs.

Similarly, at Ghazeepore, Mr. Ross kept all quiet by his bold front and active measures, though strong signs of disaffection had appeared, and the native troops had to be closely watched.

In those lower provinces no further overt action had been taken by the disaffected. The sepoys had not risen there, though along the Jumna, at Banda and Humeerpore, south of Allahabad, they had mutinied, and some of the officers had been killed. But further south no outbreak had yet occurred.

More westward, in the several stations occupied

by the troops of the Gwalior contingent, peace was at an end, and at Sangor, as disturbance and outbreak were rife on the borders of the district, Brigadier Sage occupied the fort, holding it as a place of refuge, and garrisoning it with the 31st Native Infantry, in which he had made up his mind to put his trust—a trust which was not misplaced.

In no other part of India had there yet been any rising. But there were strong signs of disaffection in the Southern Mahratta country, about Kolhapore, where the chiefs were connected with the Nana Sahib, and in the Hyderabad districts, to which a column that left Poona on the 8th June for Mhow and the north had to be diverted, to Aurungabad, to keep the cavalry there in check.

These movements in Bombay, in connection with Hyderabad and with an advance towards Indore and Agra, will be found more specifically dealt with in the preliminary part of the narrative of the Central India column in the second stage of the Campaign.

CHAPTER IX.

SOME SPECIAL FEATURES OF THE MUTINIES AND THE REVOLT.

THUS had the Mutiny developed definitely by the end of June, 1857; but the method of its spread showed that the concert about it was no greater than about the outbreak itself. It had occurred in four distinct groups, each of which, instead of co-operating with others, took its own course and line of action independently. These four were: the *Punjab;* the north-west or *Delhi* group, including Rohilkund; *Oude*, including the borders on its south and east; and the *Southern* group between the Jumna and the Nerbudda. A fifth group of mutinies broke out later to the *east* of Benares. And the areas in which these groups of mutinies broke out formed, it will be seen, corresponding theatres of war or military operations. In the *Punjab*, the rising of the sepoys had been not only checked, but checkmated, by the vigorous action of the authorities, and that province was now about to play the part, not of a theatre of war, but of the base of operations for the campaign at Delhi. In the north-west, or *Delhi*, theatre all the mutineers from between Rohilkund and Neemuch and north of that line were concentrated on Delhi. In *Oude* all the mutineers of the province, and from its immediate south and east, were at Lucknow to besiege it, or at Cawnpore to oppose the advance of the British from Allahabad. In the *south*, between the Jumna and the Nerbudda, the mutineers remained hovering about, having no enemy to contend with. The Jhansi troops alone now left that theatre and marched off to Delhi. In the *eastern* theatre the mutinies had not yet developed.

Meanwhile, the Nana Sahib and the Ranee of Jhansi were the only people of position and influence who had joined the insurgents. The great Rajpootana and Mahratta chiefs held aloof, deterred by the aspirations and intentions of the Moghul party, to which they had become alive before it was too late. But in the upper provinces the *Pax Britannica* was entirely gone; though brave and energetic civil officers, with such loyal men and police as they could muster, were ceaselessly on the war-path, scouring their districts, rescuing and helping fugitives, seizing and punishing rebel chiefs, collecting supplies for the troops, and supporting and encouraging the friendly natives.

The loyal and kindly action of the Rajpoot and other chiefs was nowhere more prominent than in Oude. The Rajahs of Bulrampore, Birhur, and Godalpore, and Maun Singh of Shahgunge, aided to safety fugitives from Fyzabad and the east; Roostum Sah of Dehra, and the Ameythee Rajah, those from about Sultanpore; Rajah Hunwunt Singh, those from Selone; and the Morarmow Rajah those from Cawnpore and elsewhere; Hurdeo Bux sheltered Mr. Edwardes and others from the North-Western Provinces; and many others who might be named, chiefs of the Byswara and other clans, were friendly and helpful.

The Mutiny, then, had developed into actual campaigns only in two out of the five theatres of operations; the British being the besieged at Lucknow, in contrast to the Delhi theatre, in which they were the besiegers.

But, in referring to the Mutiny of the Bengal army as being in five groups, it is not to be understood that the whole of the native troops in these five groups or theatres of revolt had mutinied. The Sikhs, the Punjabees, and the Ghoorkas, as a rule, held aloof—both as regiments, and also individually. The rising was almost entirely confined to the Hindoostanees, and even of them many did not join. Thus the 31st Native Infantry drove off the 42nd, and held Saugor for the Government. The 13th at Lucknow, and the 21st at Peshawur, remained staunch. The 43rd at Barrackpore held the other troops in check; Renny's native battery of horse artillery served on the ridge at Delhi throughout the siege; and numerous instances could be cited to show that by no means the whole of even the Hindoostanees of the Bengal army had joined in the revolt. Nor did the Mutiny spread beyond the Bengal army at all, though for a short time there was some uneasiness in Bombay.

The sepoys took unquestionably the lion's share in the contest; practically they bore the whole brunt of it until towards the end. In the five theatres of operations, the civil administration being virtually at an end, the criminal and predatory classes, the town ruffians, the retainers of disloyal landholders, and occasionally Mahomedan zealots, took part in the local conflicts; not doing so much, however, in the fighting line, as proving mischievous in harassing the communications.

As already stated, no members of reduced dynasties joined the enemy, except the Nana Sahib and the Ranee of Jhansi. The Nana held himself ill-used as the lineal representative of the head of the great Mahratta Confederacy, and had come under the influence of the notorious Azimoola. The Ranee was rankling under the sense of wrongs from the British annexation of Jhansi under the adoption question, in spite of the unswerving loyalty of the House. None of the great native rulers, Mahomedan, Mahratta, or Rajpoot, joined the revolt at all, though Scindia's and Holkar's people rose against the local British residents and troops. The puppet emperor at Delhi was merely a handle for the Moghul party, and not really a leader of the rebellion.

Hence, as a fact, the great Rebellion, which this rising was intended to be, and was on the verge of becoming, had drifted into a war in which the Hindoostanees of the Bengal army alone played any important part, while the Moghul party had sunk almost into insignificance, and none of the great races or chiefs joined in it at all.

At the same time, it is quite certain that only a few months before there had been unusual and bitter disaffection among the latter. The explanation of this apparently paradoxical attitude and conduct, and of the failure of the rising to develop into a great rebellion, lies in the consequences of the aggressive action of the Moghul party at Delhi. They showed their hand too soon and too eagerly, regardless of results. They evinced their determination to recover their rule and take the lead; to assert their supremacy, and set aside all other interests; not merely to subvert the British rule, but to replace it by their own. And this forcibly reminded those other races of that past which they had been forgetting under the pressure of the more recent causes of irritation. To resent the masterful and imperious policy of the British was one thing; to exchange it for what they remembered of the lawless tyranny and brutal rule of the Moghul was quite another matter. So their thoughts of joining in a blow at the English were at once checked, and they remained passive. But their temper toward the English was shown by that passiveness. None of them came loyally and actively to the support of the Government. Had there not been this bitterness and dislike to the English rule, would not the great Mahratta leaders, such as Scindia, Holkar, and the Guicowar, the great Rajpoot chiefs, such as Oodeypore, Jeypore, Jodhpore, and others, have aided the Government against any efforts at supremacy on the part of a Hindoostanee army which they cordially hated?

As to that army and its mutiny, there is every indication that its rising had neither been long premeditated nor matured. The isolated groups into which the mutineers collected, their delays, their halts, their inaction for many months in some cases, their absolute want of concert, the absence of any leaders, real or nominal—all this showed that they rose without any plan or programme; nor was there any sign that they were imbued with any real hostility to the Government before the cartridge incident. They had long been a spoilt body, their discipline had been impaired and become lax, and they had doubtless become aware of their preponderating power. Then, in 1856, the General Service Act had caused annoyance and disquietude, but had not directly angered the existing army, as it affected only the future recruits. In January, 1857, however, the cartridge question had really roused their fears and their animosity, but hardly gave time before May for working up a conspiracy.

Before quitting the subject of the part taken by the army in the organization and development of the revolt, it may be as well to point out some other general influences which affected its conduct, and also some characteristics of the individual mutinies.

In the first place the real status of the army and its traditionary position must be remembered, as well as the injudicious way in which it was treated from time to time. It has been the habit to speak of it—disparagingly—as a mercenary army. Doubtless, in the first days of the rise of the British power its native troops had been mercenaries; but certainly long before the present century the sepoy army had lost its mercenary character, and, under such a rule as the British Government had become, was more truly a national army—almost a militia—than anything else, employed for the protection of their own peaceful states, and for their defence against outer aggression. The growth of that army, both in numbers and in its fixed relations to the State, had been gradual. And whilst from the very first there had been no desire on the part of the sepoys, as recruited and enlisted, to serve outside their own peninsula, there had been repeated attempts, more or less irregularly managed, to induce them to go on foreign service. These occasions, with the attendant question of the exceptional pay when so employed, had been causes, but almost the sole causes, of any unpleasant attitude ever assumed by the sepoys to the British Government. It can hardly be disputed that they had sound ground for their objection; and, when that objection became almost chronic, the blame would seem to attach more justly and with greater force to the Government and the commanders, who tried to coerce them, than to the sepoys. Their traditional opposition to this particular coercion was, both in itself and in the laxity to which it led, the chief ground for the impression, held by many, of their having a tendency to mutiny.

In the next place, the sepoys were the one body of natives who had never suffered, but always benefited, from British rule. They were identified with it and its power and its triumphs during the whole of its rise. They were linked to it by these relations and by the fidelity of a hundred years. They looked to its service as the career for themselves and their sons after them. They were assured of pensions in their later years, and their fathers and relations were dependent on the pensions they were already enjoying. These formed ties which could not be lightly broken or easily replaced. In fact, though they had no real chance of such great aggrandizement as was possible to a very few in native states—which embittered the ambitious—there was no other service in which there was such assured certainty and prosperity and pension. Besides this, the men were, as a rule, attached—in some cases greatly attached—to their officers, and under their influence; while there also prevailed the old traditional claim of fidelity to the salt, and loyalty to the oath, which with Rajpoots, if properly kept in view, could be counted on almost with certainty. The world has shown no nobler examples of military fidelity than that of the sepoys of the Lucknow garrison.

Many of the Hindoostanee regiments, it has been shown, did not join in the Mutiny. It is quite open to question whether the delay of the British for three whole weeks in operating against Delhi did not encourage and lead many regiments to break out, which were wavering and might otherwise have kept loyal.

Further, there is every reason to believe that in most cases the bulk of the men, though angry and bewildered, were not disposed to mutiny; they were, however, excited and easily led by the more energetic spirits, who were the agents of the party of sedition. These were mostly the high caste men, the pulwans (the wrestlers and athletes), and those who were personally of a restless, ambitious, and discontented character. And when the time for rising came, these leaders generally had to shoot an officer or to perform some similar act by which the regiment would be led to believe that it had no option left it, and was committed to mutiny. It was well known that the best and the most popular officers were thus sacrificed to prevent the check which might have resulted from their influence. On the other hand, where the necessity for this was not felt, the men not only avoided molesting their officers, but escorted or helped them to places of safety. And there are numerous well-known, well-authenticated cases where they rescued ladies in difficulties, escorted them in all honour and safety to their friends, and then, deaf to all entreaties, saluted and returned to their comrades, with whom they said their proper place was.

As to the counter influences, the principal one was that the claim of the State to their fidelity had been weakened, if not annulled, by the treachery of the British, and their designs against caste; while their pride and patriotism were touched by the tale that their own tribal chiefs and the whole country were with them and expecting them to lead the way. The incitements and taunts of the bazars then added their weight; and latterly, in no small degree, the doubting and unfriendly looks, and the injudicious if not irritating talk of many of the English. It may also be remarked that, in the case of the great majority of the sepoys, the Oude Rajpoots, their childhood and youth had been spent amidst scenes of bloodshed and violence, and associated with the spirit of turbulence and contest with their rulers.

Before proceeding to the campaign or warfare of the Mutiny, we may touch on some points which have been at one time or other adduced as causes of the rising.

Had the fact that the sepoy army was not the army of her Majesty, but of the East India Company, any bearing on the matter? There seems no reason whatever for such a supposition. The discipline was absolutely in the hands of the Commander-in-Chief, who always belonged to the Royal service, and against whose judgment and authority and orders the Company's officers would have no weight whatever. This can hardly be gainsaid when the names of the British commanders are remembered, from the days of Wellington to those of Gough and Napier.

Again, the Government and policy in England that controlled the Governor-General in India had been that of the Board of the East India Company, and not that of the British Cabinet. Had this fact any connection with the rising? This much seems certain; the sudden change to earnest attention to the material prosperity of the country, combined with a comparative cessation of the old regard for native habits and prejudices, had been the main cause of the disaffection; whereas it was the old conservatism, the care for native thought, and the extreme caution about material improvements or changes which might be misunderstood, that had been the chief characteristic of the policy of the East India Company.

Had the conduct of our countrymen in India been in any way or degree the cause of the disaffection or of the Mutiny? To those acquainted with the social life of the British in India in those days, any such idea is simply ludicrous. There was absolutely not the slightest ill feeling on the part of the sepoys to their officers or to the British community. The tone that prevailed with them was precisely the opposite; their irritation, when it came, was against the Government. Eventually, when the spirit of mutiny became obvious, then, but not till then, the sense arose of division of race and of social and military antagonism. As to oppressive demeanour or conduct on the part of the British community to the native community in general, there was none whatever. Not only would the paucity of the English race make the idea absurd, but it was well known that not only in any cases of alleged oppression, but in disputes and legal differences, the civil authorities took the attitude and *rôle* of protectors of the natives; and, although the native subordinates of Government were greatly given to exaction and oppression, there has been invariable and universal recognition of the fact of the purity of the English officials, of their kind bearing to the natives, and of the trust placed by the people in them.

BOOK III.

THE VITAL STRUGGLE.

BOOK III.

THE VITAL STRUGGLE DURING JULY, AUGUST, AND SEPTEMBER, 1857.

CHAPTER I.

THE STAGES AND THEATRES OF THE CAMPAIGN.

THE war into which the Mutiny had thus developed at the end of June, 1857, lasted for eighteen months, throughout which the insurgents never appeared to be acting on any concerted plan, or under the guidance of any one ruling spirit.

The conflict of eighteen months may be conveniently divided into three periods—

First, the period of *The Vital Struggle*, in which, during the three months of July, August, and September, 1857, the British garrison of India were fighting for existence, and standing at bay, unaided by help from England. This desperate conflict ended with their victory in the three contests of the period, viz. the siege of Delhi, the defence of the Lucknow Residency position, and Havelock's advance to its assistance.

In the second period *The Decisive Contest* lasted for six months—from October, 1857, to March, 1858—during which the reinforcements arrived from England, and the insurgents, who had concentrated in full strength at Lucknow and at Jhansi, were driven out of those positions and utterly defeated, but not yet crushed.

The third stage was *The Suppression of the Revolt*, during the last nine months of 1858, when the defeated groups of mutineers were being attacked and crushed or pursued, till they eventually dispersed to their homes, the country settled down, and peace was restored.

Each of these periods forms a distinct stage of the Campaign, and its story will therefore be divided accordingly. The account of each such stage or period will be arranged under the separate theatres of operations, which coincided closely with what have been already described as the theatres of mutiny, viz. the Punjab, Delhi, Oude, the Southern, and the Eastern.

Of these five, the Punjab never became a theatre of real serious warfare at all, though the outbreaks of mutineers and occasional local risings had to be suppressed by troops. But in the importance of its bearing on the war, it was second to no province of India—if, indeed, it did not occupy the most prominent position of all—first, as the base for the operations at Delhi, and then as the source of the huge new native army that aided the British to quell the revolt.

Of the other four theatres each formed a seat of

warfare in one or more of the three stages: Delhi in the first stage, and its Rohilkund section in the third; Oude in all three stages; the other two in the second and third stages. So that Oude was the only theatre in which real warfare raged throughout the whole struggle.

In the first stage, Delhi and Oude were the seats of contest; but the warfare in Oude, though intensely interesting, was secondary in importance to that at Delhi, where the struggle was absolutely vital, the fate of India depending on its issue; for on our success or failure there would turn the question, whether the hostility with which we should have to cope would be restricted to those who were already our declared enemies, or would spread over the whole Peninsula.

CHAPTER II.

THE PUNJAB.

As the Punjab formed the base of our operations at Delhi, and the only source for the supply of all the assistance, support, and reinforcements which our force there received, we must first, before narrating the siege of Delhi, describe how the Punjab authorities managed to deal with the crisis, so as to send help to Delhi, while having to meet the dangers and secure the integrity of the province itself.

For the Punjab had three dangers of its own to face—attack from beyond the frontier, the mutineer sepoy force still left in the province, and disaffection and outbreak in its own population.

The frontier might be threatened by the inroads of the border tribes, and still further by an invasion of the Afghans in force. The latter would depend, but up to a certain point only, on the Ameer Dost Mahomed. He was showing himself to be friendly; yet, however well disposed he might be, he would probably be unable to restrain or control his subjects under excessive excitement and temptation. The independent border tribes would be certain to join the Afghans in any general invasion, but they might also be disposed to indulge in minor raids at their own caprice, irrespective of any combined attack. This tendency would be checked and controlled mainly by our own policy and bearing towards them, and by the personal influence of our local frontier officers.

Now Dost Mahomed had entered into a treaty with us, and was behaving loyally and showing himself true to the alliance; still the strain on him was very severe, if not intense, for his subjects—as described by Major Lumsden, our representative at Candahar—were keen for an invasion; and it was therefore essential, as due to the Ameer, as well as to minimize the hostility and increase the friendliness of the frontier, that we should do all in our power to lessen the excitement and temptation to attack us, show the boldest front to all dangers, and enlist the alliance and support of those who were disposed to trust to our character and prestige.

This was the policy and the spirit that guided our chief officer on the frontier, Colonel Herbert Edwardes.

It has been already shown how thoroughly he carried out this policy before the Campaign actually developed; and now he continued it still more energetically and strenuously, if possible—at any rate, with more tangible results. Through Foujdar Khan and other personal friends, levies were raised of the Mooltanees of the southern districts. The frontier tribes were invited to bring in horses for sale—an invitation they accepted freely, from their natural cupidity, and with excellent results, though they did not themselves at that time enlist as troopers. The Wahabees and other fanatic sects that tried to support the enemy were boldly met and heartily thrashed. Other tribesmen were led into checking and attacking the mutineers, till the race animosity towards them that ensued confirmed the active alliance and support of the British by the border tribes; so that before long some 2000 Mooltanee cavalry were raised, the numbers of Mooltanees in other regiments were doubled, some hundreds of Afreedis beyond the Khyber frontier who were in disgrace paid up their fines and were enlisted into new regiments, and four additional regiments were raised of Puthan cavalry or infantry. These measures and our stern dealings with the mutineer regiments successfully secured the integrity of the frontier, though Edwardes and others felt the most intense anxiety lest Sir John Lawrence should, by any chance, be allowed to carry out his idea, already referred to, of handing over the Peshawur frontier to Dost Mahomed.

The next danger to be faced in the Punjab was the large number of sepoy regiments who were still in the province, and of whom only a minority had been disarmed. A movable column had been formed, and the command of it given to Brigadier-General John Nicholson, to operate between the several stations and suppress any attempts at outbreak. It was after this column had gone far on its way towards Delhi that the regiments left at some of the out-stations broke out, the principal cases being at Jhelum and at Sealkote. In the Peshawur districts and at Jhelum the sepoys rose and endeavoured to fight the British and the troops that remained loyal, and were almost annihilated. At Sealkote, the regiment, after rising, marched eastwards, endeavouring to raise the country. The sepoys at Jullundur had mutinied and managed to escape to Delhi before Nicholson could reach them; but, after disarming the other regiments at Phillour and elsewhere, he turned back on the Sealkote mutineers, caught them at the Trimmoo Ghat near Gurdaspur, and inflicted on them a crushing defeat, leading to their practical extermination.

After this the few mutinies that occurred were not of any serious moment, and the local hostile sepoy element had become so greatly reduced that Sir John Lawrence hardly counted it now among the sources of danger.

But though the frontier tribes—all Mahomedan—were being turned into useful allies by Herbert Edwardes and his colleagues, Sir John was still watching the Sikh community nervously, especially in the *Manjha* (the Lahore and Umritsur districts), and it was not till towards the end of this stage of the Campaign, when we had taken Delhi, that he began to enlist them freely; though their attitude led him to risk denuding the country of the bulk of the existing troops. As a fact, the Sikhs never did rise nor show hostility to their British rulers, and though they delayed giving them hearty support and alliance, still many of them enlisted on opportunities occurring; while the *Malwa* Sikhs—those, that is, to the south of the Sutlej—were from the first, and continued throughout, actively friendly. Two thousand Cashmere troops also came down to Delhi, under Captain Richard Lawrence; and the only outbreak in the general community that occurred in the Punjab was among the nomadic Mahomedan tribes in the Gogaira districts, halfway between Lahore and Mooltan—an outbreak which subsided speedily under the prompt measures taken by Sir John Lawrence.

The practical result with regard to Delhi was that the reinforcements sent forward up to the 3rd July having brought the *effective* strength up to 6500 men, the arrival, early in August, of General John Nicholson's movable column made it stand at 8122, of whom 4386 were natives; and on the day of the attack it consisted of 14,225 men, of whom the effective natives numbered nearly 8000.

Remembering the losses in action, the non-effectives sent to Umballa, and some troops that had not been thought trustworthy and had therefore been sent away, it can be readily recognized what splendid efforts Sir John Lawrence had made, and at what risk, to create the army for the capture of Delhi; maintaining all the time a resolute rule in his own province, keeping inviolate the integrity of the frontier, and actually enlisting the support of the wild border clansmen.

At the same time it must be understood, in thus giving to Sir John the credit for these efforts and their results, that it is given on the ground that he was the responsible authority, and bore the burden of the intense anxiety of weighing justly and successfully the demands for aid to Delhi against the need of caution for his own province. As the fault of any disaster in the Punjab would have fallen on him, so on him must rest the glory of the success due to the assistance he sent to the force before Delhi. But the initiative in these reinforcements did not rest with Sir John; they were ceaselessly and vehemently urged on him by his chief lieutenants, and especially by Edwardes at Peshawur and J. D. Macpherson at Lahore, who were as keen and persistent in their pressure on him in regard to the levying and forwarding of troops to Delhi as he had been, and still was, in his pressure on the generals to "take Delhi." While this movable column was still in the Punjab, Sir John was saying that he had come to the end of his tether, and could not spare and would not send another man to Delhi. Mr. Montgomery in vain urged him to send Nicholson's column; but, after he had given up expostulating with him about it, Macpherson still would not cease, but continued pressing it and showing how the different points to be guarded could be held; till at last Sir John, calling him a mutineer, yielded to his importunity, and allowed Nicholson and his column to go forward to Delhi.

CHAPTER III.

THE SIEGE OF DELHI.

HAVING described the efforts and arrangements made in the Punjab for the support and furtherance of our operations against Delhi, we now turn to those operations. We left the narrative of them when the besieging army numbered 6500 men, and had settled down before the northern front, to await reinforcements and a siege train before attempting further to make any actual attack.

A glance at the map will show that the British position, being along the Ridge, had its left thrown back, while the end of the Ridge on the right was but little more than half a mile from the Moree Bastion at the north-west angle of the city walls. That part of the position, consequently, was the nearest and most constant point of the enemy's attacks. The most prominent post there was Hindoo Rao's house, which was held throughout by Major Reid, with a party of his own Ghoorkas and the 60th Rifles.

The right of the position was flanked by the Delhi canal, but this was crossed at numerous points by bridges, and so long as they existed the enemy could pass the canal readily and assail our posts. On the other hand, our position came sufficiently near them to admit of its being enfiladed with batteries near the canal, which protected the enemy from our sorties as much as it protected us against their irruptions.

At the right of our position were various suburbs of the city, which formed constant fighting ground, such as the Kishengunge, immediately on the right, but beyond the canal, and the Subzee Mundee, more in the rear, on our extreme right. Along the river bank were various buildings at intervals, such as the Koodsea Bagh, close to the city, and Metcalfe House, about a mile distant from it. And then in front of the city wall, more or less near it, between the Koodsea Bagh and the end of the Ridge, were isolated buildings and garden enclosures, such as the Custom House and Ludlow Castle. In the triangle between this line of buildings on one face, the river on a second, and the Ridge on the third face, was a large space of comparatively neutral ground.

The road to Kurnaul and Umballa ran in the rear of the position inside the canal, and was therefore tolerably secure from interruption. On the other hand, the enemy had freedom of communication all round, except along the west bank of the Jumna, and their bridge of boats across it was entirely beyond the reach of our artillery fire, affording free access to the eastern districts.

Within a few days of the 1st July the last bodies of mutineer troops arrived, bringing the rebel force up to about 30,000. On the 3rd the enemy attempted to get at Alipore, on our rear, and stop our communication with Kurnaul, but after a sharp encounter with Major Coke they returned to Delhi. The British, on the other hand, set to work vigorously destroying the bridges over the canal, thereby reducing the enemy's facilities for crossing and getting at our rear. On the 9th Barnard died of cholera, Reed succeeding.

On the 9th occurred the well-known inroad by a body of about a hundred of the mutineer cavalry. They either eluded the videttes in the Subzee Mundee, or were mistaken for some of our own irregulars, and thus managed to get sufficiently forward to charge the guns on the picket. They caused a scare, but, after losing a third of their number, they were routed and pursued out of the camp. A counter-move was then made, and the Subzee Mundee suburb was attacked and cleared of the enemy, with a loss to them of 500 men. The Irregular Cavalry, through whose negligence, or worse, the successful inroad was permitted, were turned out of camp and sent back to the Punjab. Reed being ill was now succeeded by Wilson.

On the 14th July the enemy again made an attack in force on our batteries at the end of the Ridge, but were defeated and driven back, mainly by a flank movement on their left through the Subzee Mundee, led by General Showers and accompanied by General Chamberlain. The enemy's loss was 1000 men; our casualties were 16 officers and 192 men.

On the 18th there was again another attack there,

but of less consequence, and again one from Ludlow Castle on the 23rd. Later on, the enemy made some desultory movements and slight attacks of no moment; and then, about the 10th August, they came forward in force and brought a heavy fire against the Metcalfe House post from Ludlow Castle and elsewhere, but were surprised in the early dawn of the 12th August, and driven back with severe loss.

Meanwhile, besides all the actual combats, there had been constant and heavy work in the construction of batteries and defences. There were three batteries near the end of the Ridge, a flanking battery to the right, and several batteries in the rear, besides mortar batteries, entrenched posts for pickets, and trenches of communication.

But now the tide began to turn, as General Nicholson's column arrived, bringing the numbers, including previous reinforcements, up to about 11,000 men, of whom 8000 were effective; and the siege-train also was on its way. Knowing this, a large force of the enemy marched out of Delhi on the 24th August, with the view of intercepting it. So General Nicholson was detached on the 25th to operate against this mutineer body, and after very great difficulties, met them in the afternoon occupying a strong position at Nujufgurh, where a bridge crosses the canal. He attacked and defeated them after a severe combat, driving them back to Delhi, taking

	British.	Native.	Total.
Artillery . .	548	477	1025
Sappers, etc.		673	673
Cavalry . .	485	769	1254
Infantry . .	2703	2467	5170
Total	3736	4386	8122

thirteen guns, blowing up the bridge, and forcing them to give up their scheme.

At length, in the beginning of September, as the siege-train was near at hand, it became necessary to arrange for the actual siege, *i.e.* the artillery breaching attack and the eventual storming of the city walls. Each of these points was attended with a very exceptional feature.

For a breaching attack the batteries have to be within a short distance of the walls or other defences that have to be breached. At Delhi there was only one point that was already held near which was any proper site for such a battery, and that was on the extreme right of the Ridge. The customary process would have been to construct zigzag trenches from the Ridge across the plain below it up to the sites where batteries could be constructed. Before this, such zigzags could not have been attempted, as the force was too weak for the work; nor was it now strong enough, though stronger than before. Time, in fact, was not available for the effort, as the attitude of the Punjab was critical, and every day was of consequence; and further, such approaches would have indicated the points of attack, and enabled the enemy to construct retrenchments to strengthen them. Thus regular zigzag approaches and parallels were out of the question. But Colonel Baird Smith and Captain Alexander Taylor had thought out the matter and prepared a scheme. By it the whole of the north face came under attack; but the enemy's attention was drawn by our *overt* measures to the neighbourhood of the Moree Bastion, at its west end, the nearest point in the city walls to our own position; thus leading to their neglect of any proper watch over the ground before the east, and especially the river end of the Face. On the 7th, the first battery was started, somewhat ostentatiously, opposite the Moree Bastion, concentrating the enemy's attention on that point; and then, on the 8th or 9th, the second battery was begun—not in the open, but in the grounds of Ludlow Castle—to breach the bastion on the right of the Cashmere Gate. These two batteries were seven hundred yards from their points of attack. At the same time a still more effective piece of work had been done. The water bastion was to be breached. To get a site for it Captain Taylor advanced reconnoitring from the Koodsea Bagh, and found the Custom House entirely evacuated. The breaching battery was forthwith constructed within its enclosure, not two hundred yards from the bastion, with a mortar battery behind it; and on the night when these several batteries were approaching actual completion, the guns with which they were to be armed were taken down to them and placed in position.

Thus, by Taylor's genius and audacity, the usually necessary steps for preparing to breach the enemy's ramparts and defences were dispensed with, and the chief batteries were enabled to open out with but little previous warning to the enemy.

The siege-train arrived from Ferozepore on the 6th. The two first batteries opened out on the 11th, and the other two on the 12th.

The reinforcements that had arrived had brought up the force to the strength noted in the margin.

British troops effective . .	3,300
Native troops effective . .	5,400
Native contingents effective	2,500
Total effective.	11,200
In hospital	3,000
Total before Delhi	14,200

The main part of the native contingents were the Cashmere troops, 2200 men with four guns, who had been brought down by Captain R. Lawrence, a brother of Sir Henry and Sir John.

Day and night, till the morning of the 14th September, did the batteries pound the walls of Delhi, creating effective breaches; and then, as no further reinforcements could appear, the time had arrived for the attack and storming of Delhi, if it was ever to come off at all. And this brings us to the second exceptional feature in the business.

General Wilson had always been very strongly impressed with the gravity of the position at Delhi. He knew the danger that would be involved in delay, and he knew equally well and dreaded equally, if not still more, the danger that would result from any failure in the attack. He disliked Baird Smith's scheme, and thought it likely to fail. But he could not suggest any more hopeful scheme of his own. So, on the latter ground, he sanctioned his chief engineer's proposals, yielding to his judgment, but avowing his opinion that the chances of success were unfavourable. The time having now come for the attack, it was arranged for in four parties to come off early on the morning of the 14th September. One, under Nicholson, accordingly stormed the breach in the Cashmere bastion; the second, under Brigadier William Jones, assaulted at the breach in the Water Bastion; the third, under Colonel Campbell of the 52nd, charged in through the Cashmere Gate, after it had been blown up by Lieutenants Home and Salkeld; Major Reid, who had throughout held Hindoo Rao's house and repelled twenty-six attacks, was to attack Kishengunge, and try to enter the city by the Lahore Gate; a fifth column, under Brigadier Longfield, was in reserve, and to follow Nicholson's column.

The first three columns carried out their task with perfect success, storming the breaches and entering the Gateway simultaneously; and then advanced inwards into the city a considerable way, while they also kept circling along the parapets of the city walls up to the Burn Bastion. This flank movement was to have been supported by Major Reid's party, but he was severely wounded, and his men got into disorder, and failed in their object; so that Nicholson's own column was checked and severely pressed, and he was himself mortally wounded. The fifth column, following the first, enabled the whole of the troops that had assaulted to occupy connected positions within the city; though the failure of that fourth column weakened the force, prevented for that day the full development of its efforts, and obliged such of the assaulting troops as had pressed too far forward to move back, and, so to speak, come in line with the rest. A column of cavalry and horse artillery under Hope Grant had been sent by General Wilson to the support of the fourth column, and frustrated the attempts of the enemy to take the attacking columns in flank.

Thus was Delhi stormed on the 14th September with the loss of 66 officers and 1104 men killed and wounded out of a total strength of 5160 in the assaulting columns. The situation was grave; but under the strenuous advice and resolute attitude of Generals Nicholson and Chamberlain and Colonel Baird Smith, supported by many others, General Wilson caused the position held by his force to be strengthened during the night; and the next morning the advance through the city was pressed forward and continued, step by step, the enemy steadily losing heart, till the whole place was in our possession. The River Bastion and the Lahore Gate and the Emperor's Palace were captured on the 19th and 20th, and by the 21st the old Emperor was a prisoner, and two of his sons, who were overtaken in a throng of their retainers, had been shot by Hodson.

And then, as a proper sequel and practical proof of the successful issue of the siege, a force of 2800 men was despatched from the British army at Delhi to pursue the fugitive mutineer army, and clear the Doab southwards between the Ganges and the Jumna.

Thus had Delhi been retaken by the English. What the stubborn courage was, and the skill in the siege operations, which had brought them to a successful issue, has been fully shown, and needs no repetition.

But a last word must be said to call to mind that that success would have been impossible but for the splendid courage, the sound instinct, and the untiring efforts of John Lawrence and his men to risk all in the Punjab in order to help Delhi to the utmost.

What the greatness of that assistance was may be gathered from the fact that the whole force available for the battle of Badl-ki-Serai was 3800 men, while, *after all the heavy losses incurred during the siege*, the troops present at its close amounted to upwards of 14,000 men. This has been already said; but it will well bear repeating.

Two remarks may be made before leaving this subject—the siege and storm of Delhi.

Three of the attacking columns succeeded, but the fourth failed; this is probably attributable in a measure to its brilliant leader, Major Charles Reid, having been wounded at the start. But it is also to be remembered that that point of attack was the one to which the enemy's attention had been carefully and intentionally drawn, in order to divert it from the other points; and that, in consequence, it had probably been more thoroughly provided with obstructive arrangements, and prepared for vigorous defence.

Then, as to General Wilson's nervousness about the final assault, it would be most unjust to underestimate the difficulty of his position, or the weight and validity of his grounds for hesitating to attack. On his success or failure rested, not the success or failure of an ordinary siege or battle, or even of a campaign, but the retention or loss of India; and on him personally would rest the whole responsibility for the loss, should it end in loss, while the weakness of his means was palpable. It is sufficient to compare them with the numbers soon afterwards held to be needed for much easier and less dangerous operations. But there can be no doubt of the intensity of the anxiety, or the reasonableness of the hesitation, when the decision had to be given for a hazard so tremendous.

CHAPTER IV.

THE FIRST DEFENCE OF THE LUCKNOW RESIDENCY.

WE now turn to Oude and Lucknow during the first stage of the Campaign. There two perfectly distinct operations were in progress—one the defence of the entrenched position, which Sir Henry Lawrence had been preparing at the Lucknow Residency ; the other, the successive advances and efforts of General Havelock to relieve its garrison. We deal with the former in this chapter.

The force that fought against the British at Chinhut consisted of parts of ten regiments of native infantry and two of cavalry, with two batteries, and the followers of three of the chiefs near Lucknow.

The enemy followed up the retreating British force, and closely invested the Residency the same day, but failed to cut off the Mutchi Bhown garrison, which joined it two nights afterwards. They were then joined by two other regiments, by the military police, and by all the armed Mahomedan population. All these, with the troops that had been besieging Cawnpore and others that were still on the march, constituted a very powerful army, whose situation in Oude and absence from Delhi was of the greatest importance to the vital struggle at the latter.

The Lucknow rebels after a few days formed a court, electing the boy, Birjis Kudr, as the new Nuwab in place of his father in Calcutta; with the real control lying in the hands of his mother, Huzrut Mahul, known as the Begum. Various people were appointed to nominal posts, but their functions were never carried out, the mutineer troops paying no heed to their commanders, and following their own devices. The only person of real vigour among the enemy was the moulvie, and he had no weight with the sepoys.

The defence of the Residency, which began so sadly with the crushing disaster at Chinhut on the 31st June, immediately afterwards received another most grievous blow in the loss of Sir Henry Lawrence, who was mortally wounded on the second day of the siege. But he had played his part—how nobly all the world knows. By his exceptional foresight and wonderful energy and resolution he had prepared the position for defence; and that so thoroughly that it ended with success, not only to itself, but as lightening the difficulties at Delhi. And now that he was dying, he crowned his work by his injunctions and arrangements for the conduct of the defence.

He was succeeded by Major Banks in the civil and political charge, and by General Inglis in the military command, with whom he associated Major Anderson of the Engineers to form a council. On Major Banks being killed three weeks afterwards,

General Inglis took up the political charge as well as the military.

The size and particulars of the entrenched position, which had four faces, of a quarter of a mile each, can be best understood from an examination of the map. But it may be explained that the line of defence was continuous; there were no gaps in it, however weak it may have appeared. Wherever there was not a wall or a building duly loopholed, there were scarped *revêtements* and parapets with ditches, fronted by obstructions, such as palisading, *abatis, chevaux de frise,* stakes, crows'-feet, and the like, through which the enemy were never once found to be able to force their way. The position was defended by more guns than could be properly manned and worked.

The combatants of the garrison, including officers, numbered 1700, of whom 700 were sepoys. The other inmates of the entrenchment were 700 natives and 600 Christians, total 1300, bringing the whole number to be fed up to 3000. Among the 600 Christian non-combatants, there were 240 women and 270 children, besides 50 schoolboys.

Sir Henry had stored supplies in such quantity that the cattle furnished meat up to Havelock's arrival, while the grain food fed the whole force, including Havelock's, till Sir Colin arrived and withdrew the garrison, late in November.

The water supply was good and plentiful.

The buildings and posts bordering the line of defence were called the *outposts.* Those behind them were supporting posts, or *retrenchments.* Among these the troops and combatants were distributed. In two of the outposts—the Redan and the Cawnpore battery—there were none but British soldiers. In four of them—the Hospital post, the Treasury, Germon's, and the Sikh Square—there were only native troops. In all other posts the garrisons consisted of about equal numbers of British soldiers, volunteers, and sepoys. The company of the 84th was held as a reserve in the Residency, on the roof of which was a post of observation from which the movements of the enemy were watched.

The families were distributed throughout the interior or more sheltered buildings, and were never allowed to wander from them, or go to their exposed faces. It may be of interest to describe how they were fed. A scale of rations per head—combatant, native, woman, and child—was drawn up for the guidance of the commissariat. The commandant of each post sent to the commissariat daily a return of his numbers. The total supply for his number was sent to him, and he had to arrange for its distribution within his post and for its cooking, for which practically there were but very few servants. This explains how no one had ever to search for food.

The basis of the organization of the defence lay in the responsibility attaching to the commandant of each post for its defence, and for due vigilance, care, and knowledge of everything that went on before him and on his flanks. No one was allowed to leave his post without the commandant's permission; the

Staff and the Engineers only went freely over the position.

With one exception, the adjacent buildings had been demolished, leaving only the ruins of their lower stories to act as a screen to the foot of our defences from the enemy's artillery. These ruins, however, served as shelter for the enemy's infantry, and as starting-ground for their mines. They were very close indeed, being only fifty and twenty-five yards off on the eastern face, and from thirteen to ten on the southern! The exception above referred to was Johannes's house, which was left standing by accident, but was a thorn in the side of the defence till it was blown up.

The defence of the Residency lasted till the 25th September, when Havelock's force arrived to its succour. This period of twelve and a half weeks was divided, by three general all-round attacks on the 20th July, 10th August, and 5th September, into four stages of about three weeks each.

During the first stage no marked incident of importance occurred. The enemy harassed, but did not attack in force. The defenders were vigorously strengthening their defences and organizing their arrangements, and they made one sortie. It was against Johannes's house, with the intention of demolishing it; but the enemy collected in too great force to allow them to effect their object, and the General consequently recalled the sortie. But a very important feature in the attack came gradually to notice—the enemy's artillery entirely failed to breach or seriously damage the lower parts of the defences.

On the 20th July the first great all-round attack was delivered, and as the other two were similar in their features they may all be conveniently described here. They all consisted of, first, the explosion of some mine meant to make a breach in the defences; then a nearly simultaneous effort to storm the entrenchments at the expected breach and elsewhere, accompanied by a ceaseless all-round fire of artillery and musketry. The same results followed in every case. The explosions were harmless, owing to the mines being short of their mark. The stormers failed, as they found no breach, and they rarely reached—they never penetrated through—the obstructions; the artillery fire damaged only the roofs and upper stories; the musketry did little harm, as the defenders kept well under cover; while the defenders' artillery played havoc among the stormers—as they came on in mass—and was well supported by the musketry fire through the loopholes of the buildings and parapets.

In the first attack there was only one mine exploded, and it was directed against the Redan; the points attacked being the Redan and Innes's post. In the second attack mines were aimed at the Martinière and Sago's posts, and the attacks were at the Cawnpore battery, Gubbins's post, and Innes's. In the third attack mines were exploded against the Brigade Mess and Gubbins's post, and another mine, aimed at Saunders's, had been destroyed by the garrison a few hours before the attack came off; the posts at which rushes were attempted were the Brigade Mess and the Sikh Square. One special feature of this third attack was that the enemy had constructed a battery close opposite the Bailey Guard Gate, and opened fire when the attack began. But Aitken's sepoys had noticed the work, and had built a counter-battery in their own, the Treasury post; and the two heavy guns with which it was armed at once silenced the enemy. Another special feature on this occasion was that Talookdaree troops joined in the attack for the first time.

Such were the three great all-round attacks; but during the whole period of the siege after the first attack the enemy were ceaseless in their efforts to drive mines under the defences, and it will be presently shown what these efforts were, and how they were all, with one exception, foiled.

But when the mine in the first attack was exploded, the significance and danger of this new feature in the struggle were so obvious that the utmost alarm ensued. Any single mine driven, undetected, under the defences of the outer line might make there a huge breach, which, from its suddenness, the defenders might be quite unable to block or defend, but through which the enemy, duly prepared, might rush forward in their thousands, and, in a few minutes, exterminate the garrison. Now, this might occur at any one single effort, and if the enemy were to try to mine simultaneously at several—say fifty—points (for which they had ample means), the defenders would be wholly unable to oppose them (from want of labour), except at a very few points; and the outlook would be appalling.

The steps taken to meet this danger were as follows: (1) At every outpost intelligent men were told off to listen for sounds of mining. (2) At whatever points sounds were ever heard, and at suitable spots in the more exposed outposts—such as Saunders's, Sago's, Anderson's, Deprat's, the Martinière, the Brigade Mess, etc.—defensive mines were begun by the garrison (of each post) by sinking a shaft to some six feet below the level of the ground outside, and then driving a gallery for a short distance outwards. The vigilance and the desperate energy with which this novel work was carried out ended in success. Fortunately the enemy did not try to make a simultaneous mining attack at all, or even many, points. It was equally fortunate that they had not attempted, for their first trial, an easy mine at a short distance, as at the Brigade Mess or the Martinière—but, instead, an almost impossible one (from its great distance), against the Redan. (3) The men of the several posts were trained to driving the mines, but the more dangerous work was left to Cornish miners of the 32nd Regiment.

Including the mines exploded in the three attacks, the enemy made thirty-seven distinct and separate mining attacks against the defences of the position. They will be found detailed in a table at the end of this chapter, which will show that out of the whole thirty-seven, only one succeeded in making a breach;

all the others collapsed, or were foiled by the steps taken by the Engineers of the defence, or were discovered after Havelock's arrival. From none of the last did the garrison run any serious risk.

The only mine in which the enemy succeeded had not been detected, because it was aimed at the Sikh square, in which the horses of the Sikh cavalry of the garrison were picketed, and the noise of the miners at work was smothered by that of the stamping of the horses. The mine made a breach thirty feet long in the rampart, but the enemy were not ready to storm. Fortunately it was daytime, and the square was commanded on three sides by the garrison buildings, the fire of which kept off the enemy till the breach was barricaded, and the defences there restored.

The defenders carried out only one aggressive mine. It was run out from the Martinière under Johannes's house, which had practically silenced the Cawnpore battery. But the mine brought it down in ruins, and on the 21st August, the Cawnpore battery resumed its *rôle* of protecting the southern angle of the position.

One subject of much importance in the defence of the Residency, but of still greater importance to General Havelock in his efforts to succour it, was the correspondence between him and General Inglis.

The garrison received the first intelligence from the outer world on the 25th July, in a letter from Colonel Tytler, of Havelock's staff, announcing that the force was then crossing the Ganges on the way to relieve the garrison, and expecting to reach it in five or six days. On the 6th August they learnt that Havelock had been unable to advance further, and then, on the 15th, General Inglis received a letter telling him of Havelock's return to Cawnpore.

In consequence of this intelligence, and of the tone of the letters addressed to him, General Inglis wrote to General Havelock on the 16th, informing him of the gravity of the situation of the garrison, and that, on half rations, their provisions would last till about the 10th of the next month. As it turned out, the meat lasted till the 25th September, and the grain food fed the combined force, *i.e.* Havelock's as well as the original garrison, till the 20th November. This extraordinary mistake does not seem to have ever been explained.

In September a new danger began to arise from Havelock's detention at Cawnpore, or rather from his not actually arriving at Lucknow to the relief of the garrison. This was the growing impression among the natives in it, including the sepoys, that the stories about Havelock were untrue, and that the garrison's position was hopeless. Many were beginning to think that it was time for them to shift for themselves; and, with their disappearance in any numbers, it would be impossible to occupy all the outposts, and would become necessary to retire from some of them into the inner posts, which commanded them. Besides other consequences of such a step, fresh mining ground would be given to the enemy, whose present mining attack was losing its chief danger, from there being so little ground now left available for such purposes, most of the space having been rendered unfit for further work by the effects of the previous explosions and operations.

Fortunately, however, by the time that the new danger began to get serious, the defence was really drawing to its close, with the arrival of Havelock's force. On the 22nd September, Inglis learnt of its immediate approach, and on the evening of the 25th it fought its way in, thereby averting all immediate danger of any successful irruption of overwhelming numbers of the enemy, and unquestionably further staving off the certain disaster which would otherwise have occurred. For in two or three days afterwards, the fugitive mutineer army from Delhi were beginning to reach Lucknow, and would very shortly, from their numerical strength, have rendered impossible any junction of Havelock's force with the Residency.

During the defence which had thus been brought to a successful issue by Havelock's succour, the garrison had not lost a foot of its own ground, and had considerably extended the neutral ground by driving the enemy out of it. Only one battery had ever been silenced (the Cawnpore battery), and that only for a few days, as it resumed its work on Johannes's house being blown up.

After the death of Sir Henry Lawrence, three other serious casualties occurred—one in each of the three successive stages of the siege. The first was that of Major Banks, who had succeeded to the civil command; he was shot through a loophole. The second was that of Major Anderson, whom Sir Henry had associated with Banks and Inglis in the council. The third was that of Captain Fulton, generally regarded as the most important of all, as he had been the life and soul of the defence, and had throughout initiated and supervised the Engineer and mining operations.

General Inglis held the command throughout this trying defence, and brought it to its successful close, ever calm and vigilant under its crushing responsibility and exceptional dangers, and was thoroughly supported by Wilson, his Adjutant-General.

The 32nd Regiment, the backbone of the garrison, lost 133 men during the siege, after losing 111 at Chinhut. The casualties in the 13th Native Infantry exceeded their full number, owing to many having been wounded twice or thrice. Has there ever been so great an instance of steadfast and gallant loyalty?

MINING TABLE NO. I.

TABULAR STATEMENT OF THE ENEMY'S MINES.

Arranged Approximately by Date.

General Serial No.	Post attacked.	Nature of attack.	Particulars.
	FIRST ATTACK, JULY 20, 1857.		
1	Redan	Explosion	Short : harmless.
	SECOND STAGE, JULY 21 TO AUGUST 9.		
2	Redan	Lodgment	Dislodged by artillery and musketry.
3	Martinière	,,	Dislodged by grenades.
4	Gubbins's	,,	Dislodged by sortie.
5	Cawnpore Battery	Gallery	Collapsed : too shallow.
6	Brigade Mess	,,	Stopped, on hearing countermine.
7	Sikh Square	,,	Broken into and destroyed by countermine.
8	Sago's	,,	Collapsed : too shallow.
	SECOND ATTACK, AUGUST 10.		
9	Martinière	Explosion	Short : damaged stockade.
10	Sago's	,,	Short : harmless.
	THIRD STAGE, AUGUST 11 TO SEPTEMBER 4.		
11	Sago's	Gallery	Fought and blown up.
12	,,	,,	August 29 : stopped on hearing countermine.
13	,,	,,	Sept. 1 : stopped on hearing countermine.
14	Saunders's	,,	August 23 : stopped on hearing countermine.
15	,,	,,	August 31 : blown up by countermine, Sept. 1.
16	,,	,,	Sept. 1 : blown up by countermine, Sept. 2.
17	,,	,,	Sept. 3 : blown up by countermine, Sept. 4.

General Serial No.	Post attacked.	Nature of attack.	Particulars.
	THIRD STAGE, AUGUST 11 TO SEPTEMBER 4.		
18	Anderson's	Gallery	August 13: stopped on hearing countermine.
19	,,	,,	August 23: stopped on hearing countermine.
20	,,	,,	August 18: stopped on hearing countermine.
21	Brigade Mess	,,	August 20: broken into and blown up, August 29.
22	,,	Explosion	Sept. 3: short, harmless in third attack, Sept. 5.
23	Sikh Square	Gallery	Met countermine: destroyed by its own explosion.
24	,,	Explosion	Successful: simultaneous with 23, on August 16th: made a breach in wall 30 feet long.
	THIRD ATTACK, SEPTEMBER 5.		
25	Gubbins's	Explosion	Short: harmless.
	Brigade Mess	,,	Short: harmless. (See No. 22.)
	FOURTH STAGE, FROM SEPTEMBER 6 TO SEPTEMBER 25.		
26	Cawnpore Battery	Gallery	Sept. 9: destroyed by countermine ready since July.
27	Sikh Square	,,	Sept. 9: stopped on hearing countermine.
28	,,	,,	Sept. 9: blown up by countermine.
29	Brigade Mess	,,	Sept. 10: checked by countermine.
30	Cawnpore Battery	,,	Sept. 10: checked by countermine.
31	Baily Guard Gate	,,	Sept. 10: checked by countermine.
32	Germon's post	,,	Sept. 10: checked by countermine.
33	Church	,,	Sept. 11: destroyed by sortie.
34	,,		Sept. 21: destroyed by sortie.
35	Baily Guard Gate	,,	Collapsed about Sept. 23.
	FOUND AFTER RELIEF OF SEPTEMBER 25.		
36	Redan	Gallery	Far short.
37	Church	,,	Far short.

MINING TABLE NO. II.

TABULAR STATEMENT OF THE ENEMY'S MINES.

ARRANGED UNDER THE POSTS ATTACKED.

Post attacked.		Serial No.	Approximate date.	Nature of attack.	Particulars and result.
Redan. .	1	1	July 20	Explosion	Far short.
,,	2	2	July 21	Lodgment	At foot, dislodged by fire.
,,	3	36	After relief	Gallery	Far short.
Baily Guard Gate .	1	31	Sept. 10	,,	Checked by countermine.
,, ,, .	2	35	Sept. 23	,,	Collapsed : too shallow.
Saunders's post . .	1	14	August 23	,,	Checked by countermine.
,, ,, .	2	15	August 31	,,	Blown up, Sept. 1.
,, ,, .	3	16	Sept. 1	,,	,, Sept. 2.
,, ,, .	4	17	Sept. 3	,,	,, Sept. 4.
Sago Garrison	1	8	July 29	,,	Collapsed : too shallow.
,, ,, .	2	10	August 10	Explosion	Short : harmless.
,, ,, .	3	11	August 11	Gallery	Blown up.
,, ,, .	4	12	August 29	,,	Checked by countermine.
,, ,, .	5	13	Sept. 1	,,	Checked by countermine.
Germon's post . .	1	32	Sept. 10	,,	Checked by countermine.
Anderson's post . .	1	18	August 13	,,	Checked by countermine.
,, ,, .	2	19	August 23	,,	Checked by countermine.
,, ,, .	3	20	August 28	,,	Checked by countermine.
Cawnpore Battery .	1	5	July 25	,,	Collapsed, under shell fire.
,, ,, .	2	26	Sept. 9	,,	Blown up.
,, ,, .	3	30	Sept. 10	,,	Checked by countermine.
Martinière	1	3	July 21	Lodgment	Dislodged by grenades.
,, .	2	9	August 10	Explosion	Short, but damaged stockade.
Brigade Mess .	1	6	July 25	Gallery	Checked by countermine.
,, ,, .	2	21	August 20	,,	Checked by countermine, and then blown up, August 29.

Post attacked.		Serial No.	Approximate date.	Nature of attack.	Particulars and resu't.
Brigade Mess .	3	22	Sept. 3	Gallery and Explosion	Checked by countermine, then exploded, short, harmless, on Sept. 5.
,, ,, .	4	29	Sept. 10	Gallery and Explosion	Checked by countermine.
Sikh Square	1	7	July 25	Gallery	Checked by countermine, then blown up.
,, ,, .	2	23	August 16	,,	Both destroyed by its own explosion.
,, ,, .	3	24	,,	Explosion	Successful: made 30 feet breach.
,, ,, .	4	27	Sept. 9	Gallery	Checked by countermine.
,, ,, .	5	28	,,	,,	Blown up by countermine.
Gubbins's	1	4	July 21	Lodgment	Dislodged by sortie.
,, .	2	25	Sept. 5	Explosion	Short: harmless.
Church .	1	33	Sept. 11	Gallery	Destroyed by sortie.
,, .	2	34	Sept. 21	,,	,, ,,
,, .	3	37	After relief	,,	Short: harmless.

CHAPTER V.

HAVELOCK'S CAMPAIGN FOR THE SUCCOUR OF LUCKNOW.

THE first defence of the Lucknow Residency having closed with its succour, on the 25th September, by the force led by Havelock and accompanied by Outram, we now turn to the campaign by which that succour was effected. That campaign and the defence of Lucknow began on the same date—the 30th June—the latter with the fight at Chinhut, the former with the despatch of Renaud's party from Allahabad towards Cawnpore.

No sooner, however, had Renaud started than Havelock heard of the surrender and catastrophe at Cawnpore on the 27th, which gravely altered his position. For it involved these results, besides others—that the whole of the Cawnpore rebel army was free to move towards Allahabad and attack Renaud's party on the way; and further, that the mutineers from the east (from Azimgurh, Jaunpore, Benares, and Allahabad) might co-operate in that attack. Havelock, therefore, sent cautioning orders to Renaud, and collecting such force as was available, started on the

7th July to overtake him. His brigade, including Renaud's detachment, was as shown in the margin.

English	1404
Natives	561
Total	1965
Viz.—	
English infantry	1286
Brasyer's Sikh infantry	448
Artillery	116
Volunteer cavalry . .	20
Native cavalry . . .	95

The English infantry regiments were the 64th, the 78th Highlanders, some of the 84th, and the 1st Madras Fusiliers.

Joining Renaud on the 11th, he fought and won the battle of Futtehpore on the 12th, and then the two actions of Aong and Pandoo Nuddee on the 15th. On this day Renaud, the gallant pioneer of the advance, was killed.

After the battle of Futtehpore, the native cavalry, having misbehaved, were disarmed and dismounted. At Futtehpore the enemy had expected to meet only Renaud's detachment, and gave way quickly before the larger force. At Aong they had entrenched the village, and they employed their numerous cavalry to threaten Havelock's flanks and rear. But keeping that cavalry at bay with two-thirds of his force, he stormed the village with the remainder, on which the enemy fled precipitately to the bridge at the Pandoo Nuddee, meaning to contest its passage, reinforced and helped by the Nana's followers, but intending also to blow it up in case of necessity. Havelock pursued, and, on reaching the Nullah, lined its banks, brought a cross-fire to bear on the enemy massed behind the bridge, forced the bridge before they could destroy it, and drove them in rout towards Cawnpore.

These three successes were all-important, as, in spite of the heat and losses, they roused the spirits of the troops and inspired them with full confidence in their leader just when their trust and endurance were to be put to the severest test. Havelock heard that evening that there were still a large number of English women and children alive in Cawnpore. So on to their rescue—no halt in the advance.

Next day, the 16th July, he fought the three separate actions by which he recaptured Cawnpore. His force had become reduced to 1100 British and 300 Sikhs, besides Maude's battery; it was opposed by 5000 regular troops and a mass of irregulars and of the Nana's followers, with 8 guns, of which 4 were 24-pounders. They were found drawn up in a curved line crossing the road to Cawnpore, only a few miles distant. Fronting them with his cavalry and skirmishers, Havelock led his main body, unseen, round some groves, till it emerged on their left flank, from which he swept down their line impetuously, rolling it up, and putting them to flight with the loss of all their guns.

After a brief rest, the infantry followed up the enemy, who had again collected at a village a couple of miles away, reinforced by two fresh guns. Maude's battery had been left behind, the cattle being too wearied to keep pace with the infantry, who, however, without their support again charged the enemy, and again routed them, finishing the second fight of the day.

Still onward continued the march of the British,

and now on the outskirts of Cawnpore they found the enemy drawn up a third time to oppose them, in greater strength than before; having been reinforced by fresh levies of the Nana, with a 24-pounder, and commanded by him in person. Again the British line advanced; the 64th charged and captured the gun, and on this the enemy finally fled and disappeared—the struggle was over, and Cawnpore was occupied next morning. But, alas! the Nana had already massacred his captives, and now with his followers was far beyond pursuit.

On entering Cawnpore, on the 17th July, Havelock heard of the state of matters at Lucknow, and at once took steps to cross the river and advance to its relief. By the 28th he had ferried his force over the river, a mile and a half wide, to the other side, into Oude, leaving 300 men under Neill in an entrenchment which he had constructed at Cawnpore; and he had prepared and now occupied a post at Mungurwar, on the left bank of the Ganges.

It was while the passage of the Ganges was in progress that Tytler sent to Lucknow the letter that has been referred to, which arrived there on the 25th. The hopes held out in it proved misleading, but this was due to the unexpected sickness and the later news of the 30th. Also it is to be remembered, in considering its tone, in what high and elated spirits the force was; how they had overcome every obstacle that challenged them; how steadily on the increase the enemy's cowardice appeared to be, and for what a noble goal the force was striving. Small be the blame, if they counted too certainly on immediate success.

When Havelock was now about to advance, the state of matters was this : he had in front of him the hostile force already described ; his communications to the base at Allahabad and at Calcutta were open ; reinforcements had been promised and were advancing up country ; and he had 300 men left at Cawnpore, under Neill, to protect his immediate rear ; but his base was 600 miles distant, and his own force consisted of only 1500 men and 13 field-guns—his Europeans did not muster 1200 men ! It was with this mere handful that he advanced towards Lucknow on the 29th, and on that day fought the two actions of Oonao and Busherut Gunge. The country was flooded, and he had to confine his march to the high road or its immediate borders. The enemy, fortunately, were similarly hampered in their movements, but they held their villages in force, and had to be driven out of them. The mutineers, when caught in mass on the road, were swept through and through by our artillery. Our skirmishers and guns played on the front of the villages till our infantry were close enough up to charge and storm the positions, and then they cleared them out by hand-to-hand fighting. This was the feature of both the battles, in which 19 guns were taken ; but the fighting was severe, and cholera had appeared, so that, on the following morning, Havelock found that he had lost one-sixth of his force.

And then, at the same time, came a crushing blow

in the receipt from Neill at Cawnpore of the disastrous intelligence that the Dinapore sepoys had mutinied; raising the district, and endangering the communications with Calcutta, so as to destroy any chance of early reinforcements, *e.g.* by the 5th, 37th, and 90th regiments, on which he had been counting. As the enemy in front was in full strength, an advance against them was at present hopeless. So, on the 31st, Havelock retired to Mungurwar, his post on the Oude bank of the Ganges, to await supports and keep in touch with Cawnpore.

A few days later, having learned that a strong force of the enemy was collecting at Busherut Gunge, he moved out against them on the 4th August, and again defeating them, drove them off with a loss of 300 men. But again he lost heavily from cholera, and so had again to return to Mungurwar; the more so that Neill was now reporting that Cawnpore was being seriously threatened by a mutineer army from the south side of the Jumna River, thirty miles off.

These rumours grew rapidly more alarming, and Havelock consequently wrote on the 9th to the Commander-in-Chief, intimating the unavoidable necessity, and his consequent intention, of returning to Cawnpore. Making then his arrangements for the re-passage of the Ganges, he first, in order to secure his retreat, moved against the enemy on the 11th, defeated them a third time at Busherut Gunge, and driving them well off, marched back rapidly to Mungurwar. On the next day he crossed to Cawnpore without the foe venturing to molest his withdrawal.

When halting at Mungurwar after the 31st, Havelock had received those few reinforcements, including a half battery, that had been following him up closely; and it is important to note the strength of his available force at various dates.

1. On the 29th July, when starting for the advance on Lucknow, he had 1500 men all told, of whom 1200 were English.

2. On returning to Mungurwar on the 31st July, only 850 men were available for the line of battle.

3. On his second advance, on the 4th August, his full strength was 1400 men.

4. On his second return to Mungurwar, on the 5th August, he had only the same strength left as on July 31st;

5. and under 900 men available on his third advance.

Further, his situation was this. No more reinforcements were likely to arrive for at least a month. In his front were some 30,000 men, the full force of the mutineer and rebel army as at the first, exclusive of casualties. The talookdars of Roya and Doondea Khera were threatening both flanks, but no fresh Rajpoot chiefs or clans had joined the enemy. On the west, at Furruckabad, a large body of Rohillas were massing under the Nuwab; and Cawnpore was threatened from Kalpee, to the south on the Jumna, by the Nana's followers, the Saugor mutineers, and the Gwalior contingent. Is there in the annals of our history any record of odds so overwhelming, and so undauntedly and brilliantly faced? Havelock's judgment, in this desperate plight, remained clear and unclouded. However bitter his disappointment, however deep his anguish, however intense the mortification of his men, who had fought with such heroic valour and such unvaried success, he felt that his duty and the discharge of his trust required him to turn his back on the goal for which he had been striving.

But this retirement from Oude produced a result which he had doubtless never contemplated. The talookdars openly construed it as the British evacuation of the province, and now formally recognized the rebel Durbar at Lucknow as the *de facto* Government; and though they refrained from supporting it by their own presence, they obeyed its orders, which they had hitherto disregarded, and sent to the scene of warfare the contingents which they had been called upon to provide.

When back at Cawnpore, Havelock had to take immediate action. His whole force consisted of some 1400 British soldiers and Brasyer's Sikhs, but out of this number 350 were disabled by wounds or sickness, while cholera was raging at a rate that in another six weeks would leave no fighting men available. Meanwhile, the Nana's followers had returned, reassembled about his neighbouring palace at Bithoor, and been joined by the mutineers from Saugor in the Central Provinces. So Havelock attacked that force, defeating and driving them off with the loss of their guns; but not before the mutineer 42nd Native Infantry had made a rash and disastrous attempt to cross bayonets with the Madras Fusiliers. He had then to send a body of men down to Futtehpore, the scene of the first of his battles, to repel the efforts of the rebels in Oude to cross the Ganges and intercept his communications with Allahabad.

It was now that he heard that he was to be superseded by General Outram, his old friend and commander in Persia; but he also learnt that Major Eyre had defeated the Dinapore mutineers. This cleared the communications, and gave him hopes that some of the seven battalions, which he knew to be present to the south of Allahabad, would soon be arriving to reinforce him. Hence it was with feelings little short of dismay that he learnt that Outram, who was coming up the river by steam, and was inaccessible by telegrams, was arranging to stop the advance of these troops towards Cawnpore, and to take them with himself on a line of his own through Oude to Lucknow.

By this time Sir Colin Campbell had reached Calcutta to take up the command in India; and Havelock wrote and telegraphed to him, explaining the real state of affairs. The result was that Outram gave up his original ideas, came up with the reinforcements, and made his famous surrender of his command to Havelock till he should have effected the relief of Lucknow.

But the reinforcements he brought up were only the 5th Fusiliers and the 90th Light Infantry. There still remained between Allahabad and Calcutta the 10th, 29th, 35th, 37th, and 53rd, besides drafts from other regiments. But all these, instead of being sent on to the front, were being kept in those southern districts, not by orders from head quarters, but through the interference of local officers. They were thus being diverted from their proper course and frittered away broadcast; and while Havelock's force, at the gravest scene of operations, could barely muster 1100 men, some 6000 men who might have been on their way to his support were kept pottering about to the south-east of Benares.

While Havelock was thus remaining at Cawnpore waiting the reinforcements, the Oude rebels again tried to cross over towards Futtehpore; but detachments of the advancing reinforcements caught them and punished them severely. The enemy, however, in the Kalpee direction to the south, and Furruckabad to the west, kept quiet.

Meanwhile, Havelock was filled with the deepest anxiety for the Lucknow garrison, and about the delay in relieving it; as the letters that reached him from General Inglis, especially that of the 16th August, impressed him with the conviction that the food of the garrison was being so reduced that they must be losing all vitality and powers of resistance. The straits of a garrison within sight of the last possible morsel of food are incomparably greater, and tend to demand much more desperate efforts for relief than when the exigencies are those lying only or mainly in liability to attack by overwhelming odds.

Outram joined Havelock on the 15th September; and although he handed over the formal command to him, he did not divest himself of a real lead in the practical guidance of operations, and kept up a strong pressure on him as to the plans to be adopted. Thus the passage of the river was carried out on Outram's lines, and not in accordance with the arrangements which Havelock had already started.

The passage was effected by the 20th, the force being as shown in the margin. On the 21st they attacked the rebels at Mungurwar, and drove them in flight to Busherut Gunge, the scene of Havelock's three actions in July and August. On the 23rd, the force reached the Alum Bagh, about four miles short of the Residency, and captured it, driving the enemy across the canal into the city. At the Alum Bagh, news was received of the storming of Delhi, and the force remained halted during the 24th, pending the settlement of the plans and route for the junction with the Residency.

1 Heavy battery } 2 Light batteries }	282
Volunteer cavalry	100
Native cavalry .	59
British infantry .	2388
Sikh infantry . .	341
Total	3170

Havelock's conviction had always been that the enemy would reserve their strength and their chief efforts for street-fighting in the British endeavour to reach the Residency. He had, therefore, meant to avoid entering the city of Lucknow, and to march, instead, through the more open ground, cross the Goomtee, and get access to the Residency by its river face. Accordingly he had carried with him the apparatus and means for bridging the Goomtee; but, on the 24th, it was decided that the recent burst of rain had made the open country too swampy and heavy for the proposed march, and that the route should be the one which avoided the actually open country, but entailed the next minimum of street-fighting. This was the route which crossed the canal by the Char Bagh Bridge, and then, turning east, followed the canal bank till it cleared the city and neared the river, whence it struck westwards direct towards the Residency position. This would involve only half a mile of streets of which to run the gauntlet.

Such, accordingly, was the route of the running battle of the 25th. A strong detachment was left at the Alum Bagh to form its garrison, and the force itself advanced towards the Char Bagh Bridge, capturing the Yellow House and the Char Bagh on its way. There was a street that led direct from the Char Bagh Bridge to the Residency; the Bridge end of this street being held in great strength by the enemy, whose commanding musketry fire covered a powerful battery that was itself entrenched, and so barricaded the bridge. Maude's guns were ineffective against that battery, so Neill was ordered to carry the bridge. The whole of the storming-party, under Arnold, were swept down, except two men, of whom the younger Havelock was one; but before the battery could fire a second round, the Madras Fusiliers, who were in support, had charged over the bridge, cleared the breastworks, stormed the battery, and won the Char Bagh passage of the canal. The 78th then seized and held the buildings and position at the bridge end of the street, while the whole of the rest of the force passed to the right in their rear, skirting the canal as planned, and so made its way rapidly and unchecked to the Begum's Palace and the Sekundra Bagh; whence it turned west to the Motee Mahul, where the column halted to pull itself together. The 78th had hard fighting to maintain the post at the bridge; and, at length, when all had passed on, they followed in the rear up to the Begum's Palace, and turned westward from that point instead of from the Sekundra Bagh further on, as the main column had done. Later in the afternoon—arrangements having been made for a party under Colonel Campbell to hold the Motee Mahul with the heavy guns and impedimenta, and the 78th having been seen coming along on the left flank—Havelock and Outram sallied out to the entrance of the streets running between the lines of buildings that still shut off the Residency. Outram was anxious to find a way through the buildings themselves, and searched hard for it, but as it had not been found when dusk began to fall, the force ran the gauntlet through two parallel routes, by which they in a few minutes reached the Baily Guard Gate and entered the entrenchment. The loss in the outer of the two parallel routes had been comparatively heavy, but well worth the end attained. The relieving force had reinforced the Residency position, and made it secure, rescuing its garrison from the extreme dangers—unknown as well as known—that threatened it, and averting a catastrophe, which would have been of primary weight and consequence at this stage of the war.

With this successful junction of Havelock's force with the Baily Guard garrison, and with the consequently successful close of the defence of the Lucknow Residency position by that garrison, single-handed till reinforced, ends the first stage of the campaign in Oude.

The two remaining theatres of operations, the eastern and the southern, during the same stage, now demand our brief attention, before we turn to the second stage of the Campaign.

CHAPTER VI.

EASTERN AND SOUTHERN THEATRES IN THE FIRST STAGE OF THE CAMPAIGN.

In these two other theatres there were no military operations or contests, except on a small scale, during this the first stage of the Campaign.

The Eastern Theatre.

The city of Patna had been giving trouble, but the sepoys at Dinapore, close to it, had not been disarmed; and an old Rajpoot chief of great influence in the district, named Konwur Singh, was known to be disaffected, owing to grievances of old standing. Hence General Lloyd, who commanded, was urged to take advantage of the presence of some English regiments, who were passing up the river by steam, to disarm the native regiments. But he did not do this, and adopted only half measures. This led to an outbreak, on the 25th July, both of the sepoys at Dinapore and of the cavalry at Segowlie, in the same district. These mutineers were not at once attacked and dealt with, although a British regiment, the 10th, was garrisoned there; and so they were enabled to move off—to Patna in one direction, to raise the city, and towards Arrah, the civil station, in another, to attack the English community, expecting to be there joined and assisted by Rajah Konwur Singh.

At Arrah, however, precautions had been taken by one of the residents, Mr. Boyle, an engineer of the railway (at that time in the earliest stages of construction); and this interfered with the designs of the insurgents. He had prepared his house for defence against such an attack, had stored food and ammunition in it, had obtained a garrison of 50 of Rattray's Sikhs from the Commissioner, Mr. Taylor, and was also, of course, now joined by the English residents of Arrah. A siege ensued, in which the garrison defended itself successfully against the attack of artillery as well as of musketry. On the 29th a detachment of some 400 men was sent out from Dinapore to relieve Arrah; but the force was caught in an ambuscade at midnight about a mile from the house, and was severely handled, defeated, and driven back. But rescue from another quarter was at hand. Major Vincent Eyre, of the artillery, was going up the river with his guns and some troops, and had reached Buxar, on the Ganges, about fifty miles from Arrah, when he heard of the attack on it. Acting on his own responsibility, he disembarked the guns and troops, and marched to the relief. After encountering many difficulties, he was still some sixteen miles short of Arrah on the 2nd August, when he was met by the enemy in full force, with their ground carefully prepared for a combat. After a severe struggle the 5th Fusiliers charged and stormed the position held by the enemy, who then fled precipitately. Next morning Eyre continued his march, and effected the relief of Arrah. This was, of course, most important, as well as satisfactory; but more had to be done. The rising had thrown the whole district into disorder, and caused an entire stoppage of the land communications, though the steamer route was still open; and while Konwur Singh, with his followers and other mutineers, remained unpunished, a large body of troops might have to be detained to hold the country. Some signal blow was necessary, and Eyre decided that this should be against Jugdespore, Konwur Singh's stronghold. Accordingly, by strenuous exertions he raised his own force to about 500 men, of whom 140 were Sikhs, and on the 11th August advanced towards the enemy. Next day he met Konwur Singh's army, which consisted of 1200 sepoys and 4000 of his own retainers, and routing it thoroughly, he then crossed the river and captured Jugdespore. This terminated the contest. The British were in the ascendant, and Eyre returned to Buxar, to continue his advance to Cawnpore. His defeat of Konwur Singh was synchronous with Havelock's return from Oude to Cawnpore.

Simultaneous with, or rather immediately following on, the Dinapore outbreak, there had been mutinies of detached bodies of sepoys, with consequent local disturbances, further south, at Hazaribagh and other parts of the Chutia Nagpore district. But these were met and settled either by the Madras sepoy regiments, which arrived both from Calcutta and from Cuttack, or by parties of Rattray's Sikhs.

THE SOUTHERN THEATRE.

Lastly, we turn to the southern theatre. There were no British troops there yet, nor any states of which the soldiery were in hearty alliance with the English, whatever their chiefs may have been.

At Gwalior the English community had been mostly able to collect at Scindia's palace, and make their way thence, under the escort first of his Bodyguard and then of friendly Thakoors, to Agra. But the whole of the contingent, virtually a body of British sepoys, had mutinied, with the full sympathy of the bulk of Scindia's followers, in open hostility to the English. Those who were not at Gwalior at the beginning, but at outlying stations, moved across the country towards Kalpee on the Jumna, opposite Cawnpore, which they kept threatening for many months, without taking any active steps till November. Those insurgent soldiery who were at Gwalior remained there, sulkily, as if at Scindia's orders. But on the arrival, on the 23rd September, of the news of the storm of Delhi, and Scindia's open satisfaction at the intelligence, they moved off in a body to join their comrades at Kalpee.

The other important disturbance in the Southern Theatre was at Indore (with Mhow its cantonment), the capital of the Mahratta chief, Holkar, where the

British representative was Colonel Durand. The importance of this position lay not only in Holkar's traditional power, but in its proximity to the more specifically Bombay provinces or territory; so that Durand's anxieties lay quite as much (if not more) in preventing the disaffection spreading south of the boundary river, the Nerbudda, as in controlling the local crisis. That there was disaffection among the Mahratta soldiery was very certain, and, excepting Hungerford's battery, the Mhow troops had shown that their temper could not be counted on; so Durand had called in, to strengthen his frontier, the Bheel Corps (aborigines) and the Bhopal contingent of the friendly Bhopal Mussulman state. He had been relying on the approach of the Bombay column under General Woodburn, but it had been diverted to Aurungabad, owing to threatened disturbances there. It may be here explained that the movements and operations of this column during these three months will be found more fully described, as a preliminary to those in Central India, in the second stage of the Campaign.

On the 1st July the body of Holkar's troops that were detached on duty at the Residency rose in mutiny against it, and against the officers of the Bhopal cavalry and other native troops. The Bhopal men, however, and the Bheels and others on whom some reliance had been placed, were too cowed to act against the mutineers, though they remained with the British. Holkar sent messages to say he was powerless against his followers, and there was no chance of any assistance from Mhow for many hours; so Durand, with all the officers and English families, started with such troops (and their guns) as remained friendly, taking the route for Mundlaisir, by which they might reach Woodburn's column. To move to Mhow would have been impracticable, with the enemy planted where they were. But the Bhopal escort refused to go on by the Mundlaisir route, or by any other route than to Sehore; accordingly, the march was directed on Sehore, where they were received with all honour by the Begum of Bhopal. Thence Durand made his way to Woodburn's column, now passed under the command of General Stuart, joining it at Asseergurh; and directed all his efforts towards the prevention of the spread of the disaffection across the Nerbudda. Those efforts were successful, and after the absence of a month he returned, along with Stuart's column, to Mhow on the 2nd August. Nothing more overt took place in those districts before the end of September. Prince Feroze Shah, of the Delhi family, was indeed fomenting disturbances at Mundesore, partly to interrupt the communications with Bombay, and partly to cause risings at Neemuch and elsewhere; but the consequent operations did not take place till October.

Before quitting the first stage of the Campaign, it has to be remarked that the tide had now turned; the neck of the revolt had been broken before any assistance had arrived from England; and, with the reinforcements already landed from the China expedition, and with those on their way, and with the Punjab siding vigorously with the English, the rest was likely to be plain sailing. The mutineers had thrown down the gage of battle at Delhi, and Sir Henry Lawrence at Lucknow, and at both the British had been the victors. They had taken Delhi, while Lucknow had not been taken by the rebels, but had, instead, been relieved by Havelock.

BOOK IV.

THE DECISIVE CONTEST.

BOOK IV.

THE DECISIVE CONTEST—THE SECOND STAGE OF THE CAMPAIGN.

CHAPTER I.

INTRODUCTORY—AND THE PUNJAB AND DELHI THEATRES.

THE second stage of the Campaign occupied the six months from the end of September, 1857, to the end of the following March.

Steady, heavy warfare went on in the Oude theatre and in the southern theatre. Elsewhere, the actual contests were desultory and comparatively unimportant, though the civil administration was much strained, and the police kept on the alert by the disturbed state of the country.

In the development of the mutiny, and in the first stage of the Campaign, the province of Rohilkund was included in the Delhi theatre, at the extreme east of which it lay. But, henceforward, it can be more conveniently dealt with as part of the Oude theatre, the operations in these two provinces being much intermixed and interdependent. For the mutineers of the Delhi theatre had now flocked into Oude and become fused with the mutineers of the Oude theatre, forming a huge force; practically representing the whole that was left of the old trained sepoy army of Bengal that had mutinied, except the Gwalior contingent and a few other regiments.

The *Punjab* is the first theatre to be dealt with, though there was no actual campaigning there of importance. There were two risings, or attempts at rising, one at Murree, near the Huzara Mountain country, and the other in the Gogaira district, between Lahore and Mooltan. Both were at once suppressed by John Lawrence's prompt action. The Gogaira rising broke out on the very day of the storming of Delhi.

During its siege, the strain throughout the Punjab had been growing more and more intense; but, as soon as it was captured, that strain at once subsided, and a reaction ensued. The star of the British was felt to be in the ascendant; John Lawrence was not slow to seize the opportunity. The Khalsa spirit was roused in support of Government, and vigorous recruiting for fresh levies opened over the province. Its details need not be given; it suffices to say that the force raised by the middle of 1858, and employed throughout all the theatres, was so powerful as to require careful watching.

The *Delhi* theatre continued for a brief period the scene of conflict. The mutineer army, on being expelled from Delhi itself, crossed over to the left bank of the Jumna into the Doab, between it and the Ganges; then after flying southward for a short distance, turned eastwards; and, crossing the Ganges, entered Rohilkund, where some of them remained, joining the revolted Rohillas, while the bulk of them went onwards into Oude and to Lucknow.

It was mentioned, in dealing with the Delhi Campaign, that a force had been despatched thence after the capture of Delhi in pursuit of the mutineers. This force, which was of the strength shown in the margin, started under Brigadier Greathed, and followed up the enemy, clearing and settling the country as it went along. It drove the enemy out of the town of Bolundshuhur; and having restored the civil administration there, it then occupied and destroyed Malagurh, the fort of a rebel leader, Wullydad Khan. On the 5th October, after considerable fighting, the column retook and restored Allygurh, as it had done with Bolundshuhur. By this time, it was found that the mutineers had turned towards Oude, and were no longer in front of the pursuing column; and on the 8th, being urgently summoned to Agra, it diverted its course to that station, from its more direct route to Cawnpore. Arriving at Agra on the 10th October, it was suddenly surprised and attacked by a force of about 7000 men, consisting chiefly of mutineers or rebel troops from Mhow and Indore, Neemuch and Gwalior,

2 batteries Horse Artillery.
1 battery Field ,,
9th Lancers.
500 native cavalry.
450 British infantry.
1200 Punjab infantry.
200 Punjab sappers.

who had been supposed by the local authorities to be still beyond the Karee Nullah, ten miles off. The enemy were, in fact, as much taken by surprise in meeting with Greathed's column as the latter were by the attack, and gave way almost immediately under their impetuous countercharge. The rout was thorough; all their guns (twelve) were taken, and the slaughter was very great and effective. After this, the column proceeded on its way to Cawnpore, restoring Mynpooree, and defeating a body of the enemy at the Kalee Nuddee. It was now commanded by Brigadier Hope Grant, and at Cawnpore it halted to join part of the force that was about to advance, under Sir Colin Campbell, to the relief of the garrison that was entrenched in Lucknow.

With this, ended the operations in the Delhi theatre; at least, in the early part of the second stage.

CHAPTER II.

THE OUDE THEATRE—SECOND DEFENCE OF THE RESIDENCY, AND ITS RELIEF BY SIR COLIN CAMPBELL.

IN the Oude theatre the operations were, at the end of September, concentrated at Lucknow itself, Havelock's force, on relieving the Residency, having joined hands with its garrison; and the only enemy in the field being the besieging army through which Havelock had fought his way.

As soon as the junction was effected, Outram assumed the command. He had felt very sanguine that, with the arrival of the force at Lucknow, the rebels would lose heart, and the well-wishers in the city and the district would assert themselves and assist with supplies and carriage, if not with troops; a hopeful feeling which had been increased by the news of the storming and capture of Delhi.

That this help should now be obtained from the city appeared to be absolutely essential; as the supplies in the Residency were understood to be exhausted, while those with the relieving force, except only a very small quantity, had been left at the Alum Bagh. But it was obvious, soon after arrival, that the garrison were in no very severe straits for food, and that, somehow or other, rations were forthcoming.

So Outram set to at once to pull his force together. The rear-guard left in the Motee Mahul was under a heavy fire during the 26th, but was brought in during the night without loss, under the guidance of Colonel Napier. The Residency position was extended down to the river and through the Chuttur Munzil buildings along the banks; and sorties were made nearly every day up to the 4th October to clear the adjacent ground, obtain command of the roads and streets, and get into touch with the city. But all in vain. The besieging force, though they had been entirely unable to stand the charge of Havelock's men, had suffered comparatively little in the well-protected posts which they had occupied. Though they found themselves first outwitted by Havelock's circuitous march, and then unable to check the gallant advance from Neill's gate to the Baily Guard, they were still numerous enough and in sufficient heart to cling to the buildings round the British position, and foil Outram's efforts to clear a way out from it. They were further encouraged in this by the treacherous support of such men as Rajah Maun Singh, who posed in their midst as a thorough rebel, but in his letters to Outram as a true though secret friend to Government; and then before the first week was over fugitives from Delhi, veterans by this time, had begun to arrive and swell the mutineer force very seriously.

Matters accordingly seemed to Outram, Havelock, and Inglis, to be in a desperate state owing to the assumed exhaustion of the food supply in the garrison. When, however, Colonel Napier, as Chief of the Staff, proceeded to institute proper inquiries personally, he found, to his surprise, that the stock remaining was, in fact, abundant, and that there had been no valid ground for the report of scarcity. So ample was the supply, then and there pointed out by the commissariat officers to Colonel Napier, that it fed and sustained the combined force till relieved by Sir Colin Campbell in November; whereas it had before been written of as insufficient to do more than feed the original garrison up to the 10th September!

This fact, ascertained without trouble or difficulty as soon as inquiry was instituted, altered the position entirely. Outram at once stopped the sorties and withdrew into his position, to hold on in it quietly, pending the arrival of reinforcements.

From this time the warfare became one of mines, but on quite a different footing from that of the first siege. Then the struggle had been for life or death—a single sudden success on the enemy's part might have meant the irruption of the besiegers and the extinction of the garrison; but now there was no such risk—it was a case of pure underground contest, with no specially important result hanging on the issue. But throughout it, except at the start, the enemy always failed, and the victory lay with the garrison. The locale of this contest was confined entirely to the new position. At the old position the mining-ground had been practically exhausted.

Singular to say, while all this was in progress, the small garrison left as the rear-guard at the Alum Bagh was never seriously attacked; and convoys travelled between it and Cawnpore. It maintained communication by semaphore with Outram, and the access of messengers to the Residency was much easier.

Outram kept up a vigorous correspondence with the outer world, but chiefly with the officers advancing to reinforce him. Who these officers were or would be, or what their forces, he did not know, and the rumours respecting them varied from day to day; but he invariably recommended as the proper route, the one which, with some slight modifications, Sir Colin did eventually adopt. At the same time, he kept his friends at Cawnpore carefully and correctly informed of the state of supplies and the condition of the garrison. Then, towards the end of October, he was told of the apparent massing of the Central India rebels about Kalpee, on the Jumna, opposite to Cawnpore, the security of which they consequently threatened; on which his urgent comment was that it was obviously to the advantage of the State that the Kalpee force (the Gwalior rebels he called them) should be first effectually destroyed, and that the relief of Lucknow should be regarded as a secondary consideration, and be postponed, as his food would hold out till the end of November. This advice, however, it will be seen, was not acted on. Outram meanwhile kept on the defensive, preparing to aid the relieving force, when it should appear, by clearing its front and flanks as it approached.

The officer who was to relieve him was none of those who were now in the neighbourhood, nor any of commonplace experience, but the Commander-in-Chief himself, Sir Colin Campbell, a veteran of the Peninsula, of China, of the Sikh War, and of the Crimea. Arriving in Calcutta in August, he had been strenuously organizing the arrangements at the base, and for the despatch and care of the troops; and as these were now sufficiently advanced, he determined to take the field, and for this purpose to proceed to Cawnpore, where he would deal personally with the burning questions of the relief of Outram's position and the operations against the Gwalior contingent. Nothing else was of so much importance; for though many districts were disturbed, the Delhi theatre, excluding Rohilkund, was now in the possession of the British, and all anxiety was at an end regarding the Punjab, which was beginning to help actively, and to produce a veritable army of friendly levies.

In the operations about Cawnpore the state of matters was this: At Lucknow was collected nearly all the mutineer army of the Delhi and Oude theatres, but it was a defeated and depressed army, its strength lying mainly in its numbers. At Kalpee, threatening Cawnpore, was a well-organized and well-trained force of fully 5000 men, with a powerful artillery, and supported by a like number of irregular troops; and in Rohilkund were numerous gatherings of the Rohillas under their own chiefs, watching the flank of the operations between Cawnpore and Lucknow, but not likely to advance beyond their own province. The forces Sir Colin had available at hand for his operations about Cawnpore were these: some 5000 men present there, free for field operations, chiefly from Delhi; besides 1000 in garrison at Cawnpore, and 2500 in garrison at Lucknow; while there were advancing to Cawnpore, and arriving there daily in detachments, the second half of the China force, and several battalions of the reinforcements from England. Sir Colin, on getting to Cawnpore, arranged with General Windham, who commanded there, to leave with him 500 British and 500 Madras troops, with power to retain such of the troops daily arriving from Calcutta as he might think necessary for the security of the position.

With these arrangements settled, Sir Colin crossed the Ganges, and, on the 9th December, joined the force collected at Buntheera under Brigadier-General Hope Grant for the movement on Lucknow. On the 12th he reached the Alum Bagh. At starting his force was about 3800 men, consisting of the column from Delhi and two of the regiments from Calcutta, besides detachments; but when he moved forward, fresh troops that arrived increased his numbers to 5000.

He adopted as the route for his advance to the relief virtually the one recommended by Outram. But this route was strongly opposed by his Chief

Engineer, Major Goodwyn, who felt certain, from his knowledge of the natives, that the enemy would have prepared strong obstacles and opposition along it, as being partly the route the previous force had taken; and he urged vigorously the adoption of that which Havelock had originally meant to take, but which had been set aside owing to its bad condition after the heavy rains. Goodwyn's views, however, were overruled, and his persistent advocacy of them led to his being removed from his post; but they proved correct as to the opposition that would be encountered. The route adopted had been strongly prepared for defence by the enemy, with the result that, as will be seen, Sir Colin met with strong resistance and heavy loss.

Having reached the Alum Bagh on the 12th, he left it on the 14th, garrisoned by 400 men, and moved to Dil Khoosha and the Martinière. There he halted for a day, and on the 16th advanced to the relief with 4200 men. Crossing the canal near its entry, into the Goomtee, he moved by a line of strong and strongly defended positions, including the Secundra Bagh and the Shah Nujeef, where the fighting was desperate, till little was left between him and Outram except the Motee Mahul and the old 32nd Mess House. Outram had in the same afternoon exploded the mines he had prepared, and opened out with his batteries to clear Sir Colin's front and flank. Next day, the 17th, the intervening posts were captured, and the junction of the two forces effected. On the 18th the order was given that the Residency position was to be evacuated, and to be replaced by the Alum Bagh, as the post which was to proclaim to the enemy that the British were not surrendering their authority in Oude. From a purely military or strategic point of view, the measure was probably a sound one; but it is open to question whether its advantage was not counterbalanced by the elation of the enemy, and their political interpretation of the withdrawal from the representative seat of British authority, and the hauling down of its flag.

It occupied five days to evacuate the Residency, and five days more, *i.e.* till the 27th, to concentrate on the Alum Bagh and start from it for Cawnpore. Outram was left with 4000 men at what was henceforward called the Alum Bagh position, with the old Alum Bagh post at its apex, to menace and watch the city; while Sir Colin moved to Cawnpore, with the rest of the force and the rescued families that had been shut up in the Residency for the last six months.

It was at this, a fit and touching juncture, on the 24th November, when these families were safe under the protection of Sir Colin's army, and about to leave for peaceful homes, that Sir Henry Havelock calmly breathed his last, worn out by hardship and illness; a true, heroic, stern, God-fearing old warrior, rejoicing in the successful issue of his glorious struggle, and happy in the knowledge that his deeds had stirred to the depths the hearts of his Queen and country.

CHAPTER III.

OPERATIONS PRELIMINARY TO THE ATTACK ON LUCKNOW CITY.

SIR COLIN left the Alum Bagh on the 27th November for Cawnpore, but the very next morning he heard, at Bunnee, disquieting rumours about the situation there, and pushing forward as rapidly as possible, crossed the Ganges the same evening with some of his cavalry and joined General Windham.

What had occurred was this: Tantia Topee had, as already shown, been at Kalpee on the Jumna watching Cawnpore when Sir Colin had passed through it to the relief of Lucknow. No sooner was Sir Colin fully committed to the operations there than Tantia crossed the Jumna, was joined by the Nana's followers and all the disaffected in the district, formed a line across the Doab to the Ganges, and was there further reinforced by rebels from the west of Oude. With his army thus expanded, he swept down on Cawnpore from its west. Windham, doubtless unaware of this vast increase, had been sending forward to Sir Colin the various detachments that kept on daily arriving from Calcutta, and the force he now had left with him to meet this large array was much too weak to cope with it. Still, as he had to prevent their artillery getting too near the bridge, he moved out to check them, and then, on the 26th, met and repulsed Tantia's right wing, capturing three guns. But the centre and left wing were advancing unopposed, parallel to the Ganges, on the city; and next day, by noon, Windham was attacked on his whole front, and driven back, step by step, by the superior force and artillery fire of the enemy to his outposts, some 400 yards in front of his entrenchment. Next day, the 28th, Tantia's attack was pressed on, and he was getting dangerously close to the fort—and, what was of more importance, to the bridge—when Sir Colin arrived in the evening.

Sir Colin's presence at once altered the aspect of affairs. He ranged Peel's naval guns along the north bank of the river next morning, and drove off the enemy that were nearing the bridge, and then the whole force and the rescued families crossed over to the south, to the road leading to Allahabad. On the 3rd the families were despatched to Calcutta. On the 6th Sir Colin attacked the enemy, who were holding the city as well as their own camp to the west, between it and the canal. Drawing their attention to the river face by a cannonade from the fort, he sent forward Walpole's brigade along the south wall of the city so as to command its gates and prevent any egress of the hostile force within it. Then with three brigades and the cavalry he advanced against the enemy outside the city, and, driving them back between it and the canal, gradually turned their retiring movement into a precipitate flight, which eventually took the Kalpee direction. The whole of their artillery and camp was captured, and Hope Grant kept up the pursuit and slaughter for many miles. While their force outside was being thus disposed of, the enemy inside the city began to withdraw from it westwards, and Sir Colin, on reaching the camp, directed his victorious brigades to the right, under Mansfield, to catch the city enemy on the flank and annihilate them.

This was not successfully carried out, but the failure was retrieved the next day by the pursuit being taken up by Hope Grant, who overtook the enemy at Sheorajpore, and drove them across the Ganges with heavy slaughter.

His success was complete. The enemy never reappeared in these districts, and Tantia Topee's army remained on the south of the Jumna, not venturing to recross, though always on the watch.

Sir Colin had now two large bodies of the enemy before him to deal with decisively: one, the rebels in Rohilkund, chiefly the Mahomedan followers of the Rohilla chiefs; the other, the mutineer army in Oude, mainly about Lucknow, supported by the contingents of clansmen demanded by the Lucknow court from the Rajpoot chiefs. Sir Colin wished to clear Rohilkund first, and then concentrate on Oude. But in this he was overruled by Lord Canning, who decided that the city of Lucknow must be first attacked and taken, hoping apparently that, with its capture, the war would come to an end.

Meanwhile more and more troops were now continuing to move on Cawnpore, both from Calcutta and from the Punjab. So, partly in accordance with the above decision, and partly as a necessary preliminary to any plan that might be adopted, three columns were employed during the rest of 1857 in clearing the Doab, *i.e.* the country lying between the Ganges and the Jumna. One, under Seaton, two thousand strong, came south from Delhi, and after defeating various bodies of the enemy, reached Bewur. Another, under Walpole, went up the left half of the Doab till it joined Seaton at Bewur. The third, under Sir Colin's personal command, moved against the enemy about Futtehgurh and Furruckabad at the boundary point on the Ganges, between Oude and Rohilkund. He first routed the army of the Nuwab of Furruckabad; then, on the 2nd of January, he seized the fortress of Futtehgurh; and was next day joined by Seaton's and Walpole's columns.

Sir Colin's objective, as now decided, was Lucknow; but, of course, his plans were unknown to the enemy. Still, they felt assured that Lucknow would be a principal point of attack, and were erecting massive defences on the route by which Sir Colin had effected the relief, and by which they consequently, as usual, expected him to advance again. Their proceedings were always well known to Outram at the Alum Bagh, and through him to Sir Colin.

After some changes, the troops that Sir Colin decided on using for the attack on Lucknow were—

1. Those already with him in the Doab.

2. The additional troops from Calcutta.

3. The siege-train from Agra, and such troops from the Punjab as might then be available.

4. Outram's force at the Alum Bagh.

5. A column from the east, or Benares, districts, then being collected under General Franks, partly British, partly Nepaulese.

6. A Nepaulese force from the same direction, under Jung Bahadur.

A seventh force was to remain on the Delhi side of Rohilkund.

From the positions and movements of these several troops the enemy would remain in the dark as to the scope and direction of the contemplated attack, till the time should arrive to deliver it.

The plan now adopted by Sir Colin for the operations at Lucknow was prepared by Colonel Napier; and in conformity with Lord Canning's views, it avoided any complete investment. The scheme was to attack Lucknow directly from the east; to blockade the south; to advance along the north bank of the Goomtee, so as to enfilade and turn the enemy's flank in concert with the direct frontal attack from the east; and to leave the west free for the enemy's retreat, when they should then be caught in the open.

Of the six forces which were to act against Lucknow, only Outram's and the two from the east had any serious fighting before the concentration.

Meanwhile Outram had been feeling his own position at the Alum Bagh to be defective, if not absolutely a false and dangerous one. He was practically liable at any time to an unexpected attack—a surprise—by the whole force of the enemy at Lucknow; which, as he knew authentically, numbered fully 90,000 trained men, made up of mutineer sepoys and Oude troops, besides bodies of Nujeebs and the Rajwara contingents (*i.e.* the Rajpoot clansmen), of whom the bulk were kept in the outlying districts to check any movements of troops there. To oppose this vast army he had only 4000 men, and was, moreover, tied to a position which was so close to Lucknow that, on the one hand, he was always liable to sudden and unforeseen attacks in force, and on the other he had no room left for a telling pursuit and punishment after repulsing the enemy. He pointed all this out to Sir Colin, repeatedly and clearly, but without effect. He was not permitted to change the site of his camp and position.

In the course of the three months, from the latter end of November, 1857, to that of February, 1858, during which he held this position, Outram was attacked six times—on the 22nd December, the 12th and 16th January, and the 15th, 21st, and 25th February. The first attack, made by 4400 men and 4 guns, endeavoured to get at the south of his position by circling round his right flank; but he drove them to flight by turning their rear and threatening their line of retreat. The second attack was in great force, some 30,000 men, in two bodies, attacking respectively the right and left of the position, but avoiding the Alum Bagh post at the apex. They were allowed to come somewhat near, and were then received with such a powerful fire of artillery and musketry as to drive them back speedily. This was done twice; afterwards the enemy concentrated against the Alum Bagh post, and were there finally routed by the fire of heavier metal.

The third attack was similar to the second, but in smaller numbers, and the enemy were, consequently, still more heavily punished. The fourth attack, led by the moulvie, though most desultory and weak, lasted longer, and led to their occupying posts much closer to the British position, enabling them to attack still more suddenly than before. The fifth attack was on the front and both the faces; but Outram had now been joined by additional troops, including cavalry, and while the front attack was kept in check, the flank attacks were in turn assailed on their own flanks, and suffered very severely.

The sixth and last attack was the strongest of all; but Outram had been still more reinforced, and had prepared for it. Checking the rest, he sent out two large bodies of cavalry and light troops to the right and left of the body of enemy on his right, and then getting at their rear caused them to fly precipitately, and inflicted very heavy loss. After this final victory, he was practically left undisturbed by the enemy; the Alum Bagh becoming the scene of the concentration of the various columns and troops from the south and west for the impending siege.

On the east, General Franks's force gradually grew

till it contained three British regiments—the 10th, 20th, and 97th—six Nepaulese battalions, two field batteries, and a few detached guns; but there was no cavalry at first, except a few that were useful for orderly work. After coercing some refractory villages and forts in the Benares districts, Franks was at length directed to cross the borders of Oude, and advance on Lucknow by the Sultanpore Road. He entered the province on the 19th February, and on that day fought two actions, defeating the enemy at Chanda and Ameerpore, and then driving off a third force which arrived too late to take part in the second action. On the 21st he surprised the rebels at the strong pass and fort of Budayan, which he secured without any real struggle, and two days afterwards fought the battle of Sultanpore against the whole concentrated rebel army of the east of Oude. Their former leaders, Mehndee Hussun and Bunda Hussun, were now superseded by General Guffoor Beg of the Oude Artillery, who had drawn up his line to hold a deep ravine which the road crossed. But, keeping their attention fixed on a demonstration on their front, Franks led his main force round the right flank of the enemy, by the upper end of the ravine, and suddenly appearing on their rear, put them to immediate and precipitate flight without any loss to his own force. All his fighting was carried out in skirmishing order, and he took thirty-four guns. The want of cavalry prevented his pursuing or punishing the enemy, although the very next day, just too late, three bodies of newly raised cavalry from the Punjab joined him. His march onward was unmolested until he reached the rear of his camping ground at Lucknow; when he was obliged, in order to secure his position, to attack a fortified village, in doing which he met with some slight loss.

This successful march, if the enemy's forces are properly considered in detail, as well as their leaders, and the resistance they made, points to some significant conclusions. It is quite certain that the bulk of the enemy consisted of matchlockmen, Rajwara, or talookdaree troops, and that they did not fight well; in fact, hardly fought at all, except when forced to stand at bay. Moreover, during the whole of this advance, not one of their leaders was of their own race—Hindoo Rajpoots; they were all Mahomedans and ex-officials of the Lucknow court, such as Mehndee Hussun, Bunda Hussun, Guffoor Beg, Fuzl Azim, Mahomed Hosseyn, and so forth. In fact, the conduct of the Rajwara men under these circumstances—very different from what it was on other occasions when led by their own chiefs—seems to point irresistibly to the conclusion that those chiefs held aloof from the hostilities, and that the men were, in their hearts, with their chiefs, and joined grudgingly in the fighting.

General Franks's march, besides being important in itself, was valuable from its clearing the way for Jung Bahadur following in his rear. He had, early in the winter months, sent down in advance various bodies of Nepaulese, which, as already described, had been of material help in clearing the Goruckpore and Azimgurh districts, and had latterly detached six battalions to form part of Franks's force. He had followed himself, with additional troops, at the end of December, and now crossed the Gogra into Oude on the 25th February with some 9000 men. He first attacked and captured the fort of Ambarpore, and then marched forward steadily to Lucknow, his progress being undisturbed by the enemy, of whom Franks had cleared the road. But he did not reach the camp at Lucknow and take part in the operations there till the 11th March, four days after the siege had begun in full vigour.

Practically, when the troops that Sir Colin had sent forward from Cawnpore to the Alum Bagh had collected there by the end of February, and Franks had joined on the 4th March, they, with Outram's force, which had been holding the Alum Bagh, began operations on the 5th March.

CHAPTER IV.

THE SIEGE AND CAPTURE OF THE CITY OF LUCKNOW.

THE city of Lucknow, which the enemy now held in force, and which Sir Colin was about to attack, had been prepared strongly for defence according to the enemy's lights. Putting aside the idea of an attack from the westward, they had protected the city along the canal face, from the Char Bagh eastwards round to the Goomtee, and also for a mile or so to the west of the Char Bagh. Along that part of the canal to the east which was bordered by dense city—that is, up to Banks's house—the defences were comparatively slight; but from Banks's house to the river there was a line of massive earthwork ramparts, with bastions and batteries at close intervals. This was their first or outer line of defence.

Behind that line lay the broad plain, narrowing to the west, by which both Havelock and Sir Colin had advanced to the relief of the Residency, bordered on the north by the Goomtee, and on the south skirting a series of palatial buildings, ending with the Kaiser Bagh. Over this plain were dotted the several enclosures and buildings that had given so much trouble to the relieving force, such as the Barracks, the Secundra Bagh, the Shah Nujeef, the Mess-House, or Koorsheyd Munzil, the Motee Mahul, and others. The second line of defence crossed this plain, starting from the Emambarah (one of the row of palatial buildings), connecting it with the Mess-House, and then going on to the Motee Mahul and the river. The third line, at right-angles to the other two, merely covered, at a close distance, the entire front of the Kaiser Bagh.

The enemy had not constructed any defences on the north side of the Goomtee, but had contented themselves with occupying it with a considerable body of troops, chiefly cavalry.

The numbers of the enemy were believed to be much the same as had been there during Outram's occupation of the Alum Bagh position; but all the sepoy troops had been called in from the outlying districts, and replaced there by the Rajwara troops. The enemy had made up their minds that Sir Colin would attack them on the eastern portion of the canal, and prepared accordingly; but Sir Colin proposed, while gratifying them so far, to attack that position not only on its front, but also on its flank, from the north. His dispositions and arrangements were these:—

His force on the 2nd March was about 19,000 men and 120 guns. Franks's column was due in a couple of days, and Jung Bahadur's a week later; and these two would bring the total strength up to 31,000 men and 164 guns.

At first his force was formed up in three divisions—*Outram's* at the Alum Bagh ; behind it, echeloned on the Cawnpore road, *Lugard's ;* and then *Walpole's*, with which was the siege-train. The cavalry were under Hope Grant and Brigadier Campbell. Sir Colin now rearranged this. He placed under Outram only a part of his own division, but all Walpole's division, with Hope Grant's cavalry ; and he left the rest of Outram's division as a brigade, under Franklin, at the Alum Bagh. The new disposition he arrived at was to send Outram's force, thus organized, across to the north side of the Goomtee ; to place Lugard's division opposite the Dil Koosha portion of the canal ; to leave Hodson's Horse as a connecting link between it and the Alum Bagh ; and to give to Brigadier Campbell and his cavalry the task of holding the ground to the west of the Char Bagh and Alum Bagh. Franks's column, on arrival, was to form up, at first in support, and afterwards on the left of Lugard ; while Jung Bahadur was to come into line on the left of Franks, so filling up the gap to the Alum Bagh.

Sir Colin began operations on the 2nd March by moving out from the Alum Bagh position to its right, and circling round Jellalabad towards the Dil Koosha. The force he took was Hope Grant's cavalry, a body of artillery, and Lugard's division. Driving in the enemy's outlying pickets, he advanced to the Dil Koosha plateau, seizing the two posts of the Dil Koosha Palace and the Mahomed Bagh, where, in order to reply effectually to the enemy's guns, he constructed two powerful counter-batteries. These, opening fire next day, silenced the enemy; and on the 4th, Walpole's division, with the rest of the siege-train, moved over from the Alum Bagh, and encamped on the Dil Koosha position, where, at dusk, Franks's column also marched in from the east and joined.

The same evening two bridges were begun from the Dil Koosha position across the Goomtee to the east, near the village of Beebiapore. By next morning, the 5th, one of them was finished, and its bridge-head begun. On the night of the 5th the bridges and the necessary arrangements were completed, and the whole of Outram's force crossed over by day-break. Until that force had advanced sufficiently to the west in its turning movement—that is, until the 9th—Sir Colin's troops at the Dil Koosha designedly remained inactive, not even attacking the Martinière, which continued to worry them with its fire; but Franks's column, meanwhile, moved up from the rear and replaced Walpole's division on Lugard's left.

Outram's column, after crossing the Goomtee, first cleared the ground to the north, to Chinhut, on the Fyzabad road, and there turning to the left, swept westwards. On its reaching Ishmaelgunge (the site of the battle of the 30th June, with which the siege of the Residency began), the enemy's cavalry were met, attacked, and driven back. This was the first occasion on which the Queen's Bays had ever been in action, and the men were eager to be the first for its baptism of fire.

At Ishmaelgunge, Outram was still considerably short of the distance he had to advance in order to turn the enemy's first line of defences; and before him, and protecting their left flank and rear, lay a small but strong post called the Chukkur Kothi (race-stand). Outram halted at Ishmaelgunge during the 7th and 8th. On the 7th he was attacked in force, but defeated and drove off the enemy. On the 8th he received his siege-guns (twenty-two), and began, and during the night completed, two powerful batteries; one to enfilade the enemy's first line of defence and take the Martinière in rear, the other to batter the Chukkur Kothi, and clear the left bank of the Goomtee.

Next morning, the 9th, the batteries opened, the enfilade fire began, and Outram attacked and captured the Chukkur Kothi; then he advanced up the left bank of the river till he held the Badshah Bagh, and was able to sweep the flank and rear of both the first and second line of the defences, up to the Kaiser Bagh Palace itself. On the enemy being thus driven from the northern end of the first line of their defences, a gallant feat was performed by Butler, of the 1st Fusiliers, who swam the Goomtee, climbed the enemy's parapet, and there signalled to Adrian Hope, who was leading Sir Colin's attack, to show that these works had been evacuated by the enemy.

On this day, the 9th, the time had come for Sir Colin, after about five days of inaction, to make a move, deliver his frontal attack on the enemy's first line of defences, and then proceed to capture the great row of palaces along the Huzrutgunge, as well as the posts between them and the river. The troops he used for this purpose were Lugard's division and Franks's, which had stepped into the line before held by Walpole's. At first Lugard led and Franks was in support.

The first move was against the Martinière, which was in front of the canal, on which Sir Colin opened a very heavy fire from the Dil Koosha early in the morning. At two o'clock Hope's brigade, supported by the rest of Lugard's division, advanced and captured it without any real contest, the enemy flying at once, mostly across the river. Hope's brigade continued the advance towards the right front, saw Butler's signalling, crossed over the enemy's earthworks at the river end, and having thus gained them, then turned to the left, swept down to the other end, near Banks's house, and thus, on the 9th March, secured the whole of the enemy's first line.

Next day, on the *left*, Sir Colin attacked and captured Banks's house and some of the houses and enclosures along the Huzrutgunge, thus securing the basis of his further advance on that line. On the *right*, on the north of the Goomtee, Outram was attacked by the enemy, whom he defeated and drove off, as usual; and then, while using his cavalry to patrol and clear the ground to his west and north, constructed gun and mortar batteries against the posts which lay in the line of Sir Colin's attack; thus fully and effectually carrying out his *rôle* of flanking and furthering the main advance and struggle under Sir Colin.

On the 11th, marked and important progress was made. Batteries had been constructed and guns placed in position at Banks's house, which in the morning opened a powerful fire on the Begum's palace, the first of the strong positions along the Huzrutgunge. By the afternoon it had been breached, and was accordingly stormed, Hope's brigade leading. The contest was severe, the enemy were resolute, and the positions were strong; but the 93rd Highlanders and the 4th Punjabees, working together as if one regiment, expelled the enemy, 600 sepoys' corpses being left within the walls. This struggle was marked by the death-wound of the famed Hodson, an ideal leader of cavalry, whose services—whatever his faults, real or alleged—had been simply invaluable throughout the war.

While this was going on, Lugard advanced on the right of the Huzrutgunge against the detached posts in the plain; seizing, without opposition, first the Secundra Bagh and then the Kuddum Russool and the Shah Nujeef, the scenes of the conflict of the 16th November—now specially important from their close proximity to the enemy's second line of defences.

While Sir Colin's troops had thus been gaining ground on the south of the Goomtee, Outram had been operating up the northern bank; on the right sweeping up to the cantonment, and on the left reaching the iron bridge and securing its northern end.

On the 11th, then, the Begum's palace had been secured, also the Secundra Bagh and the Shah Nujeef, and Outram had advanced, and was holding the left bank as far as the iron bridge; and the day was further marked by the arrival of Jung Bahadur's army.

During the 12th and 13th the Engineers worked their way through the palaces up to the Emambarah, the troops simultaneously attacking, occupying, and securing them; and Jung Bahadur, crossing the canal on the left, worked through the city on the flank of the advance through the palaces.

On the 14th the lead of that advance was transferred from Lugard's to Franks's division, and the situation was this: Sir Colin's main column had penetrated and sapped through the palaces up to the Emambarah, and had made a breach in its walls; on its left the Nepaulese were working through the ordinary city; on its right he held the position in front of the enemy's second line of defences. On the other side of the river Outram had turned that second line of defences and seized his end of the iron bridge.

On that day he asked leave to force the iron bridge, and operate against the enemy's posts behind their second line, but he was prohibited by an order *not to do so if it would cause his losing a single man.* The bridge was blocked by a battery and held in force by the enemy; so he had to remain passive.

Not so Franks at the range of palaces. The

breach having been made in the wall of the Emambarah, Sir Colin gave the order for the storming of that position. The stormers, after a sharp struggle, made good their entrance and drove out the enemy, who fled precipitately, and streamed off towards the Kaiser Bagh. The attacking party followed, not in direct pursuit of the fugitives, but flanking them by a line parallel and close to their route into the next palace; from which they found they could command both the second line of entrenchments, and also the third in the immediate front of the Kaiser Bagh. Bringing a musketry fire to bear on their bastions, they drove the enemy off and forced them to quit the nearest positions. By this movement their second line of defences was obviously taken in rear at this end, after it had already been turned by Outram's operations at its river end, and was practically no longer tenable. So the enemy retreated into the buildings and enclosures which still lay between the second line and the Kaiser Bagh. But Brasyer, with his Sikhs, followed them up into that intervening position, and being supported, cleared it entirely of the enemy.

This was the limit of the programme assigned for the day, but circumstances sometimes destroy the value and the real practicability of such limits in military operations, especially in dealing with Asiatics. Once get them on the run, and it is as dangerous and mischievous to halt in the advance as it is advantageous to press it on. So Franks's men followed up the enemy into the Cheenee Bazar, which skirted the

Kaiser Bagh and lay inside the *third* line of defences, and thus turned that line.

By this time the enemy, who had been still holding the middle of their second line of defences with the Tara Kotee and the Mess House (the Koorsheyd Munzil), and were in great strength, finding that their position had been turned on both flanks, and that they were in danger of being cut off from their line of retreat, were retiring rapidly, and pouring down towards the Cheenee Bazar and the Kaiser Bagh, some 5000 or 6000 in number. Then Franks's Sikhs, entering and seizing the bastions in the third line, turned their guns on that body of the enemy flying from the second line, and checked and drove them off, turning their flight in the direction of the Chutter Munzil buildings.

On this the supports (of Franks's column) followed up and secured the posts in the *third* line which had thus been seized, and sent word to our troops who were holding the Secundra Bagh and other posts on the right, in front of the enemy's *second* line, that that line was clear; and these forthwith advanced and captured the Motee Mahul, the Mess House, and the other intervening posts in the plain.

At the same time Franks sent forward his own division into the courtyard of Saadut Ali's mosque, one of the chief buildings of the *third* line, from which they stormed the enclosures and gardens of the Kaiser Bagh itself, and cleared it of its defenders; so capturing and securing the very heart of the enemy's position.

Numerous had been the rumours of the desperate measures and arrangements that the enemy had adopted for the defence of the Kaiser Bagh; and Sir Colin was much discomposed and disturbed on hearing of its sudden capture and occupation, fearing that there would be great explosions of mines and the like. He is believed to have even sent orders to evacuate it, and to have received from Franks in reply the English, or rather the Irish, equivalent of the famous "J'y suis, j'y reste." But thus it was that, on the 14th March, Franks's column in the one day captured the whole of the enemy's positions from the Begum's house, whence it started, to their last real stronghold, the Kaiser Bagh; considerably anticipating Sir Colin's programme.

Next day, March 15th, the two cavalry brigades, Hope Grant's from near the iron bridge, and Campbell's from the west of the Alum Bagh, were directed to pursue the fugitive sepoys along the Seetapore and Sandeela roads respectively—the routes by which they were assumed, incorrectly it seems, to have fled.

On the 16th, Outram was directed to recross the Goomtee to its south bank and join in the operations there. This, with the error in the direction of the pursuits ordered on the 15th, led to two important events. First, a great mass of the enemy—taking advantage of the gap, or unprotected space on the north of the Goomtee, caused by Outram's movement, combined with the absence of Hope Grant's cavalry on the Seetapore road—forced their way across the stone bridge, and escaped by the Fyzabad road unmolested into the open country, there to reassemble shortly and continue the war. And next, the enemy made an attack in force on the Alum Bagh, knowing it to be for the time unsupported by Campbell's cavalry, thus threatening the communication with Cawnpore. Outram, having according to orders crossed the Goomtee, advanced to the Residency, and capturing it at once, followed on the heels of the enemy, and stormed first the Mutchi Bhown, and then the great Emambarah.

The enemy's attack on the Alum Bagh was in great force, their infantry threatening its front, and their artillery and cavalry its left. But they were repulsed by Franklin, and retired without our infantry having been at all seriously engaged.

Meanwhile Jung Bahadur, with his Nepaulese, had been clearing the city between the palaces and the canal, though his progress had not yet reached so far as the road from the Residency to the Char Bagh.

Thus closed the proceedings of March 16th, after which the operations lay simply in driving the enemy westwards through and out of the city. On the 17th and 18th Outram's advance took him past the Hooseynee Mosque and the Dowlut Khana, up to Shuruf-ood-Dowlah's house, and near Ali Nukkee Khan's, while Jung Bahadur had also worked along the left. It was known that the relics of the enemy, still forming a considerable force, and consisting of its most resolute troops, meant to make a final stand at the Moosa Bagh, on the extreme west of the city; animated by the presence of the Begum, the young

Nuwab, the moulvie, and all the other leaders of the rebel party except the Nana. So Sir Colin arranged for an effective finishing stroke. Outram was to attack the position, aided by flanking fire from the north of the Goomtee, while Hope Grant's cavalry on the right (to the north of the Goomtee) and Campbell's on the left should catch the enemy as they were driven out. Outram carried out his part of the programme thoroughly, capturing the position and clearing it of the enemy, who fled in large masses along the road where Brigadier Campbell was to have caught them. But the brigadier failed, and the enemy escaped with but slight loss, when Sir Colin had them practically in his grasp.

Thus Lucknow had been taken, but the foe had not been crushed, nor even punished, and they were free to reassemble elsewhere in their thousands and tens of thousands.

So Sir Colin lost nearly the whole of the hoped-for fruits of his capture of Lucknow, owing first to his checking Outram on the 14th; then to his misdirected pursuits of the 15th; and finally to the failure of proper leading for his splendid force of cavalry at the most opportune and critical moment of the war.

Thus ended the second stage of the war in Oude. The British loss in the capture was 127 killed and about 600 wounded.

CHAPTER V.

THE EASTERN AND SOUTHERN THEATRES.

In the eastern theatre the operations, during the decisive contests that were raging in the Oude and the southern theatres, were comparatively slight and unimportant. Small bodies of troops or of volunteers were everywhere vigorously at work dealing with each outbreak, and keeping the districts under control. The most important proceedings were in the Goruckpore districts on the east of Oude, following on the approach of the Nepaulese troops of our ally Jung Bahadur. Several regiments had been sent forward in advance in September, and contests in which they were invariably victorious ensued between them and bodies of insurgents. There was one combat on the 19th September at Manduri, ten miles from Azimgurh. Then they took the Forts of Mubarukpore and Atrowlea, on the Oude borders. On the 19th October they defeated an Oude force at Kudja, and on the 30th they fought and won the battle of Chanda (the same town at which General Franks fought his first action in his march to Lucknow), defeating 5000 men, and taking four out of seven guns. These advanced troops were then reinforced by a detachment of the 10th Foot, and kept those districts suppressed until the operations began, which have been already described, for the concentration on Lucknow.

Another force under General Rowcroft operated in western Behar. It consisted of the seamen and marines of the *Pearl*, some Nepaulese, and police. Its principal action was at Sobhanpore, near Chupra, which helped to clear the way for Jung Bahadur's army.

No other operations of any special consequence occurred during this stage in the eastern theatre.

We therefore turn to the southern theatre, where the operations had heretofore been but slight, but were now to play a prominent part in this Campaign; especially those of the Central India column under the leadership of Sir Hugh Rose.

It may make the story of the operations in this theatre more clear if they are dealt with in three groups:—

1. The earlier operations connected first with the march from Bombay up to Mhow, and then with the clearance of the districts there and to the north, in the direction of Neemuch and Rajpootana, principally under General Stuart.

2. The march, in two columns, from Mhow on Jhansi, and the siege and capture of Jhansi, under Sir Hugh Rose.

3. The operations of the eastern or Madras

force, chiefly the Kamptee column, from Nagpore to Jubbulpore, Punnah, and Banda, latterly under General Whitlock.

The earlier operations of the first force (General Stuart's)—*i.e.* up to the end of September—have been already attended to, but only briefly, and will be now described more fully.

The second, or combined, movement had not then begun, as the 2nd Brigade, forming part of the column, had not yet joined.

The Kamptee column had relieved Dumoh, which had been threatened by mutineers.

Sir Hugh Rose had arrived at Bombay on the 19th September, and he was presently appointed to the command in Central India. But, as will be seen, he did not join his troops at Mhow till the middle of December, or take the command in the field till the beginning of January—a long lapse of time in entering on field operations.

In dealing with the earlier proceedings of the Bombay column, it may be observed that at first, on the outbreak of the Mutiny, it had been arranged to give the Central India command to General John Jacob, the famous ruler of Scinde, and commander of the Scinde Horse. But after Outram left Persia it had been found to be imperatively necessary that Jacob should remain on there to bring the settlement of affairs after the war to a satisfactory conclusion; so Sir Hugh Rose had been nominated to the command.

As Rose did not take the command in the field till the beginning of January, the story of the operations till that date—*i.e.* for the first three months, the first half of the second stage of the Campaign—does not include his active career in Central India.

The first movement towards Mhow from Bombay had been made by General Woodburn, who left Poona on the 9th June, in command of a force consisting of the 14th Light Dragoons, Woolcombe's Field Battery, the 25th Bombay Native Infantry, and a Pontoon train. On his reaching Ahmednugger applications came from every direction to the General to go to the assistance of threatened districts. He was to have been joined there by the 1st Hyderabad Cavalry from Aurungabad, but that regiment had refused to march. This mutinous conduct led General Woodburn to turn aside to Aurungabad; and eventually his column, which arrived there on the 23rd June, and drove the 1st Cavalry out of the station, did not leave it till the 9th July. It then marched on to Asseergurh, which it reached on the 22nd, where it was joined by Colonel Durand and by Brigadier Stuart, who had been sent forward to command it. Asseergurh, which had been in a critical state from the mutinous tendencies of a sepoy regiment in its neighbourhood, had been secured, being occupied by some Bheel troops through the vigorous and timely efforts of Lieutenants Keatinge and John Gordon. On the 24th July, the column left Asseergurh with its face towards Mhow; four days later it was joined at

Simrole by the 3rd Hyderabad Cavalry, under Captain Orr; on the 2nd August it entered Mhow; and on the 5th was reinforced by a wing of the 86th, which had left Malagaon on the 23rd July.

From this date till the end of September it had been practically doing nothing beyond watching the district and Holkar's troops at Indore.

The troops that were engaged in the operations heretofore were mainly those that had come up country with Brigadier Stuart—some 240 of the 14th Light Dragoons, a wing of the 86th Foot, two batteries of artillery, the 25th Bombay Native Infantry, the 3rd Hyderabad Cavalry, some Madras and Bombay sappers, and a few native troops who had joined from time to time. Then, after the rains had ceased and the ground became fit for marching, the balance of the Hyderabad force had joined, as also the 3rd Bombay Fusiliers, and the rest of the troops now present.

But there were two or three points in which the conduct of operations and the difficulty to be overcome differed from the conditions that prevailed in the other theatres of operations. The enemy comprised very few sepoy troops; they were mainly the followers of native chiefs. The 50th and 52nd Native Infantry seemed to be the only *regiments* that were ever met in conflict till towards the end; and the hostile artillery included but little British ordnance.

Early in October the brigade at Mhow, under the control of Durand, was still watching the Indore army, and had not disarmed it, while it was now being threatened both from the east and the west by bands of Vilayutees, or soldiers of foreign origin; and Shahzada Feroze Shah was making himself the centre of a strong gathering. So Durand decided on taking active steps, first against the Fort of Dhar to the west and then northwards against Mundesore, whence he could move to relieve Neemuch. The garrison that had to be left at Mhow reduced to 1500 men the force available for field operations. The immediate neighbourhood of Mhow, including Mundlaisir, was first cleared of scattered parties of rebels; and a battle was fought on the 22nd October before Dhar, in which the enemy were well beaten, and driven into the Fort, which was then invested and besieged. A practicable breach was made on the 31st, but that night the enemy evacuated both it and the neighbouring Fort of Anjhera. Durand, reinforced by some fresh troops from Hyderabad, occupied these forts, and on the 8th November advanced on Mundesore. On the 13th a strong force of the enemy, who were retiring from Mehidpore, were encountered by the Hyderabad cavalry and driven to flight, with the loss of all their guns (eight). On the 21st they approached Mundesore. The rebel force, chiefly Vilayutees, came out, and drew up in array; but they were first shaken by the British artillery, and then charged by the cavalry and driven into the city. Marching past the city, and so getting between it and Neemuch, Durand met the enemy who had been besieging Neemuch at the village of Goharia. Here there was a most obstinate contest, the Mundesore rebels coming out again and attacking the rear.

But the latter were again driven back into the city, which they finally evacuated during the night; while those of the enemy who had concentrated in Goharia were almost annihilated, only 200 surrendering next morning. These blows crushed the enemy in those districts, led to the dispersion of the Shahzada's army, and at once relieved Neemuch. In the course of this campaign forty guns had been captured.

Durand then circled back to Indore, and, from the effect produced by these victories, made Holkar, on the 15th December, disarm his troops without further hesitation.

And now his task at Indore was over. Sir Hugh Rose and Sir Robert Hamilton arrived on the 16th December, and Durand handed over his charge, and left.

Sir Hugh's instructions were to clear the country, and operate towards Jhansi, but not to move forward for that purpose except in concert with General Whitlock, who had been appointed to the command of the Madras column, which was to operate on his right. This delayed and prevented his moving till towards the middle of January.

Rose divided his force into two brigades. The left, or No. 1, at Mhow, under Brigadier *Steuart*, consisted of—

English.	Native.
14th Light Dragoons.	One troop 3rd Bombay Cavalry. Two regiments Hyderabad cavalry.
86th Regiment.	25th Bombay Native Infantry. One regiment Hyderabad infantry.
Three field batteries.	A few Sikhs.

No. 2, or the right brigade, at Sehore, under Brigadier *Steuart*, consisted of—

3rd Light Dragoons.	3rd Bombay Light Cavalry.
	One regiment Hyderabad cavalry.
3rd Bombay Fusiliers.	24th Bombay Native Infantry.
	One regiment Hyderabad infantry.
Three batteries artillery.	Siege-train and sappers.

So that the whole force contained, besides the Bhopal contingent, one British cavalry regiment, four native ditto; two British infantry regiments, four native ditto; six batteries and siege-trains, two companies of sappers; and also some loyal troops of Scindia's attached to the 1st Brigade.

The left brigade was to operate up the trunk road towards Agra, under its brigadier, while Sir Hugh Rose proposed to accompany the 2nd Brigade and operate on the right, relieving Saugor and then advancing towards Jhansi. In conformity with his orders respecting concert with General Whitlock, he did not leave Mhow to begin operations with his 2nd Brigade till the 8th January. With these operations we will deal presently, having first to describe those of the 1st Brigade till it eventually joined Sir Hugh.

Not being allowed to advance from Mhow till the 21st Company of Royal Engineers and the rest of the 86th should join it, the brigade did not start till the 6th February. It marched on the road to Agra, clearing the country as far as Goonah; Orr and Keatinge also moving there from Mundesore, where they had been left, and restoring the postal arrangements. From Goonah, in consequence of the accounts of the movements of the rebels, Stuart turned to the east, towards Esaugurh and Chandeyree, coming to Khakwaree, six miles short of Chandeyree, on the 5th March. A reconnaissance pushed forward next day cleared the jungle that intervened, and stormed an external line of defences that had been erected about one and a half miles off the fortified city itself—a place of great size and old renown, but now much ruined by Mahratta oppression. The Fort itself was four miles in circumference. A ridge commanding the city was seized, and a road made along it with breaching batteries under heavy fire from the city walls. Breaching commenced shortly after the 10th March; on the 16th, the remainder of the 86th joined the camp, and on the 17th the assault was delivered at two points with entire success.

After the completion of this, the special part it had to play, the 1st Brigade moved on to join the 2nd Brigade, the 14th Light Dragoons going ahead on the 19th.

To the movements of that 2nd Brigade we now turn. On the 8th January Sir H. Rose had left Mhow to join it at Sehore, and so had the siege-train. On the 15th the latter arrived, and next day, the 16th, the brigade advanced towards the Fort of Ratgurh, on its way to the relief of Saugor, and arrived before it on the 24th. Ratgurh was then invested. On the 26th the town was occupied; on the 27th the breaching batteries opened fire on the

Fort; on the 28th the enemy made a vigorous sortie; and next day they were found to have evacuated the Fort.

The force then advanced to Saugor and relieved it on the 3rd February. From this point the march would, under ordinary circumstances, have been northwards towards Jhansi, the objective of the Campaign. But on the eastern flank, opposite Saugor, lay the very strong fort of Garrakota, held by the mutineer sepoys of the 50th and 52nd, and by the rebels; and its capture was essential. On the 8th the force moved against it, drove in its garrison, and began to breach it; on the 13th the enemy evacuated it, and, leaving a detachment of the loyal 31st Native Infantry (who had held Saugor) in charge of the Fort, the force returned to Saugor on the 17th February.

But it did not leave Saugor for its advance on Jhansi till the 27th February. A short distance ahead of the force a range of hills would have to be passed over, on the other side of which the 1st Brigade was operating. Accordingly, Rose had sent instructions to that brigade to advance by Chandeyree, to facilitate his own movements. As he approached the hills and the passes through them, where he knew he would meet with strong opposition, he began the manœuvres on the 3rd March by despatching a small force of all arms under Major Scudamore towards the Malthon Pass on the left; to divert the enemy's attention there, while he took the remainder of his division towards the main group of those passes

—the Narut, the Mundenpore, and the Dhamoni. The Narut Pass was the most difficult, and was held by the Rajah of Banpore. Mundenpore, twenty miles from it, was the least difficult; it was held by the 50th Native Infantry and the Rajah of Shahgurh, with a number of Bondeelas. Leaving alone Dhamoni, which lay on the right, Rose feinted with his whole force on Narut, and then countermarching to the right with his main body, attacked and forced the Mundenpore Pass, driving the enemy from the hills that successively commanded it. This victory paralysed the enemy; and then the forts of Sorai and Manora were captured. On the 17th the brigade crossed the Betwa, while Chandeyree was being taken by the 1st Brigade, whose artillery they heard. On the 21st the column, without any further fighting, appeared before Jhansi. On that night the cavalry of the 1st Brigade arrived, followed, on the 25th, by its main body. On the 23rd the enemy's position was invested, and so the siege began.

At this juncture it is expedient to advert to the movements of the Madras column which General Whitlock had been appointed to command in November. It was at Jubbulpore on the 6th February, and its task was to advance northward on Rose's flank, protecting it from the enemy there, and supporting the friendly chiefs. But on the 17th March, the day of the capture of Chandeyree and of Rose's advance from the passes towards Jhansi, Whitlock was still halting about Saugor and Dumoh; where he received direct orders from the Governor-

General to carry out the instructions he had received, advance towards Banda, and act in concert with Sir Hugh. But it was now too late for him to help in any way in the operations at Jhansi; and thus Rose was left unaided to his own force for the siege and capture of that fortress.

It was high and commanding. Except on the west and part of the south, it abutted on the city, which was surrounded by massive bastioned walls, varying in height from 18 to 30 feet. The garrison was said to be 11,000 strong.

The breaching batteries were begun on the 22nd, and opened out as they each got completed and armed. As the plan shows, the attack was directed on the city in two parts, the right against the north-east face, the left against the south-east, which was on very high ground.

Whilst the breaching was in progress Sir Hugh heard, on the 31st March, that a force of 22,000 men, consisting of the Gwalior contingent, and other troops from Kalpee, under Tantia Topee, had marched south to attack him and raise the siege, and were about to cross the Betwa on the east. Sir Hugh arranged to avoid disturbing the course of the siege operations and bombardment, and to take with him only such troops as could be spared—some 1500 men—to meet Tantia Topee and drive him back across the Betwa. His aim was to turn the enemy's right. Brigadier Steuart was sent forward that night to the banks of the Betwa in that direction, while Rose, having marched out, lay all night in front of the rebel army. Tantia Topee had formed it in two lines, a mile and a half apart, with jungle intervening. In the morning of the 1st April the battle opened with artillery from both sides. Rose then sent all his Horse Artillery and a large portion of his cavalry under Lightfoot to the right flank of Tantia's first line, while he advanced against it in front. The enemy's object was to take advantage of their numerical strength to outflank and overlap him, but Lightfoot's enfilading attack on their right disconcerted them and threw them into disorder, which was converted by the frontal attack into flight.

Tantia Topee found his first line thus flying back, routed, on his second line, when now, at the opportune moment, on *its* right, appeared Brigadier Steuart's force. This second flank attack terminated the combat. The whole of Tantia's force fled precipitately across the Betwa, leaving all their guns, and being for the time dispersed.

Sir Hugh returned at once to Jhansi, where the bombardment, which had been going on vigorously, was continued during the 2nd and the 3rd. Jhansi was then stormed at four points; escalading was tried at three of them; at one it failed from the ladders being too short, but everywhere else there was success. Thus was the city taken, and Sir Hugh at once proceeded to concert measures for the attack on the Fort. But the Ranee saved him this further trouble by evacuating it on the night of the 4th April, and flying with her defeated troops towards Kalpee. With this capture of Jhansi, Sir Hugh's decisive campaign in Central India may be held to close. The subsequent operations were for the suppression of the rebellion.

Meanwhile, on his right, but much in the rear, Whitlock had been advancing to Punnah, and there remained halted. His campaign, however, was not over. The Banda Rajah still held the field in his front. Advancing on the 3rd April (the day of the capture of Jhansi), he reached and re-occupied Chutturpore on the 9th. Moving on then towards Banda, he was nearly taken by surprise at a place called Kabrai, where the Rajah had secreted a force in ambush; but, defeating that attempt, he pushed on, and met the whole force of the enemy drawn up in array in difficult ground, full of ravines, in front of Banda. By a combined attack on the enemy's right and front, and by judicious leading, ravine after ravine was carried; and the Rajah, leaving all his guns, fled with his army to Kalpee.

And thus ended the decisive struggle in the southern theatre.

BOOK V.

THE SUPPRESSION OF THE REVOLT.

BOOK V.

THE SUPPRESSION OF THE REVOLT.

CHAPTER I.

GENERAL, AND IN OUDE.

BY the beginning of April the decisive contest stage of the War of the Mutiny was over; the Punjab was actively and heartily on the British side; Delhi and the other districts of the upper provinces, except Rohilkund, were no longer at the mercy of insurgents and predatory tribes; Lucknow was now entirely in our possession, and our troops had overrun the Central India districts and taken Jhansi.

But there still remained to be subdued, before the revolt could be thoroughly suppressed, the mutineers and rebels that had escaped from Lucknow—the Rohilla and other bands that held Rohilkund—and the Central India rebels who had been driven out of Jhansi and other positions, and were now reuniting under Tantia Topee about Kalpee, on the Jumna. These three bodies will be separately dealt with in two theatres, Oude and the Southern respectively;

and, as will be seen, now that the hot weather had begun, the suppression was, practically in Oude, markedly carried out in two successive parts or campaigns, in the hot weather and the cold weather respectively.

But the eastern districts now became a theatre of serious, prolonged, and troublesome warfare, as the enemy there, hitherto passive, became active. Moreover, the hostility in Oude was no longer restricted to the mutineers and the adherents of the rebel court, with some contingents of no great account, but embraced the whole body of talookdars and their clansmen, now greatly excited. This was due to a proclamation issued on the 20th March by Lord Canning, generally known as the Confiscation Proclamation. By it all the chiefs, except some half-dozen men of no importance, were declared to have been guilty of rebellion and of waging war against the Queen, and to have consequently forfeited all their proprietary rights. The chiefs at once realized that their position was desperate, and they rose *en masse* in active rebellion, which they certainly had not done before.

It was a singular act on Lord Canning's part, because he seemed to stand almost alone as its author, and alone in his insistence on it. He was strenuously opposed by Outram, who prophesied of it precisely what happened. It was condemned by every authority and every class in India. It raised a storm of surprise and indignation in England, and caused the severest crisis in the fate of the English

Ministry. Its policy was defended with his utmost ability by Lord Canning; but however just and sound theoretically, results showed that it was practically a blunder, and led to the very widespread increase which has been mentioned in the hostility of the country.

This story has shown that the mass of these talookdars had, since Sir Henry Lawrence's arrival, and owing to his line of action, refrained from a hostile bearing to as great a degree as could be expected, or as was possible, under the despotic native rule and powerful army that dominated the situation at Lucknow and throughout the province. They had aided the fugitive residents of out-stations at the outbreak; they had helped Sir Henry Lawrence with supplies; with three exceptions, they had held aloof from joining the rebel army, either personally or through their retainers. They continued this loyalty till Havelock evacuated Oude territory and returned to Cawnpore; even then they sent to the rebel camp only such contingents as were demanded, and personally remained passive; and throughout the rest of the campaign they had abstained from any harassing of the British troops—in marked contrast, it will be seen, with their conduct after this Proclamation was issued. Was it reasonable and fair to class them not only with all other rebels, as equally open to punishment with them, but as worse than most? Was it not reasonable, on the other hand, that they should disavow being rebels at all, having been tricked out of the promises made them when they became her Majesty's subjects? or that they should actually revolt when they found their exceptional friendliness and good conduct ignored, and believed themselves to be tricked a second time?

But the proclamation had a still deeper and more widespread effect than on the talookdars alone. It was viewed by the country at large as a declaration of the British Government that, on becoming sufficiently powerful, there was no despotic action which it would not take if it so willed, and as confirming the truth of all the worst charges which the malcontents had been in the habit of making respecting the intentions and aims of the British.

CHAPTER II.

THE OUDE THEATRE—HOT-WEATHER CAMPAIGN.

THE enemy in Oude now consisted of four actively hostile parties—

1. The mutineer sepoys.
2. The resuscitated forces of the Nuwabee—the Begum's troops, as they may be conveniently called.
3. The Mahomedan followers of the Fyzabad moulvie; and
4. The talookdars, and their retainers and clansmen.

The numbers of the parties one and two had now diminished considerably. They had taken the leading part in all the military operations heretofore, had been now thoroughly defeated, and were somewhat sick of the struggle. But the moulvie's force was becoming a more prominent factor in the struggle, and was acting as a focus of Mahomedan hostility; while the Rajwara men under their chiefs, all over the province, had started their old style of guerilla warfare; which lay, not in aggressive and combined movements against the common foe, but in stopping and cutting off supplies, checking and harassing the movements of the troops and emissaries and officers of Government, making and threatening local attacks, frustrating every effort to introduce civil administration, and encouraging marauders and brigandage.

The talookdaree gatherings and warfare were mainly in Byswara and the south-east of Oude, but the three other parties collected in two groups: one on the north-west of Oude, towards the Rohilkund border, under the leading of the moulvie; the other on the north-east. This consisted of all the *four* classes of rebels, who formed themselves into four separate bodies, though keeping together without any one recognized chief, while a large number of persons exercised more or less influence and command over the several sections; such as the Begum, Mummoo Khan, Jeylall Singh, the Nana's brother, various officers of the sepoy troops, and the like. These three gatherings came to a head not simultaneously, but at different and successive periods—the north-west first, then the talookdars in Byswara in May, and afterwards the north-east gathering in June.

Before dealing with these hostile bodies, Sir Colin arranged for securing proper command of Lucknow itself by constructing a large fortified position on the south bank of the Goomtee, facing the stone bridge, called the Mutchi Bhown Fort. It was about half a mile each way, and included within its *enceinte* the old Mutchi Bhown citadel at one angle, and the Great Emambarah and other large edifices at other points; and was bordered by a large clear esplanade on its landward faces, which had involved a sweeping demolition of the denser part of the heart of the city. Also the old Residency position was now surrounded with ramparts on a more correct trace, and formed a separate detached fort.

While these were in progress, and before dealing with the threatening gatherings in Oude, Sir Colin sent off troops to Rohilkund and also to Azimgurh, in the eastern theatre, which had been attacked, and was in difficulties.

The column directed against Rohilkund was commanded by Walpole, and was to sweep up the left bank of the Ganges to clear and settle those districts first. The part it played was important, and requires description. Walpole left Lucknow on April 7th, and in a fortnight reached Rhodamow, near which was the jungle fort of Roya, held by a talookdar named Nirput Singh. He was not a man of any power or following, but his father, Jussa Singh, though he had not fought against the English in Oude itself, had been a staunch friend of the Nana, had joined him at Bithoor, and had been killed in one of his combats with Havelock. The son had followed in his father's footsteps, and had given a home and shelter in Roya to the Nana when driven out of Bithoor. Nirput Singh was now holding out in Roya, and had to be attacked. The fort was small—not, like some others, many miles in circumference. Its strength lay in its thick earthen walls and deep ditch, surrounded by an almost impervious thicket of bamboo jungle; which, however, as was the case with all such forts, was not equally strong all round, but had some faces weaker than others, and also gaps here and there by which access was easy. Putting aside the more powerful modes of attack, in which artillery and mortars come into play, the recognized and well-known mode of capturing these places without serious loss was to discover the weak points and gaps, and then force an entrance.

Now, General Walpole would not adopt any such plan. He had a splendid little force, the Highland Brigade (42nd, 79th, and 93rd), the 4th Punjabees (old comrades of the 93rd), the 9th Lancers, and a Punjab cavalry regiment, with two batteries of Horse Artillery and some heavy guns and mortars. But he would not take advantage of the opportunities such a body of troops gave him. He did not reconnoitre. He did not listen to the information tendered him. He simply sent his Highland regiments forward to pierce through and storm the defences at the strongest points. The result was a heavy loss in men and officers, especially in the death of that ideal soldier, Adrian Hope, and a positive repulse, inasmuch as the British force was withdrawn from the attack. Nirput Singh evacuated the fort during the night, and Walpole proceeded on with his force into Rohilkund; but this episode of Roya had a most serious effect. Its fame, as a matter of course, spread with exaggerations throughout the province, and emboldened the talookdars. So Sir Colin presently proceeded to conduct and control the operations in Rohilkund in person.

Hope Grant was left in command in Oude to

meet and suppress whatever efforts the enemy might make. It was, doubtless, hoped at first that the enemy would be gradually scattered and dispersed; but it soon became evident that this could not be effected in this hot season, and that the organized and thorough crushing out of the rebellion must be deferred to the cold weather, present efforts being confined to the attack and dispersion of important gatherings. The first movement for this object was made on April 11th, when Hope Grant led a force by the Seetapore road against the party of Mahomedan rebels, the north-western group, at whose head was the moulvie. These men were really in touch with the insurgents in Rohilkund, but at present were still in Oude in the Mahona direction, at Baree, about twenty-five miles from Lucknow. Grant's column was about 3000 strong, with some eighteen guns, and contained British and native troops of all arms. As they neared Baree, the moulvie tried to turn their flank and get at the baggage; but the flanking movement was detected and defeated, chiefly by the charge of the 7th Hussars. After this the moulvie's men would not bide the British attack, but evacuated the village which they had occupied as their stronghold, and then withdrew in retreat and disappeared into Rohilkund, to form part of the gathering with which Sir Colin had to deal in that province.

From Baree, Hope Grant turned to the right to Mahomedabad and the Gogra, hoping to catch the Begum at Ramnugger or Bithoolee. But she fled on his approach, and so his immediate task was to co-operate with Jung Bahadur's army, which had started on its return to Nepaul.

Next, the gatherings on the north having been cleared off for the present, he returned to Lucknow, and then dispersed a party of the enemy which had collected on the south; taking several of their forts.

But other clansmen gathered under an able chief, Beni Madho, who avoided any serious engagement, adopting instead the ubiquitous tactics of genuine guerilla warfare—skirmishes and surprises; ceaselessly harassing and then eluding the British troops which he could easily do, as his followers (of whom he is said to have had over 80,000, chiefly matchlockmen, scattered over the district) knew every inch of the ground. Hope Grant was not long in seeing that against such an enemy as this our troops must during the summer heats and rains remain comparatively passive and on the defence. So leaving others for the present to maintain that attitude towards the enemy in Byswara, he started early in June to attack the hostile force; which had again gathered in the north-east, and, advancing from the Fyzabad direction, had concentrated at Nuwabgunge, eighteen miles from Lucknow. As already shown, this enemy was made up of four different parties, each under a separate leader, and was without much cohesion in the parties or unanimity and concert in the chiefs. There were sepoys of the regular army, troops of the old court of Oude, talookdaree troops, and such of the Mahomedans as had not followed the fortunes of the moulvie into Rohilkund. These four groups kept more or less apart, instead of acting in unison under one acknowledged leader. Hope Grant had a strong division—two British and one Punjab infantry regiments, three batteries of artillery, some six squadrons of British cavalry, and 900 native cavalry. He marched against the enemy at night, turned the right of their position, and took them by surprise in the morning. They fought well, especially the talookdaree troops, who routed Hodson's Horse; but after three hours of hard combat they had to fall back, leaving 600 dead on the field. This victory dispersed the enemy, and had also the effect of checking and turning back other additional hostile bodies that were in motion to concentrate on Nuwabgunge. The defeated enemy had fled in different directions—some to Gonda, some to Fyzabad; but apparently the largest column turned towards Sultanpore.

Shortly before this, Maun Singh, the Brahmin talookdar and ex-amil, who had hitherto tried to play a double game, and to stand well with both the British and the rebels, had openly proclaimed his allegiance to the Government, and held his fort of Shahgunge in their interests. The enemy had appeared before his fort and besieged it, but now, on Hope Grant's approach to Fyzabad, they dispersed and disappeared. Maun Singh being thus relieved, Hope Grant moved on to Sultanpore, and here occurred the last real combat in the summer. The enemy were in considerable strength, 14,000 men, with 15 guns; and to attack them the Goomtee had to be crossed, as they were on its right bank. This operation occupied from the 25th to the 27th August, but at last it was effected, and the battle came off on the evening of the 28th. The enemy were the assailants, but they were checked in their attack, then driven back, and finally put to flight, leaving Sultanpore in Hope Grant's possession.

During the next six weeks the operations were desultory and isolated, being directed chiefly to clearing and strengthening the posts which were to be used as the starting-points for the cold weather movements.

The enemy in Oude now consisted mainly of the talookdaree troops, followers of such chiefs and leaders as Beni Madho, the Rajah of Ameythee, Hunwunt Sing, and the like. Sir Colin determined to reserve his real attack on them till the winter, and meanwhile to save his men as much as possible from further exposure during the trying heat and malarious rainy season. The mutineer sepoys, who had belonged to the two northern gatherings, had now in great part disappeared and dispersed. Their cause was gone, and they had to make the best of their plight. But the Mussulman fanatics, and the adherents of the Oude Durbar, and of the Nana, were still in force. Moreover, the whole country population of the province was in dogged rebellion, and had to be subdued; and Sir Colin was planning to effect this during the coming winter.

CHAPTER III.

THE ROHILKUND CAMPAIGN.

WE turn, meanwhile, at this period, to Rohilkund on the west. It has been told how Walpole's division had been sent there shortly after the capture of Lucknow, and how its commander had blundered on his way, at Roya, and raised the spirits of the enemy. Sir Colin had then left Oude to conduct the campaign in Rohilkund in person, and proceeded by Futtehgurh to join Walpole. It has also been shown that the rebel body which had collected in the north-west corner of Oude under the moulvie had crossed into Rohilkund to take part in the struggle there. The enemy, consequently, to be dealt with in those districts consisted of the moulvie's force, of a large body of mixed troops under Prince Feroze Shah, of Rohillas under Khan Bahadur Khan, and of the gathering, as of old, under the Chief of Furruckabad. Sir Colin arranged for this campaign that four columns should converge on Bareilly, clearing the country as they advanced, viz. one from Lucknow, under Walpole (as already referred to); one from Roorkee, in the north-west—the opposite direction—

first under Coke, and afterwards under Jones; one from Futtehgurh, under Sir Colin himself; and the fourth from Budaun, on the west, under Penny.

Sir Colin joined Walpole's column; which he led to Shahjehanpore, and then to Meranpore Kutra, without any serious fighting. There, or *en route*, he was joined by Penny's column, which had had a skirmish, in which Penny had been killed. On the 4th May he reached Faridpore, a march short of Bareilly, where Khan Bahadur Khan had collected round him the bulk of the insurgents. On the 5th was fought the battle of Bareilly. Though the force on the British side actually engaged in that battle was that under Sir Colin's own command, the enemy was embarrassed by the approach from the opposite direction of the Roorkee column, which arrived and fought on the following day, the 6th; and the movements of that column will be now first dealt with.

It was commanded by General John Jones, with the advanced brigade under Brigadier Coke, one of the most brilliant of leaders, and a man full of resource. It started from Roorkee on the 17th April, and had its first action at Boginwala, where it routed the enemy, who were pursued and severely punished by Cureton's newly raised Mooltanee Horse. Continuing the advance, Jones found the rebels on the 21st, numbering 10,000 infantry and 2000 cavalry, with 15 guns, posted strongly on the canal at Naghina. Sending a strong force to cross the canal on his left, and then turn down on the enemy's right flank, Jones charged in front on their making their appearance; and the enemy, upset by the double movement, offered no real opposition, fled precipitately, and were again severely punished by the Mooltanee Horse; with the loss of their leaders, their guns, and their elephants. After this the column moved on, with little opposition, through Bijnoor to Moradabad, where, on the 26th April, it captured 21 of the Rohilkund ringleaders; and then forward to Bareilly, to co-operate with Sir Colin. The whole of that further march, till the city was reached on the 6th May, was one continued series of successful and effective skirmishes.

On the 5th May Khan Bahadur Khan, knowing that Sir Colin was close at hand and preparing to attack him—while Jones, with the Roorkee column, was still at some distance—arranged to contest that attack, instead of slipping out of the way. He drew up in two lines on the banks of Natia Nullah, but without destroying the bridges over it. So Sir Colin passed his guns over one of the bridges, and, getting on the enemy's flank, raked them with his artillery, while his infantry kept pressing on in front. Now occurred the very well-known incident of the splendid attack by a body of fanatical Ghazees on the 4th Punjabees and the 42nd Highlanders, which tried the mettle of those gallant regiments, but ended with the result that not a Ghazee survived. The force then advanced, but Sir Colin did not think it prudent to enter the city that day, as the men were exhausted and suffering from sunstroke and other causes. Hence Khan Bahadur and his following escaped during the night, and moved towards Philibeet. Some of his cavalry, however, remained near the field of action, harassing the camp and baggage and pickets all through the night; and they also met the Roorkee force as it approached next day from the opposite direction, and did not leave till after a smart skirmish with it.

So Bareilly was taken, but the bulk of the rebels in Rohilkund were still at large. Khan Bahadur was near Philibeet, where he was free to escape into Nepaul, and the moulvie, who had been hovering not far from the borders of Oude, had taken advantage of this concentration of the British force on Bareilly to move again on Shahjehanpore. He was now speedily joined by the neighbouring rebel parties on the Oude frontier. Colonel Hall, who commanded the party left at Shahjehanpore, heard of his approach, and moved into the gaol which he had prepared against such an attack; and this he held against the moulvie's bombardment without any difficulty. On the 7th Sir Colin had directed Jones to proceed to relieve Shahjehanpore, where he arrived on the 11th. The enemy's cavalry was too numerous to allow of his attacking and defeating them in the field, so he manœuvred to drive them out of the suburbs and city into the open country, effected a junction with Hall, and then sent back word to Sir Colin for reinforcements to deal effectively with the enemy. From the 11th to the 14th the opposing forces faced each other, the moulvie being joined meanwhile by Prince Feroze Shah, the Begum, and all the other leading rebels in the neighbourhood. On the 15th the moulvie, thus reinforced, attacked Jones, but in vain, being steadily repulsed. Meanwhile, after despatching Jones to Shahjehanpore, Sir Colin had scattered the troops he had had with him at Bareilly, leaving some there under Walpole, sending others to Oude and to Meerut, and a brigade under Coke in pursuit of Khan Bahadur Khan towards Philibeet; starting himself on the 15th with a strong force towards Futtehgurh. But on receiving Jones's message he had to counter-order these movements. He at once sent back to Bareilly for reinforcements, and turning himself towards Shahjehanpore on the 18th, was there attacked by the moulvie; and though he duly repulsed him, he sent messages to Coke to leave his original route and join him, in order to deal effectually with the enemy, who had now obviously massed in his immediate front. On Coke's arrival the moulvie's whole force was driven from Shahjehanpore and out of Rohilkund to Mohumdee in Oude, where it broke up and scattered. With this ended the campaign in Rohilkund, contemporaneously with the cessation of the hot weather struggle in Oude; so that when the contest was resumed there at the end of the rains and the beginning of the cold weather, Rohilkund gave comparatively little trouble, the enemy in it merely being those hovering on the borders of Oude, and being driven northwards by our flanking columns. It may be added that shortly after leaving Shahjehanpore the moulvie was shot at Powayn in endeavouring to coerce that fort, on the borders of Oude and Rohilkund; and with his death disappeared one of the most resolute of the rebel leaders.

CHAPTER IV.

FINAL WINTER CAMPAIGN IN OUDE.

HAVING held his hand during the hot weather and rains of 1858, in order to save his troops, Sir Colin had determined that, during the coming winter, the Province of Oude should be thoroughly subjugated; and the general outline of his scheme was this: The Gogra, running through the province somewhat parallel to the Ganges, divided it into two parts, north and south, the southward part being itself subdivided into two, east and west, by the line of road that ran from Cawnpore to Lucknow and onwards. Each of these three parts was to form a separate theatre of operations. The two to the south of the Gogra were to be attacked first, and simultaneously; and such of the enemy in them as were not crushed were to be driven into the district north of the Gogra, which would thus form the final seat of operations. The flanking districts of Rohilkund on the west, and Azimgurh on the east, were meanwhile to be held in force by our troops.

In the two theatres south of the Gogra, Sir Colin had three lines of Oude troops with which to operate.

On the west was the Rohilkund line ; on the east was the Azimgurh line, besides those remaining in those districts themselves ; and in the middle was the Cawnpore and Lucknow line, with Lucknow as the great centre of all. The troops in the two outer lines were to advance inwards, beginning at their southern ends, and so gradually to edge the enemy off to the north, and then drive them across the Gogra. The middle line at the south end was held by Evelegh, who was to operate to the east or west according to the exigencies of the occasion.

Now, the region north of the Gogra, lying between it and the Nepaulese Himalayas, into which the enemy were to be driven, is a triangle, with its apex at the west and its base at the east, where the space is wide and the mountains are distant from the river. As the mountains run westwards, they incline towards the river, till at length they meet it at its debouchure, forming the apex of the triangle. Sir Colin's plan, in this final part of the war, was to guard the Gogra strongly so as to prevent any slipping back of the enemy into the southern districts ; and then, having formed a line, so to speak, at the base of the triangle on the east, to sweep upwards through the narrowing districts, forcing back the enemy before him till they should be dislodged, or captured, or driven into Nepaul.

Further, in the eastern of the two southern parts, Sir Colin had to deal with a crowd of large jungle forts, and with the clansmen of the district ; he therefore determined to hem these in and coerce them locally as much as possible. So the lines from Lucknow round by the Gogra to Fyzabad, and along the Goomtee, were very strongly held ; and, in attacking any fort, he designed to concentrate on and around it, so as to make escape almost hopeless, and lead, if possible, to its surrender without fighting. Afterwards, as he drove the enemy before him, and captured their towns and positions, he proposed to occupy them with police, and so re-establish civil administration.

In October the operations began; and first of all in the western district south of the Gogra, for here the ball was opened, not by the British, but by the rebels. The enemy collected in force, 12,000 men with twelve guns, and marched on our post at Sandeela in the heart of that district, on the 3rd October. On the 6th, its garrison, which had shut itself up in the Fort, was relieved by a small party under Major Maynard, which forced the enemy off for some four miles ; and then, on the 8th, Brigadier Barker with a strong brigade arrived from Lucknow. Barker, after a fierce fight, in which he lost eighty-two men killed and wounded, defeated the enemy thoroughly; and a few days afterwards he turned the tables, attacking and taking their Fort of Birwah.

The projected movement inwards into that part of Oude from the Rohilkund side began on the 18th. Under the orders of General Seaton, who kept watch over Rohilkund itself, two columns penetrated Oude; one under Colonel Hall from Furruckabad at the south end, towards Roya and Sandeela; the other under Brigadier Troup from Shahjehanpore, further north, towards Seetapore.

While Hall advanced from the west, Evelegh cleared the ground along the Ganges towards him from the south end of the middle line up to Sandeela. Then Barker, co-operating with Hall, captured Roya on the 28th October; and thus the south part on that western theatre was cleared of the enemy, and held by our own police; while the Ganges became free for navigation.

Brigadier Troup, on the north, when desiring to move from Shahjehanpore on Seetapore, found that he had first to deal with the Rohilla chief, Khan Ali Khan, who had remained at Philibeet; so he began by defeating him and driving him across the Gogra. Having thus gained the clear command of that frontier, at the extreme west of Oude, he then crossed the boundary into Oude, and took the fort of Mithoolee.

In the next month (November) Brigadier Barker advanced *northwards* from Sandeela, clearing the country right and left, and at the end of the month secured Khyrabad and Biswah; leaving, however, a gap on the Lucknow side, though nearing Troup on the other flank. To co-operate with him, Brigadier Troup, after capturing Mithoolee, also moved northwards in advance of his left; driving the enemy before him to Aligunge, near the Gogra, across which most of them were forced after a sharp action on the 17th. Then he turned to his right, marched along the right bank of the Gogra, and reaching Biswah on the 2nd December, effected his junction with Barker.

At this time Evelegh, in the middle line, had been directed to operate on the north-west of Lucknow, to fill up the gap between Lucknow and the site of Barker's operations. In doing this he took the fort of Oomeria, on the 2nd December.

So that now all that western district had been subdued, and all its rebel troops, with one exception, driven across the Gogra by Barker's forward and Troop's flank movement. That exception was that Prince Feroze Shah, when being hemmed in on the Gogra near Biswah, dodged and escaped through our troops with some 1500 men, and, doubling back south by Sandeela to the Ganges, crossed it and then the Jumna, and finally joined the Central India rebel army; so disappearing from the scene in Oude.

Thus was the western district cleared and subdued by the beginning of December; and we now turn to contemporary operations in the eastern district, which were conducted under the personal guidance of Sir Colin Campbell.

Before they were begun, our troops held in force the line from Sultanpore *viâ* Pertabgurh to Allahabad, and also from Sultanpore north to Fyzabad; but, since it was essential to prevent any opportunity for the enemy to escape eastwards across the Sultanpore-Fyzabad line into the Azimgurh districts, Sir Colin began his operations by strengthening the Sultanpore position, and detaching Hope Grant to his eastward flank to co-operate with a column which he directed to advance under Colonel Kelly from Azimgurh into Oude. This Colonel Kelly did, driving the enemy before him, and securing Akbarpore, and then Tanda, near which he halted, on the 30th October, to watch and guard that flank during the ensuing operations.

The flank within which he wished to hem in the enemy being thus provided for, Sir Colin's first step in his direct operations westwards was to send forward a brigade under Wetherall towards Rampore Kussia, the stronghold of the Khanpooria clan, and there to co-operate with Hope Grant in capturing it. But Wetherall did not wait for that co-operation, and finding the weak point of the Fort in an otherwise almost impregnable triple circle of defences, attacked and stormed it on the 3rd November, with a loss of 80 men.

Continuing westwards, the next point to be attacked was Ameythee, a very strongly fortified position belonging to its powerful chief, the Rajah Lal Madho Singh, who had been conspicuously friendly at the outbreak, and instrumental in aiding English families and escorting them into security. To operate against this fort, three columns concentrated on it—on its east, Pinckney's (Sir Colin with it) from Pertabgurh; on its south, Wetherall's from Rampore Kussia; and on its north-west, Hope Grant's. While thus concentrating, Sir Colin summoned the Rajah to surrender, which he did eventually on the 10th November; not, however, till he had seen, from the strength of the attack by which he was menaced, that resistance was hopeless. But though he surrendered personally, most of the garrison, some 4000 men, of whom 1500 were sepoys, had evacuated the fort and escaped during the night.

The next move, still westwards of course, was against Shunkerpore, the stronghold of its chief, Beni Madho. The three columns that had taken Ameythee were to concentrate on it on its north, east, and south; while Evelegh's brigade, from Poorwa on the Lucknow-Cawnpore line, was to advance on it from the west. But the latter was delayed by the resistance he met with on the way. As with Ameythee, so Sir Colin summoned Beni Madho to surrender. The Fort was a huge one, some eight miles in circumference, but its defences were incomplete and full of gaps; and Beni Madho, who was a soldier of ability, knew he could not hold it. He replied accordingly that he would evacuate the Fort, but would not surrender personally, holding himself a subject of the Nuwab of Oude, and not of the British Government. So he and his followers, said to be 15,000 men, with several guns, marched out of the Fort on the night of the 15th, taking their route to the west towards Doondea Khera. On their way, however, they were met by Evelegh, on the 17th, and defeated, with the loss of three guns, though their escape westwards was not averted.

On becoming, next morning, aware of Beni Madho's flight, Sir Colin sent off (1) Wetherall's brigade, now Taylor's, towards Fyzabad, to prevent his circling round to the east, and to keep that line secure; and (2) Hope Grant to Roy Bareilly and Jugdespore, to its north, to get into more immediate contact with

Beni Madho, if he should be trying to escape in that direction. After leaving a detachment to destroy the Fort, Sir Colin himself followed on to Roy Bareilly with Pinckney's brigade to effect a junction with Evelegh. On the 19th he heard of the successful combat of the 17th, and gathered that Beni Madho had been effectually kept to the south between Doondea Khera and the Ganges. To hem him in, he continued his march westwards parallel to the Ganges, up to Buchraon, between Doondea Khera and the river. There he turned, on the 21st, to his left, and bore down on Beni Madho on the morning of the 24th. He found the opposing force drawn up in line of battle, with its back to the river, and its front protected by a jungle of thorny scrub, which had been filled with skirmishers. Sir Colin advanced against Beni Madho in line; infantry in the centre, cavalry on the flanks, guns between the infantry and cavalry, and the whole preceded by skirmishers. These last forced the opposing skirmishers back through the jungle; and on the latter emerging from it defeated, the enemy's entire line broke and fled along the banks of the river, without ours having to come into action at all. Beni Madho escaped along the river bank, then turned and fled north; and eluding the several columns that met, but only checked, his progress, he crossed first the Goomtee and then the Gogra.

Meanwhile the troops that had been all along left on the Lucknow-Fyzabad line had tackled and defeated all the local gatherings, and gradually driven them all to the north of the Gogra; including the Begum, Mummoo Khan, Nirput Singh, the Nana, and the rebels that followed them. Thus by the end of the month the eastern district of Oude south of the Gogra had been cleared of the enemy, and police posts and civil administration established; while the precisely similar measures, already described, were being carried out in the western district.

And now the last part of the programme, the finale, the subjugation or expulsion of the enemy in the triangular tract on the left of the Gogra, had to be carried out. A necessary preliminary to this end was the construction of a bridge at Fyzabad, the point on which the line that had to sweep up the district must turn. This had been effected by the strenuous exertions of Lothian Nicholson, R.E., with the support of the Fyzabad garrison, against the persistent fire and opposition of the enemy on the opposite bank. These were under the command partly of the ex-amil Mehndee Hussun, and partly of the Gonda Rajah, the recognized head of the federation of the whole of the Rajpoot clans on the left of the Gogra. The arrival of Taylor's brigade (from Shunkerpore), and afterwards of Hope Grant's column, enabled action to begin at once. And so, on November 25th, Hope Grant had crossed the bridge, had attacked and routed the Gonda Rajah's and Mehndee Hussun's following, and had thus secured the means for starting the required movements and operations.

Here Hope Grant remained till about December 6th, clearing the line across the districts to the hills as well as he could, capturing Bunkussia and other forts belonging to the Gonda Rajah and other chiefs, and awaiting the arrival of a column from Goruckpore under Rowcroft, which was to take part in the final operations.

After defeating Beni Madho, Sir Colin had returned to Lucknow; and now, on the 5th December, he started thence with a very strong column—an infantry division, a cavalry brigade, and some fourteen guns—*en route* to Fyzabad *viâ* Nuwabgunge Barabankee. But on reaching this latter point he heard that the enemy, under Beni Madho, were encamped at (another) Nuwabgunge, on the other side of the Gogra, close at hand, at its passage at Byram Ghaut, and were holding the Fort of Bithoorlee, and threatened to recross the river southwards. So Sir Colin halted to protect that passage, and sent orders to Hope Grant to advance (up the left bank of the Gogra) to Secrora, which lay on the east, close to Bithoorlee. This movement led to the enemy's evacuation of the position they were occupying; and accordingly, leaving a sufficient force to hold the Byram Ghaut and construct a bridge there, Sir Colin proceeded with the rest of his column to Fyzabad.

On the 14th the active operations began. Sir Colin's column advanced from Fyzabad to Secrora; Rowcroft's column, which had come up on the right, was directed northward across the Raptee, and then turned to the left to Toolseepore, whither also Hope Grant was detached to co-operate with him; while Evelegh's brigade followed in the rear, as a reserve, and to stop any doubling back of the enemy.

Rowcroft, on the right, then advanced against Toolseepore, captured it, and was there joined by Hope Grant, whose cavalry prevented the enemy doubling back. From this point they were instead driven steadily forward towards Bhinga, till at length, in the first days of January, the insurgents were forced across the frontier and took refuge in Nepaul, leaving all their guns in Hope Grant's possession.

Meanwhile the main column, under Sir Colin, had advanced from Secrora on the 15th December against Baraitch, where the Begum and the Nana were, with the troops that still adhered to them. It reached Baraitch, which the enemy evacuated on its approach, retreating towards Nanpara and Pudnaha. From Baraitch a force had to be detached under Colonel Christie to move close up the left bank of the Gogra, to aid our posts on the other bank in preventing a repassage by the enemy; with whom it had a smart action on the 23rd December. Sir Colin was somewhat delayed in his advance from Baraitch, partly from having to wait till Hope Grant came sufficiently forward on his flank, and partly to enable the police arrangements to be properly organized; on the 23rd, however, he made his advance toward Nanpara. On arriving there he found it deserted; but the enemy were said to be at Burgidia, a short distance ahead, and he moved on it on the 26th. Finding them drawn up for action, he formed up his troops on their front, and then suddenly moving on their left, he attacked them on that flank; on which they fled precipitately, abandoning their guns. Next day, the 7th December, the force advanced on the neighbouring Fort of Musjidia, which was shelled for three hours, and was then found to be abandoned. These forts were all in a corner or neck of the triangle in which the space between the river and the mountains was of the narrowest.

During the 28th and 29th the enemy were being pressed up further and further towards the hills into the narrow space where the Raptee debouches from the mountains and reaches the plain; till it became known that they were massed at a spot called Bankee, and meant to make a last stand there. Their position was at the edge of forest ground. Sir Colin moved his force forward during the night, attacking them in the early morning with his Horse Artillery and cavalry, and then with skirmishers. The enemy never made any attempt at a resolute stand, but kept retiring before the skirmishers, who, with the guns and cavalry, advanced, following them up. At length they were forced back from the jungle into more open ground, with the Raptee behind them. Thereupon the 7th Hussars and 1st Punjab Cavalry charged them, driving them headlong into and across the Raptee. With this episode, in the last day of December, 1858, ended the long-sustained war in Oude.

CHAPTER V.

THE EASTERN THEATRE.

WHEN Franks's force left the Benares districts, towards the end of February, for their march through Oude to Lucknow, in the decisive contest, the disaffected who were there already, and the insurgents who were defeated by Franks, collected and formed a camp at a place called Belwa, near Goruckpore—which was occupied by Brigadiers Rowcroft and Southeby—with the intention of raiding Azimgurh, Jaunpore, and perhaps Benares. Thereupon Rowcroft moved with his force to Amorha, close to Belwa, and so drew the enemy out, on the 5th March, for a combat. Defeating them, he drove them back, with the loss of 8 guns and 400 men, the volunteer cavalry pursuing them into their entrenched camp. Twice again afterwards, on the 17th and 25th March, while waiting for reinforcements, he encountered and defeated them.

Meanwhile, a new and important enemy had appeared in the field in these districts. Rajah Konwur Singh, who since his defeat at Arrah and Jugdespore, had been hitherto unable to enter on any active measures, now took advantage of the absence of the British troops in Oude to come to the front, crossed the Ganges, and with his own followers and sepoys, as well as a part of the Belwa men, began by occupying the Fort of Atrowlia. Leaving this on the 22nd, he attacked and defeated a detachment under Colonel Milman, and followed it up to Azimgurh, beleaguering it two days later in the gaol entrenchments there. But during these two days, Milman was reinforced by some 300 men from Ghazeepore and Benares, and was thus enabled to hold his own. Then, on the 6th April, Lord Mark Kerr arrived with a force from Benares, and after a prolonged and severe fight, of which the issue was for many hours in doubt, at length drove off the enemy from his line of advance, and relieved Azimgurh and Milman's garrison. But the relief was almost similar to Havelock's relief, *i.e.* only ensuring the safety of the garrison, the enemy being still in very preponderating strength. Substantial aid, however, under General Lugard, was already well on its way from Lucknow, and the Azimgurh garrison received from Sir Colin strict orders to remain on the defensive until relieved by it. Lugard had left Lucknow with a strong brigade, on the 29th, with the intention of going direct to Azimgurh; but on reaching Sultanpore, on the 5th, he found that, as the bridge there had been destroyed, the passage of the Goomtee, which lay in that direct route, would delay him a week; so, instead of adopting that line, he continued his march by the right bank of the river, when his route would be by Jaunpore. On the 10th, near that city, at the village of Tugra, he attacked and put to flight a body of the enemy under Gholam Hussun, and then relieving Jaunpore, pushed on for Azimgurh, and came before it on the 15th. But Konwur Singh, feeling that he would not be able to deal successfully with the large force concentrating there, went off with the main body of his own troops towards the passage of the Ganges at Ghazeepore, and left a small picked body to hold the bridge over the Tons, by which Lugard's access to Azimgurh lay. His men did their duty well; they held out as long as was necessary, and then followed up their leading column, holding the rear, and keeping the pursuing cavalry at bay very effectively. But Azimgurh was relieved.

Still it was essential to give no breathing time to Konwur Singh. So Brigadier Douglas was despatched next day with a strong force to overtake the advanced cavalry and continue the pursuit of the fugitive rebels. This was conducted as rapidly as the marching powers of his men permitted, and Konwur Singh was allowed no rest. There were fights at Naghai on the 17th, and at Manohur on the 20th; but Konwur Singh, who always managed to outwit his pursuers by misleading reports, eluded their efforts, and, on the 22nd, crossed the Ganges at Seopree Ghat, seven miles from another passage, to which Douglas had gone in pursuit of him. But during the passage of the river, he was wounded, and next day, the 23rd, he was attacked by the Arrah garrison, under Le Grand; who seemed to be succeeding against him, when, by some blunder which has never been traced, the retreat was sounded, and the British force, in dispersed order in the jungle, got bewildered, and was defeated and pursued, with very heavy loss. The district, of course, at once collapsed into disorder. But, on the one hand, Douglas now again resumed the pursuit, with Lugard advancing in the rear to his support; and, on the other, Konwur Singh died under the operation which his wound had made necessary. The lead was now taken by his brother, Ummur Singh, a man of equal energy, but less ability and skill.

Lugard crossed the Ganges on the 3rd May, and on the 9th encountered Ummur Singh, driving him off from Arrah, and capturing Jugdespore. From this date he pressed the enemy steadily, having daily encounters with them, and, on the 27th, retaking the guns which had been lost by Le Grand. But now Ummur Singh organized a system of pure guerilla warfare, dispersing his followers into small parties, which, avoiding conflict and evading the cavalry, kept harassing the troops, attacking the baggage, and cutting off supplies. Lugard met these measures by cutting roads through the jungle, and establishing posts by which the enemy were forced more into the open ground. But, by the middle of June, illness obliged him to resign the command. Douglas, then succeeding him, pursued the same tactics; but, though he held the enemy in greater check, he was unable, now that the rains had begun, to prevent the district continuing in a very disturbed state. On the subsidence of the rains, Douglas began on the 9th

October a converging movement of seven columns to drive all the enemy into Jugdespore, and there finish the Campaign. But the failure of one of them under Colonel Walters frustrated this scheme. Now, however, proposals that had been previously made by Major Havelock, the General's son, to employ *mounted* infantry, were accepted and adopted; and this resulted in immediate success. The ubiquitous infantry, supported on suitable ground by cavalry, allowed the enemy no rest, and followed and headed them everywhere; till at length finding themselves getting shot down and destroyed without the power of retaliation, they gradually gave up the contest; the district quieted down; and so, by the end of November, peace was restored in the eastern theatre.

CHAPTER VI.

THE SOUTHERN THEATRE.

THERE remains the southern theatre, in which, about the beginning of April, Sir Hugh Rose had stormed Jhansi, and Whitlock had captured Banda. But the fugitive rebels were collecting towards Kalpee, which was already held in force by the Nana's nephew; and Central India generally was still in a very unsettled state.

On the Ranee of Jhansi and Tantia Topee arriving at Kalpee, the force there consisted of several regiments of sepoys, and others from the Gwalior contingent, the fugitives of the Jhansi garrison, the contingents of many rebel chiefs, and the Nana's own people. Tantia Topee was appointed to the command and led the bulk of the force back some forty miles to Koonch on the road to Jhansi, and there halted and entrenched.

Meanwhile, Sir Hugh Rose, having detached two advanced parties under Majors Gall and Orr to clear the flanks, left Jhansi for Kalpee, on the 25th, with one brigade; the second following two days later. The whole force, further strengthened by the 71st

Highlanders, was collected on the 5th May at Pooch, about fourteen miles short of Koonch, and Orr and Gall were sent forward in advance, the former towards Koonch, and Gall towards the fort of Loharee, ten miles ahead, which he attacked and took, destroying the whole garrison.

On the 6th May, Sir Hugh advanced against Koonch, and, after a march of fourteen miles, formed up on the left and left rear of the entrenched town, turning its strong defences, and at the same time masking its Jhansi front. On his opening fire from the flank, the enemy found that their communications with Kalpee and their escape thither were threatened, and at once began to evacuate. As they streamed off in good formation towards Kalpee, at first in good order, they were steadily pursued, pressed and charged by Rose's cavalry, and at last they broke into a confused mass during the rest of the retreat, in the course of which nine of their guns were captured. But the heat was intense, the British suffering more from sunstroke and heat than from the enemy. In following up the fugitives, Sir Hugh sent one brigade on the direct road to press their retirement, and with the rest edged to the right to Golowlee, on the Jumna, opposite to where General Maxwell's division was encamped on the left bank. On the 15th May the junction was effected. On the 19th the 2nd Brigade joined.

Now, the main strength and defensive power of Kalpee lay in the ravines around it, all leading into the Jumna. So, on the 22nd, the Kalpee garrison, stealing up through these ravines, made a fierce attack in full force on Sir Hugh's position; but they had at last to retire before the charge of Ross's Camel Corps from Maxwell's camp, and were then caught by the cavalry. This defeat caused the evacuation of Kalpee the same night; and next day it was held by Rose's troops, the aim of the campaign having been thus successfully attained.

The evacuation was carried out by the Ranee, and her flight was westwards. It was a comparatively free direction; but even there her course now seemed hopeless. Troops from Rajpootana were advancing towards her, besides those that, set free by the British successes, were closing in from the east and south. Still she had one more card to play, and, aided by Tantia Topee who now again joined her, she played it skilfully and boldly. Her design was to march on Gwalior; call on Scindia to join; and, with or without his co-operation, to seize his fortress and raise the whole Mahratta country and race in the name of the Peishwa. She knew that the Gwalior men would certainly join her in preference to supporting Scindia in any adherence to the British. On the 1st June, she appeared before Gwalior, and her plans proved successful. Scindia drew out his army to oppose her, but it deserted to her *en masse*, and he had to fly to Agra. On this she immediately seized the Fort, made the Rao Sahib its Governor, and retaining the command, proclaimed the Nana as Peishwa. Meanwhile, Brigadier Smith, of the Rajpootana force, was marching towards her from

Goonah; Colonel Riddell lay on the banks of the Jumna, the brigade at Agra were on the watch ready to check her from the north, and Colonel Robertson, with a strong pursuing column, which was also being reinforced as he proceeded, was following her from Kalpee. Then, on the 4th June, Sir Hugh Rose heard of the Ranee's seizure of Gwalior. He at once, with the rest of his available troops, marched off thither, and, as he neared it, was joined by General, now Sir Robert, Napier. The Hyderabad troops, and others who were dispersed on their way to other stations, rapidly rejoined him. On the 16th June, he reached Bahadurpore, five miles from Gwalior, along with the troops already sent forward with Robertson and Steuart. Four miles to the south was Smith's, or the Sipree, Brigade, which had been also reinforced by detachments from Calpee and Jhansi, and on the north lay Riddell's column from Agra. Beginning his reconnaissance and fighting on the 16th, Rose pushed on his combined operations vigorously. On the afternoon of his arrival he began by attacking the cantonments of Morar, driving out the main body of the enemy, and then holding the position, which was useful as shelter for his own troops as well as on other grounds. Next day, the brigade moved up to Kotah ke Serai, five miles from Gwalior, through a defile and ground full of ravines, driving forward the rebels who held it, and ending in a pursuit, in the course of which the Ranee of Jhansi was killed.

On the 18th, a junction was effected between

Smith's brigade and Sir Hugh's army, and arrangements were made for a strong advance. The successive points to be carried were a line of hills; a plain, on which at one end stood Scindia's palace; the city; and the Fort. Next morning, the hills or heights were attacked and carried, and all the enemy's guns there were taken. Smith's brigade then turned the position held by the enemy in the plain, who withdrew from it into the city; the palace was seized without bloodshed through the influence of Captain Meade, who was personally known to its defenders; and Scindia, with rejoicing, reoccupied it. The force then advanced into the rest of the city, and held it without serious opposition. Next morning, the 20th, Steuart's brigade moved against the Fort; and Lieutenant Rose, of the 25th Bombay Native Infantry, on the right, catching sight of a gate into it in some hollow ground, stormed it with his skirmishers, and the Fortress of Gwalior was captured.

The routed and flying enemy were forthwith pursued by a light column under Napier, who next day, the 21st, overtook them at Alipore Jowra, drawn up 12,000 strong in two lines. Holding his cavalry in hand in their front, but sheltered from them by intervening high ground, he sent the Horse Artillery to enfilade their lines from their left flank. This speedily shook and began to roll up their lines, when the cavalry were let loose and made a frontal charge. On this the enemy broke and fled, losing twenty-five guns, all their equipment, and 300 killed. The rout was complete; and from that time—the end of June —Tantia Topee's force was a fugitive one; but it gradually dwindled away, though it never surrendered.

This flight of Tantia Topee's * was continued till the following March, and though his following was no longer strong as a fighting body, it was mischievous from the ceaseless excitement and anxiety its movements and its presence created; and its action may be briefly described. The area of its wanderings ranged from Ulwur on the north, to Beytool, south of the Nerbudda; and from near Oodeypore on the west, to near Saugor on the east. After Jowra Alipore, he moved north-westerly to Jeypore. Headed there by Roberts, and pursued, he turned south to Tonk, and thence south-east to the Chambal. Unable to cross it, he fled westward, and was attacked and punished by Roberts at Kotaria and Sanganeer. Pushing eastwards, he was headed by Parker, and bending more to the south, crossed the Chambal, and moved by Jhalra Puttun to Rajgurh. There he was met and defeated by Michell, who had succeeded Roberts. Flying by zigzag routes eastwards, and passing Chandeyree, he was again beaten and turned by Michell at Mungrowlee, and then at Sindwaho. Turning north to cross the Betwa, he was again headed, and now fled due south. At Khoria he met with a fresh attack and defeat, and his right wing was dispersed; but this did not prevent his continuing his flight southwards with the rest till he reached and crossed the Nerbudda and tried to raise the

* See map of Central India.

Mahrattas, causing much excitement and great anxiety in Bombay. But there, headed from the south by a force from Nagpore, he turned and pushed westwards; and skirting the Nerbudda, recrossed to its north bank and moved to Chota Oodeypore, where, being again met and defeated by Parker, he dashed into the Banswara jungles. Moving north, he emerged thence at a point where he threatened both Oodeypore and Neemuch, but being headed, he turned eastwards to Zeerapore, and then more northwards to Burrode, where he was joined by Prince Feroze Shah. Thence he swept northwards till he approached Ulwur, whence, being headed by Showers, he turned west. Again headed by Holmes at Seekur, he eventually turned southwards, with only a very small following; and passing close to Neemuch, fled thence eastwards to Seronje. By this time he had traversed upwards of 3000 miles; and now, while hiding with but a few devoted followers in the Seronje jungles, he was betrayed by the Rajah of Paoree to Major Meade on the 7th April, was tried for his complicity in the Cawnpore massacre, and hanged. With this episode flickered out the last embers of the great fire of the revolt.

BOOK VI.

SUMMARY AND COMMENTS.

BOOK VI.

SUMMARY AND COMMENTS.

CHAPTER I.

SUMMARY.

HAVING brought the story in detail up to the complete suppression of the revolt, and the restoration of peace and order and of the *Pax Britannica*, a brief summary may now be given with advantage.

There was ever prevalent a grave amount of disaffection towards the rule of the alien British. But it generally remained latent, in consequence of their superior and more civilized characteristics, and their avoidance of measures that might be repugnant to the native races generally, and tend to unite them in a common cause against the State.

But in Lord Dalhousie's time, his very extensive annexations excited alarm and created much general ill feeling ; the annexations of feudatory states, based on the refusal to recognize adopted heirs, gave rise to intense and widespread animosity, so that the disaffected were encouraged and became active. The annexations had led to the increase of the native army to a dangerous preponderance; of which the seditious took advantage to tempt it to revolt, but for a time in vain. Then came the annexation of Oude, well managed at the time, but followed by grave mismanagement, which alienated a powerful people, among whom lay the homes of the great majority of the sepoys, and who had hitherto been friendly. This was followed by the General Service Enlistment Act, which severely strained the loyalty of the native army; and then, in January, 1857, by the cartridge incident, which led to the revolt, started by those who came under the influence and guidance of the Moghul party—a party that had ever been working for this end. They seized Delhi, and made it the gage of battle, proclaiming the restoration of Moghul rule.

But the army was not prepared, had not concerted any general plan, for a mutiny; and the higher classes of the native population drew back from joining in any revolt at all on seeing the dominant attitude of the Moghul faction.

Consequently, there was a halt of three weeks before any spread of the mutiny began beyond the neighbourhood of Delhi. These three precious weeks gave a breathing-time to the British to prepare for the storm, but not nearly to the extent that was needed. In the Punjab the British army was much stronger than elsewhere, both actually and in comparison with the sepoy force, and the people of the province were friendly; so there the native army was suppressed, and the British troops, with local regiments, kept the province quiet, and became available for operations against Delhi.

The Commander-in-Chief gathered as strong a force as he could, some 3800 men, about Umballa and Meerut to move against Delhi; but he was desperately hampered by the defective military organization for transport and supplies, which had been prescribed by Government, and reduced, in the interests of economy, to the requirements of times of peace; so that mobilization, especially for siege purposes, was unavoidably a slow business, even though required, not for foreign war, but for the very centre of the Empire.

In Oude, Sir Henry Lawrence at once resolved on holding to Lucknow, and prepared there for the construction of entrenchments and a vigorous defence, retaining a large quantity of treasure—a sure magnet to all local enemies.

The Calcutta Government sent forward up country such few troops as they could spare at once, and took energetic measures for obtaining reinforcements for India from all directions; and the authorities in Madras, Bombay, Scinde, and Central India, took effective steps to prevent the rising from extending south of Upper India.

But at the end of May the Mutiny began to spread over the upper provinces, and in another month the war had begun. The mutineers were in five groups: in the Punjab, in the upper provinces, in Oude and on its borders, in the eastern districts, and in the southern provinces of Central India and Bundelkund.

In the Punjab they were overmastered. In the upper provinces they rallied to Delhi; in Oude to Lucknow and Cawnpore. In the east they remained localized, disturbing the country, but not, at first, coming to any head. In the south there were no English troops; still the mutineers remained there, instead of joining any of the other groups, until towards the end of the year. The five groups consequently led to five corresponding theatres of operations.

But at first the belligerent bodies of mutineers were limited to those at Delhi and those in Oude; where the struggle was a vital one, and lasted until the end of September, when the British in India began to receive reinforcements from England. Between September and the end of March, 1858, the contest was brought to a decisive issue; and during the remainder of the year 1858 the defeated mutineers and rebels were being pursued and dispersed, till peace and order were restored. The vital struggle closed with the British capture of Delhi, and Havelock's succour of Lucknow, the contest having been confined to these two theatres, and the British at Delhi being aided from the Punjab. The decisive contest lay, chiefly, in Oude and in the southern theatre. In the one Lucknow was captured, and in the other Jhansi; and the rebels were dispersed into small groups, while a new native army was being recruited, mainly from the Punjab.

But an ill-considered proclamation raised a fresh and powerful body of rebels in the Rajpoot chiefs and people of Oude; so that it took all the rest of that year for Sir Colin, with a very large army, to subdue that province, and the neighbouring one of Rohilkund. Similarly, in the Eastern district, Konwur Singh so roused the people into revolt, that it was only after he had been killed and his followers paralysed by the use of mounted infantry, that that district was quieted. And in Central India, Tantia Topee and the remnants of the rebels there kept those provinces in a fever of trouble and anxiety, while he was zigzagging throughout their length and breadth for distances exceeding three thousand miles, ever pursued, and being constantly headed, till his followers dwindled away, and he was betrayed, captured, and hanged.

CHAPTER II.

REMARKS AND COMMENTS.

THE prominent names among the leaders of the enemy were—the Nana Sahib, as the titular but deposed head of the Mahratta community — the Ranee of Jhansi, whose family had been deprived of the right of succession—the Begum of Oude, a wife of the deposed monarch, and the mother of his elected son—the Fyzabad moulvie—Rajah Konwur Singh—Tantia Topee—and Prince Feroze Shah of Delhi.

Not a single representative of the sepoy army ever appeared, or was even named as such; which would certainly have been done if the army had been the inciters to the revolt. Except in bearing the brunt of the fighting, the army never showed that its cause was the cause of the revolt. Nor did any of the real native potentates, such as Scindia, Holkar, or the Nizam, join in it. Only the Delhi imperial faction took the lead and guidance at the outset, and, by openly showing their hand, choked off those other races and communities that had been irritated with the British rule, but had no desire to revert to the Moghul rule in its place. In fact, in this tragedy, the Moghuls played the part of Iago, the army that of Othello.

The Nana, the Ranee, the Begum, were all under the influence of real or imaginary wrongs. The Moulvie was a fierce Mahomedan bigot, a zealot against the Christians, and a loyal subject to the Emperor and the Nuwab of Oude. Konwur Singh was a sufferer from the alien novelties of English land policy and English law courts.

Though the leaders named were all in earnest and energetic, there was only one of them, Tantia Topee, who possessed real ability; and he was not a soldier in heart.

It is impossible to avoid recognizing what the force and position would have been, and may at any time be, if we so act as to raise a common Cause, and excite a racial antipathy towards the British rule, and have opposed to us any leaders of ability, character, influence, and resolution.

The mutiny was confined to the Bengal army. It did not spread to the Madras army or the Bombay army, and reasons for this have been mentioned. Their essence lay in their being separate and disconnected armies; still, they were not so perfectly disconnected as they might have been, inasmuch as their recruiting grounds were not confined to their own areas—though the administrative arrangements were absolutely separate, to the grave disadvantage of the public service. One of the lessons of the mutiny seems to be that, while the whole army should be under one control and supreme command, it should be formed of several component armies, differing in race, in hereditary feelings, and in historical traditions. And one feature that might be usefully guarded and cared for in this arrangement is the retention and *effective* employment of those classes and races, whom it is now the fashion to make light of, but whose repute for real gallantry, chivalry, and devotion to their duty have been stamped in the pages of history in the days of Clive, and Lake, and Wellington, and in the defence of Lucknow. Stalwart physique and fierce valour are great qualities in a soldier ; but they are not everything. And there are many races in India, which are now passed over as unsuitable for warlike material, whose hereditary qualities have a sterling value, especially in a good and honourable cause, that only need opportunity to become properly recognized.

The revolt of the army has been traced back frequently to the first Afghan war, when great weakness was manifest in British conduct, and after which Brahmin and Rajpoot sepoys were outcasted in consequence of the violations of caste requirements to which they had been subjected. These features have been explained in our pages in the references to Sir Henry Lawrence's Article, and to the attitude of the sepoys in respect to the General Service Enlistment Act, and to compaigns involving a sea-voyage.

The revolt was characterized by murders, but rarely by worse atrocities; it is to these features, however, that the attention of the public has generally been drawn. But it is more pleasant to remember the facts that tell the other way—the equally numerous cases in which English lives were saved by the active help of the native chiefs and people, as more fully described in the "Development" chapters. India is not exceptional as regards the outbreak of crime and horrors, and the license of malignity and brutality, when civil rule has been lost, and the criminal and disaffected classes can run riot unchecked.

In looking back to the outbreak, the most startling fact—for fact it seems unquestionably to be—is that no one in authority, except Sir Henry Lawrence, realized up to the last moment that a momentous and possibly desperate crisis was at hand. That is the only excuse, at all valid, that is urged by the defenders of Lord Canning and General Anson. It does seem almost incredible. In Calcutta, where Lord Canning was, there were the intrigues that were being daily detected, and thwarted mainly by Cavanagh and Wauchope, in connection with Scindia's visit, with the King of Oude's Alsatia, with the Barrackpore threatenings, and the like, as well as the rumours rife in the mercantile community of the cessation of all up-country business. In Umballa, at General Anson's own camp of exercise, with shrewd men like Chester and Norman at his elbow, there were the nightly incendiary fires and seditious meetings, and other occurrences, that were unquestionably brought to notice. And there was the certainty that the sepoys felt gravely the General Service Act, that they were a body keenly sensitive at all times on the subject of caste and creed, and that they were now dangerously excited and suspicious in consequence of the cartridge incident, and of the discovery which it seemed to imply of a foul and treacherous plot.

Next, had the police failed everywhere in their detective and loyal duty? Had they kept the superior civil authorities ignorant and blind to the sedition at work, or had those authorities blundered, treated the reports as moonshine, and withheld these clues from the Government?

Lastly, was not the manifest tendency in the army to display their irritation, sufficient to make it incumbent to improve the military position and secure the strategical points?

Can the answers to such queries as these be in any doubt?

In considering the actual war, there seems to be a marked contrast between the characteristics in the conduct of the vital struggle on the one hand, and in that of the subsequent operations on the other. In the first, we admire the vigour in the Punjab, and the wise and noble resolution of its men to incur danger to their own province rather than increase the risk at Delhi; the boldness and the endurance in the siege of Delhi; the grand heroism with which it was stormed; the genius of the measures by which its walls were breached, and the brilliant and invaluable services of the handful of cavalry there; the wisdom and foresight of Sir Henry Lawrence; the strategical effect on Delhi of holding fast at Lucknow the sepoy army that besieged it, and the unique and continuous success of the defenders in the prolonged and desperate mining warfare there; Havelock's unparalleled campaign for the relief of Lucknow against overwhelming odds, with the never-ending difficulties and fresh dangers daily cropping up. All these indicate features which, without any disparagement to the later campaigns and the valour of the troops engaged, had no real parallel in them except to a slight degree; for, in fact, there was not the same crisis.

In the vital struggle, the struggle was for existence; danger lay in delay, in caring for odds. The great necessity was to create the conviction, and make it unmistakable, that British character and courage would take no denial, and must win, whatever the opposition. Afterwards the problem was to conquer solidly and effectually, and restore peace and tranquillity, to ensure success rather than accept every challenge.

No one can doubt the sound generalship and the great qualities of that grand old veteran, Colin Campbell, Lord Clyde. Yet it does seem open to question whether his concentrated attention on the securing of ultimate success did not lead to a slowness of movement which emboldened the enemy and gravely delayed that ultimate success; whether this was not at variance with his own character, and largely due to his deference to other influences; and whether, under those same influences, he did not seriously undervalue the importance of the earlier stages of the war, and of the work of certain branches of the Service.

As to Sir Colin's slowness, compare Havelock's leaving Mungurwar on the 21st September, and entering the Residency on the 25th (total four days), with the times of Sir Colin's relief, when there was great reason for his speedy return to Cawnpore. Three days' halt at Buntheera, two at the Alum Bagh, two fighting to the Residency, total seven days. Then eleven days more to evacuate the Residency and return to Cawnpore, leaving Outram at the Alum Bagh.

The new name that came forward most conspicuously in the decisive contest was that of Sir Hugh Rose. His brilliant leading and fighting, and the quickness and weight of his blows against the enemy, will ever bear their mark in history; but the tone of most of the comments on them, and especially those of the officers of his own force who have written on the subject, claim for him and for their deeds a unique superiority over all else in the war. This has no solid ground; its chief basis is the quickness and boldness with which he fought when he did take to fighting, and on the exceptional difficulties of heat and climate with which he and his force had to struggle. Let us analyse this. His force was in the field from January to, say, the end of June, 1858, but so was Sir Colin's also; and further, the exposure and privations of that period cannot be held to throw into the shade those of the Delhi force and Havelock's in the previous year. He was, without doubt, quick in absolute action, but not equally energetic and pressing in his arrangements and preparations. The characteristic of his methods seems more theatrical, in fact, than genuine. It is to be remembered that he arrived in Bombay, for the command of the Central India operations, in September, but he did not join his head quarters at Mhow till the 16th December, and he did not begin his advance from Sehore till the 16th January. There does not seem to be any adequate reason for ignoring the significance of these much greater delays and prolonged periods of inaction, more than in the case of Anson and Wilson at Delhi, which Sir John Lawrence so loudly condemned, or of Sir Colin's successive operations for the relief of Lucknow, and for the suppression of the revolt in Oude.

The time, too, thus taken up by Sir Hugh Rose in the preparation for action must be reckoned in the account when calculating or dealing with the rapidity with which he dealt his eventual blows. The space crossed from Sehore to Jhansi was two hundred miles, and this occupied two months.

He was fortunate also in having, in the 14th Light Dragoons and Orr's and Gall's regiments, a cavalry force which no other commander, except latterly Sir Colin himself, with his widely extended operations, had at his disposal; and the enemy opposed to him were not mostly trained sepoys, but Rajwara troops.

And, in the end, was his generalship really successful? He let Tantia go free first from Jhansi, then from Kalpee, and finally from Gwalior; when, with the reputation and position he had established, he could command for the operations against Gwalior all the forces in that direction—his own, the Agra, the Rajpootana, and the northern Bombay troops. Still he failed to make the combinations requisite to check Tantia properly, and Napier's brilliant action at Alipore Jowra was, in consequence, comparatively fruitless, because it was "in the air."

Of his dash and spirit there can be no question; but his own letters, and those from his force, show that he assumed the sole possession of these qualities, and wished to teach the other generals and leaders in India how to fight the rebels. Nothing apparently had been done before, whether at Delhi, Agra, or Lucknow; by Havelock, Nicholson, or Eyre.

In contrast with the inclination to extol Sir Hugh Rose's vigour, there seems to be a tendency to treat lightly the achievements of General Havelock. This is due probably to his return to Cawnpore, and perhaps also to the hopes that had been raised by Tytler's sanguine letters. A word may therefore be said to recall the fact that Havelock's strength, compared with that of the other prominent forces, was insignificant, constantly dropping to 1000 men only; and that his failure to carry out the expectations under which he first crossed the Ganges, was owing to the rising at Dinapore, and the consequent stoppage of the reinforcements which had been promised, and on which of course he had counted.

Before concluding, it is but just to refer to one point which has not been noted with sufficient prominence in dealing with the period involved—the development of the revolt.

The most important of the native potentates at that juncture was Scindia. He was the bearer of an historic name; the successor, and a powerful successor, of the greatest of the opponents of the rise of British power in India. He was the chief of a race that were still enthusiastically hostile to the English, and, with him at their head, would have turned out a strong army. The whole Mahratta race would have followed him, and the Gwalior contingent, that gave General Windham and Sir Colin so much trouble at Cawnpore, would have supported him strenuously. He was close to Agra; and had he turned rebel, he would have been the champion of the revolt, and would, with his army, have at once turned the tide at Delhi, and stopped the siege. His abstention from this course was not due to any personal liking for the British, but to his intellectual convictions, based on the lessons steadily instilled by his minister, Rajah Dinkur Rao, and the Government agent, Major Charters Macpherson. Nor was there any one of high standing, who, throughout, more strenuously and correctly pressed upon the Government the true character of the crisis. Scindia's loyalty saved India for the British.

In dealing with such a war as that of the Mutiny, in which the leaders and generals, and those who were specially concerned in the more stirring and important incidents, are necessarily those whose names are most prominent in the record, it would be unjust to omit notice of the invaluable work done by the staff, and especially by one whose name is ever acknowledged as foremost in Sir Colin's ranks—Henry Norman. He was only a subaltern during the whole period of the war, but he was throughout the right hand of the general holding the most important command in the field, first of Wilson at Delhi, and then of Sir Colin for the rest of the war. His astounding memory obviated the need of reference to papers; the clear and ample map of the position of forces and detachments, which was ever kept up to date and held before his mental eye, enabled his chief to make at once and without hesitation the fresh combinations necessary to meet any unexpected news or juncture. More might be said; but there is no doubt of the concensus of opinion that, in these invaluable qualities, Norman was without a rival.

But the Mutiny and all its circumstances contain a lesson which should never be lost sight of. We must ever be on guard against any measures that can tend to excite a universal animosity or suspicion against the British, either by interference with the creeds or caste, or traditional codes of honour and practice of the native community, or by injustice in financial arrangements when their interests and those of the ruling race appear to be in antagonism. We must never give room for temptation to the disaffected by allowing our military strength and position to be unduly weakened. A steady watch should ever be maintained over all causes, fanatical or other, of social irritation tending to lead to such local animosities as may extend into widespread strife.

Sound sources of information and advice, and a favourable state of public feeling, should be encouraged and utilized; while, on the other hand, inflammatory publications and seditions should be open to repression in the British territories, where they would not be tolerated in the adjacent native states. Until the people became suspicious of the designs of the state, no active sedition existed. Until the army were alarmed in regard to their caste requirements, they identified themselves with the British rule, though their discipline was lax, and their demeanour sometimes querulous.

Good faith, genial rule as well as just, sound military organization, the avoidance of wanton innovations, the protection of the ignorant—these are the necessary elements for our successful and peaceful tenure of India, and in defects in those elements lay the initial causes of the Mutiny.

MAP

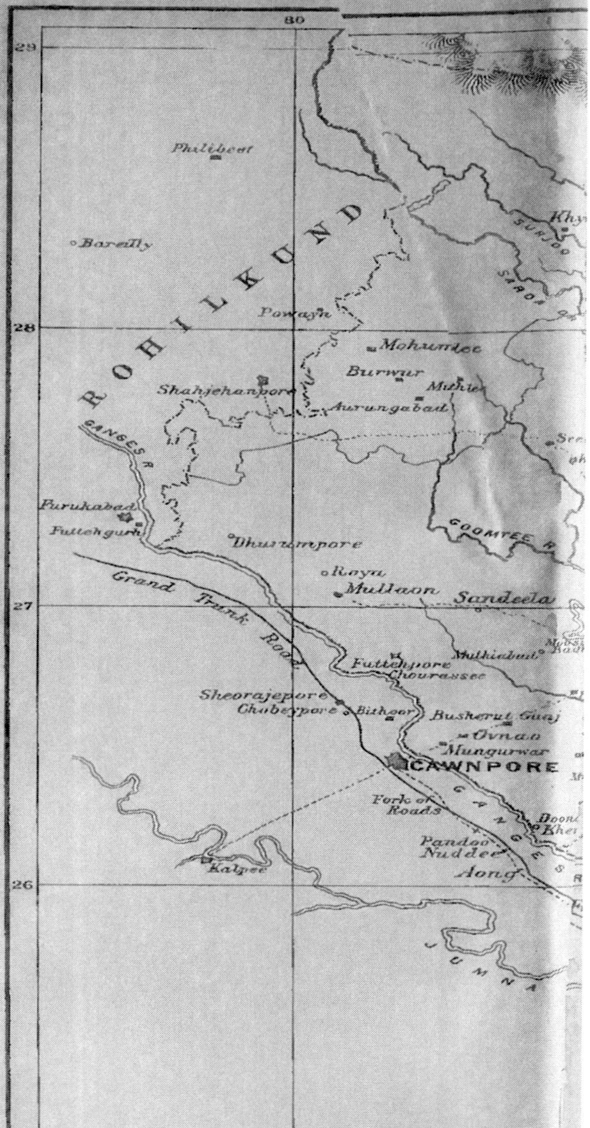
80
29
28
27
26
25
Philibeet
Bareilly
ROHILKUND
Powayn
Mohumdee
Burwur
Shahjehanpore
Aurungabad
GANGES R
Furukabad
Futtehgurh
Dhurumpore
Roya
Mullaon
Sandeela
Grand Trunk Road
Futtehpore
Chourassee
Sheorajepore
Chobeypore
Bithoor
Busherut Gunj
Ovnao
Mungurwar
CAWNPORE
Fork of Roads
Pandoo Nuddee
Aong
Kalpee
JUMNA
GOOMTEE R
SURJOO
GANGES R

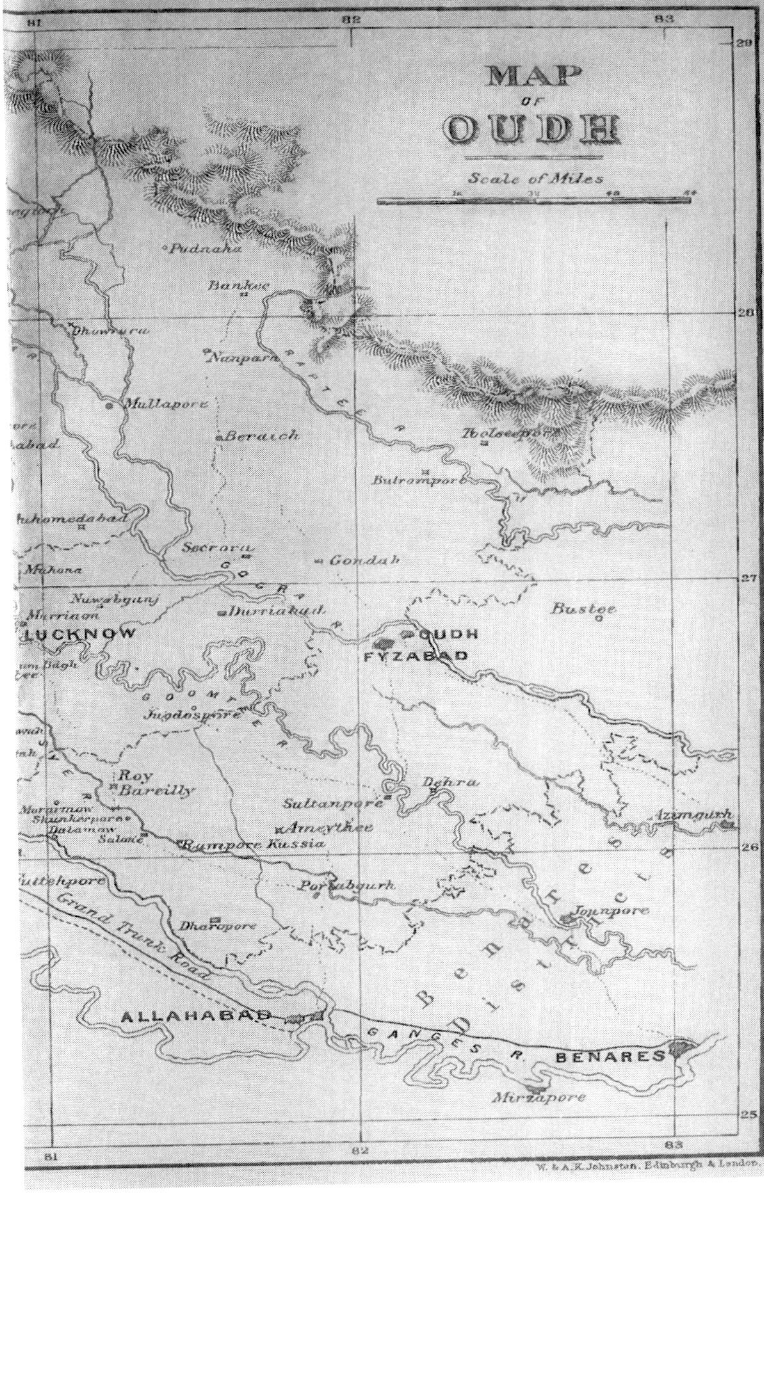

MAP OF OUDH
Scale of Miles
Pudnaha
Bankee
Dhowrura
Nanpara
Mullapore
Beraich
Tolseepore
Bulrampore
Muhamedabad
Seerora
Gondah
Mahona
Nuwabgunj
Murriaon
Durriabad
Bustee
LUCKNOW
OUDH
FYZABAD
GOOMTEE R
Jugdespore
Roy Bareilly
Dehra
Sultanpore
Ameythee
Azimgurh
Shunkerpore
Dalamow
Salone
Rampore Kussia
Futtehpore
Purtabgurh
Jounpore
Grand Trunk Road
Dharopore
Benares District
ALLAHABAD
GANGES R.
BENARES
Mirzapore
W. & A.K. Johnston, Edinburgh & London.

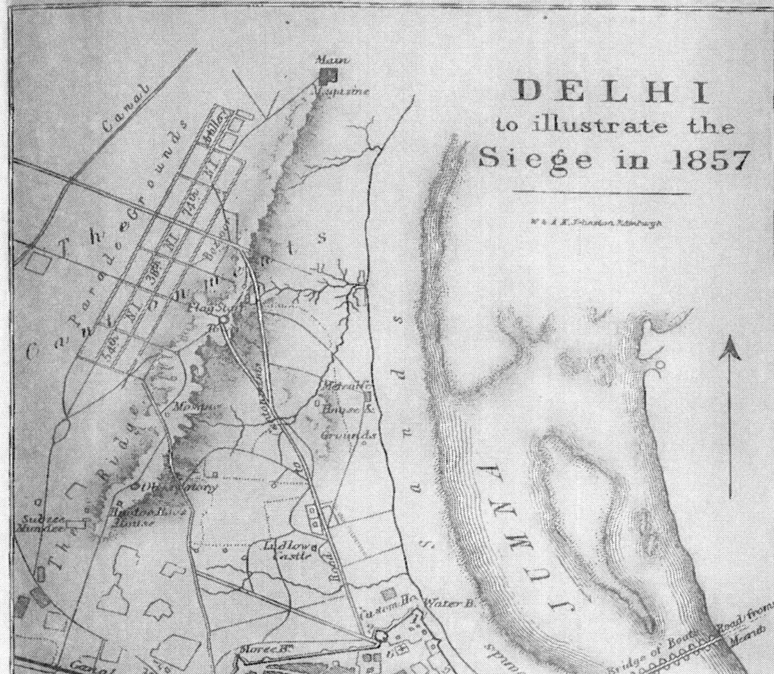
DELHI
to illustrate the
Siege in 1857
Main Magazine
Canal
Flag Staff Tower
Mosque
Observatory
Metcalfe House & Grounds
Ludlow Castle
Custom Ho.
Water B.
Moree Bn.
Kishen Gunge
Cabul G.
Burn B.
Lahore Gate
CITY
King's Gardens
OF
DELHI
Calcutta Gate
KING'S PALACE
Bridge of Boats
Road from Meerut
JUMNA
RIVER
Sands
Jail
Ruins of Ferozabad or Ancient Delhi
1 Kutcherey
2 Cashmere Gateway & Main Guard
3 Burial Ground
4 King's Garden
5 College & Gardens
6 Church
7 Delhi Bank
8 Kotwallee
9 Jumna Musjid
10 Main Gate of the Palace

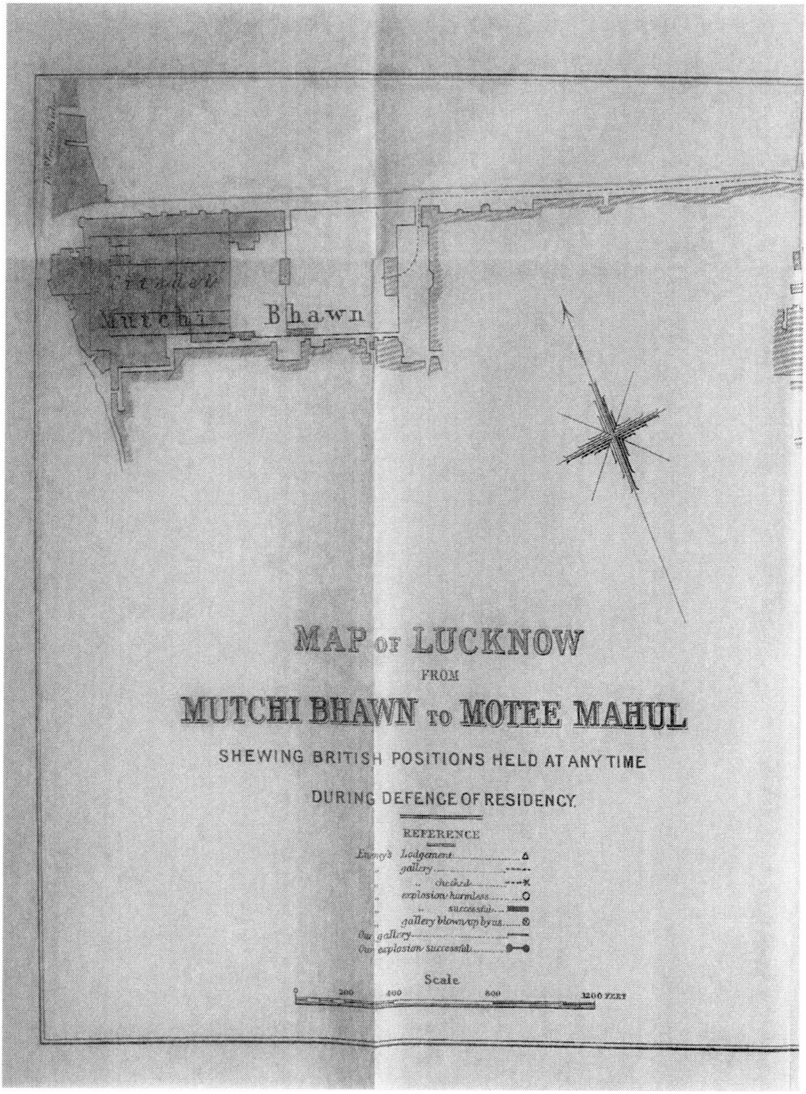
Citadel
Mutchi Bhawn
MAP OF LUCKNOW
FROM
MUTCHI BHAWN TO MOTEE MAHUL
SHEWING BRITISH POSITIONS HELD AT ANY TIME
DURING DEFENCE OF RESIDENCY.
REFERENCE
Enemy's Lodgement
gallery
checked
explosion harmless
successful
gallery blown up by us
Our gallery
Our explosion successful
Scale
0
200
400
800
1200 FEET

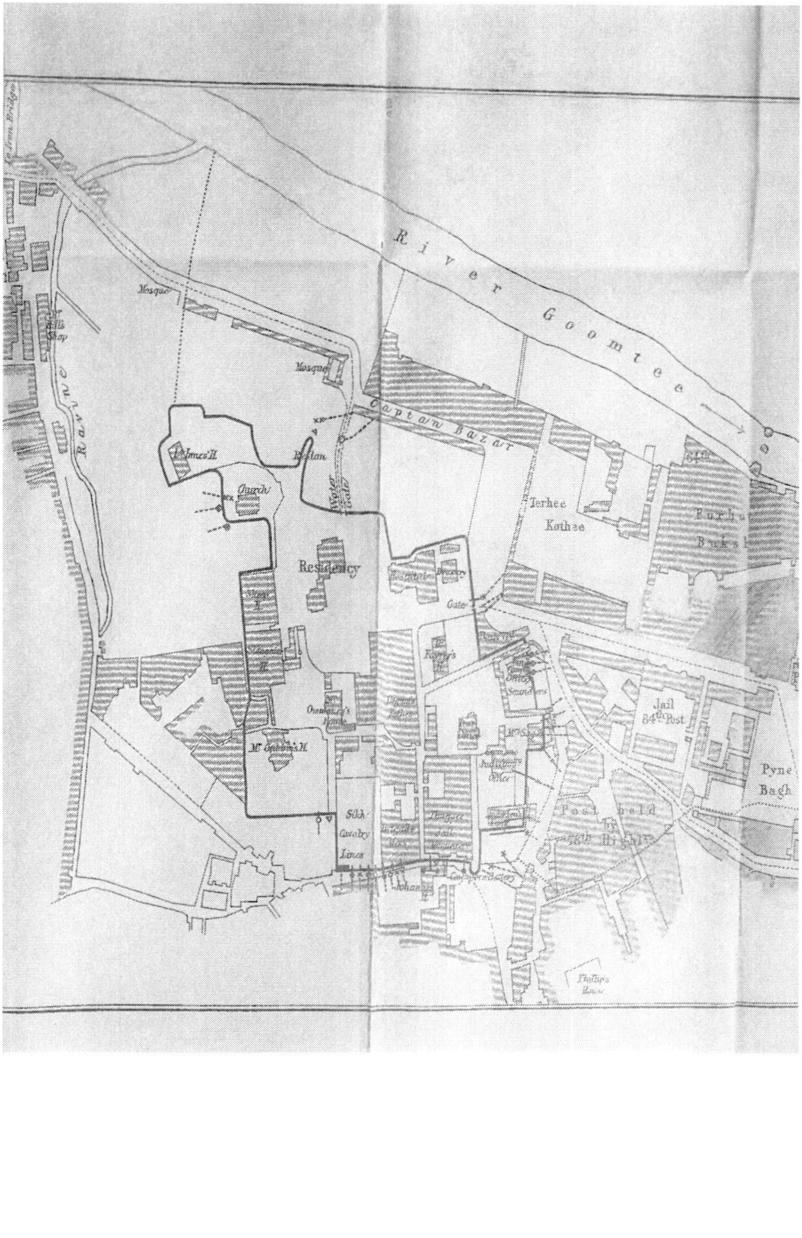

River Goomtee
Captan Bazar
Ravine
Mosque
Mosque
Church
Residency
Terhee Kothee
Gate
Jail
84th Post
Pyne Bagh
Sikh Cavalry Lines

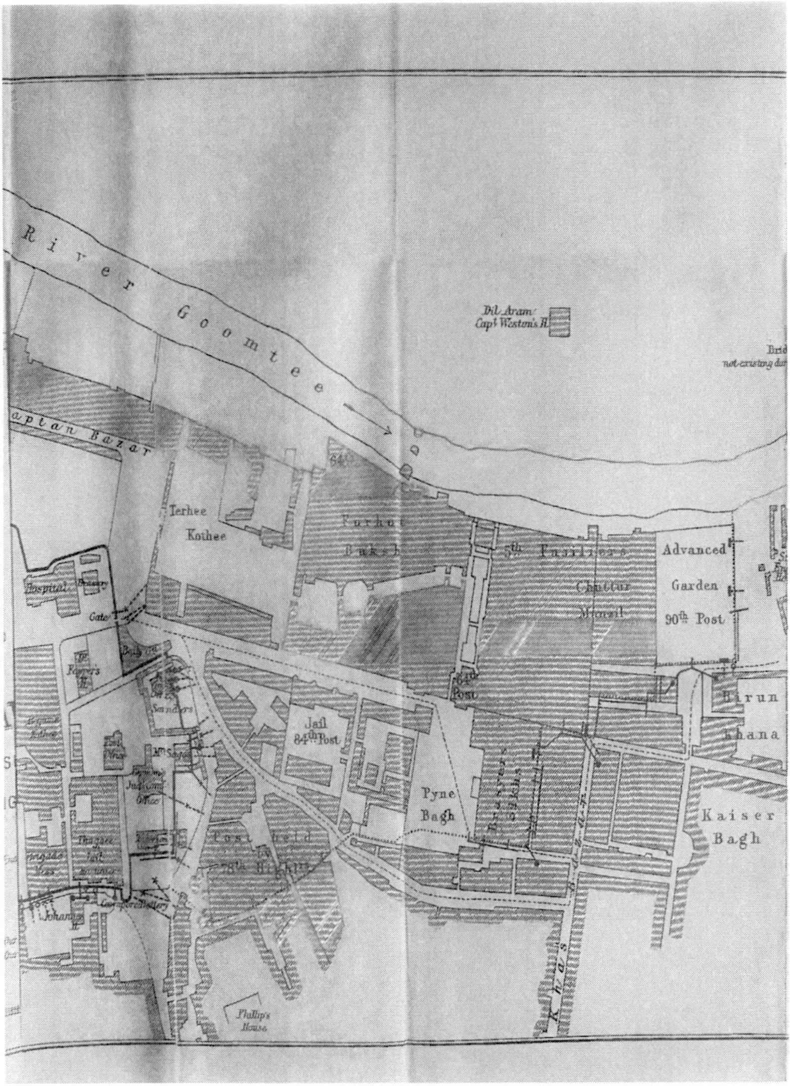
River Goomtee
Dil Aram
Capt. Weston's H.
Captan Bazar
Terhee Kothee
Furhut Buksh
5th Fusiliers
Chuttur Munzil
Advanced Garden 90th Post
Hospital
Gate
Jail 84th Post
64th Post
Pyne Bagh
Kaiser Bagh
Khana
Phillip's House

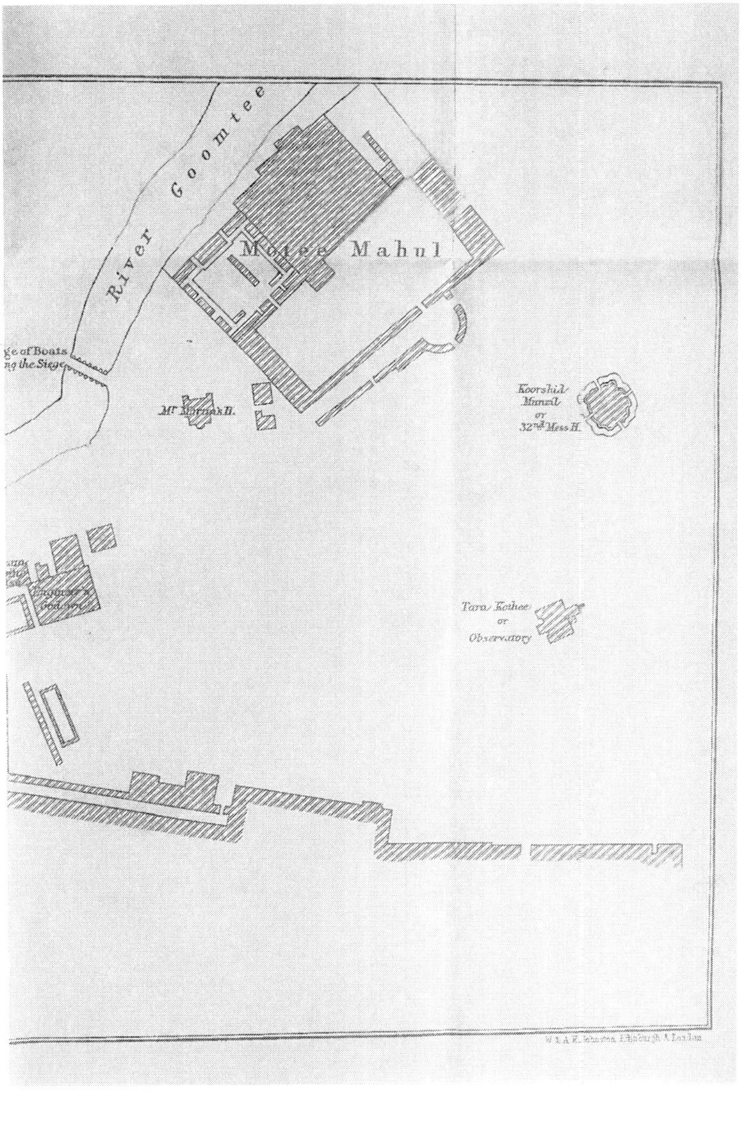
River Goomtee
Motee Mahul
ge of Boats
ng the Siege
Koorshid Munzil or 32nd Mess H.
Tara Kothee or Observatory
W. & A. K. Johnston, Edinburgh & London

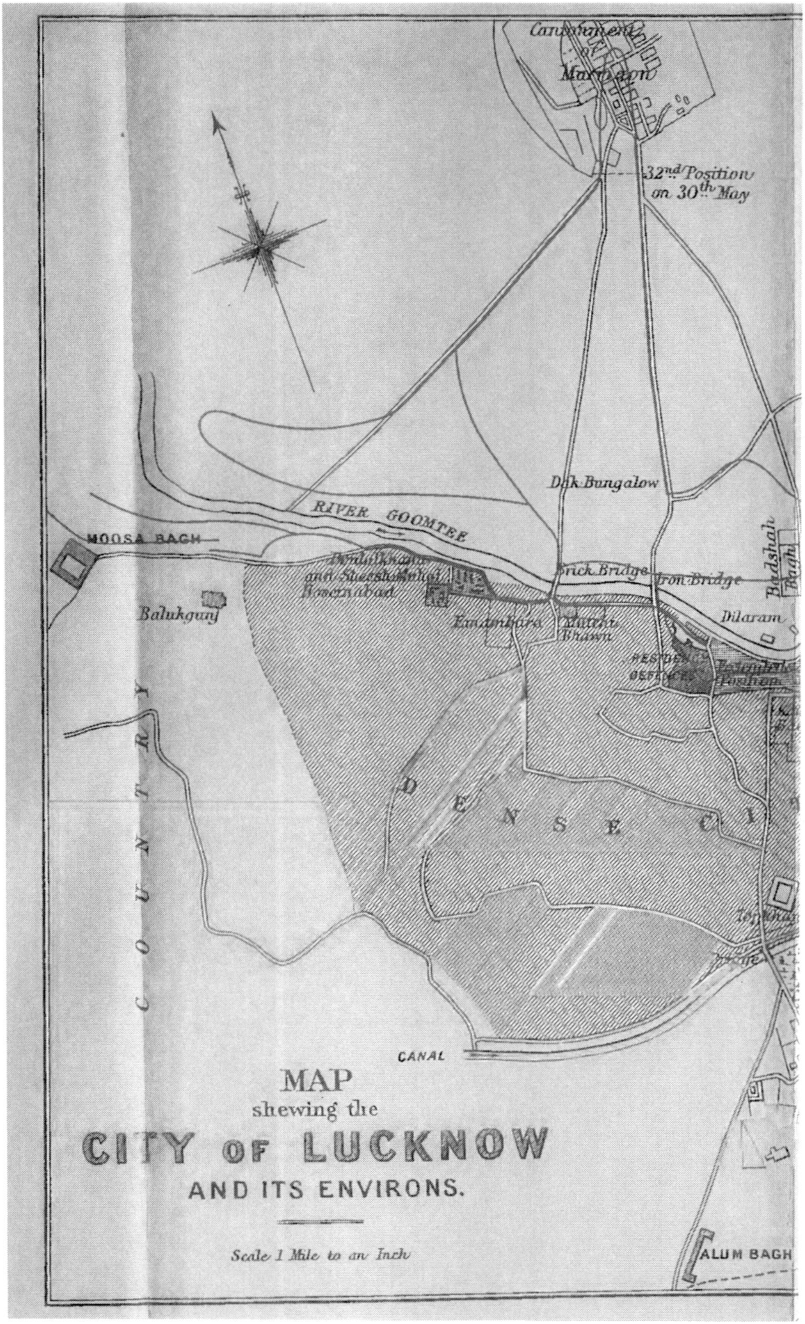

Cantonment of Mariaon
32nd Position on 30th May
Dak Bungalow
RIVER GOOMTEE
MOOSA BAGH
Brick Bridge
Iron Bridge
Badshah Bagh
Balukgunj
Emambara
Muchhi Bhawn
Dilaram
COUNTRY
DENSE CI
CANAL
MAP
shewing the
CITY OF LUCKNOW
AND ITS ENVIRONS.
Scale 1 Mile to an Inch
ALUM BAGH

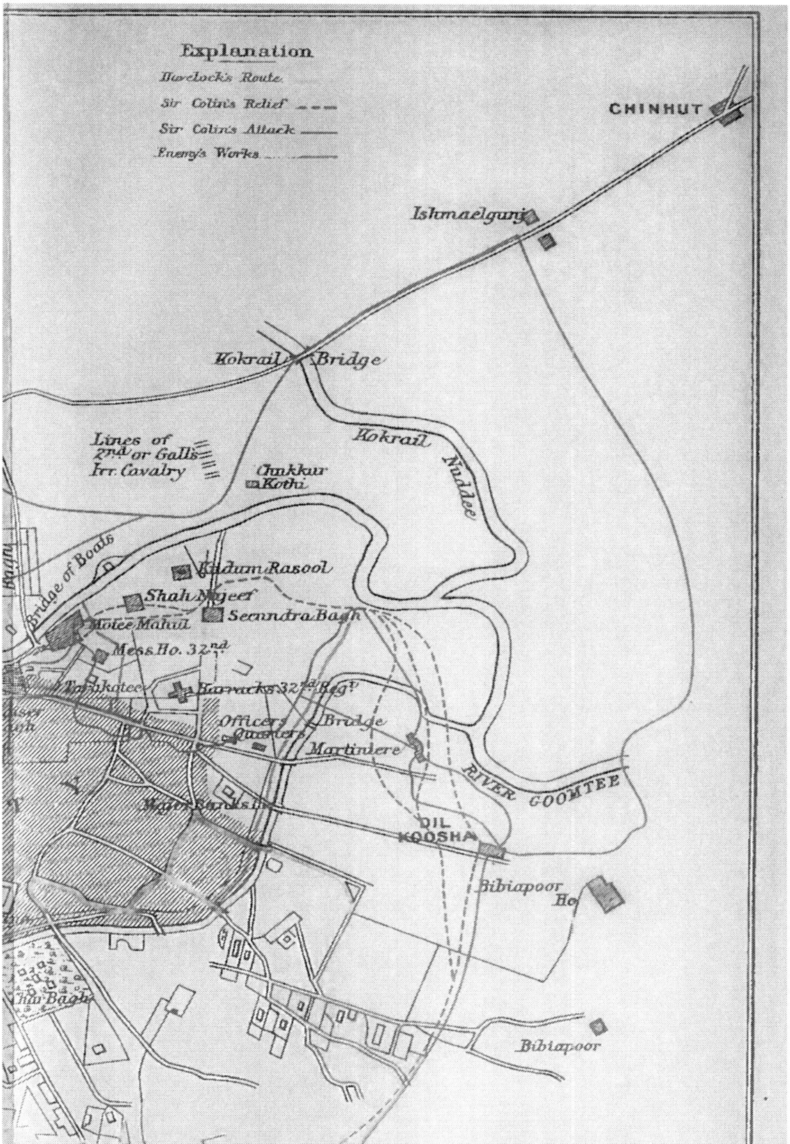
Explanation
Havelock's Route
Sir Colin's Relief
Sir Colin's Attack
Enemy's Works
CHINHUT
Islmaelgunj
Kokrail Bridge
Kokrail Nuddee
Lines of 2nd or Galls Irr. Cavalry
Chukkur Kothi
Bridge of Boats
Kudum Rasool
Shah Njeef
Secundra Bagh
Motee Mahul
Mess Ho. 32nd
Barracks 32nd Regt
Officers Quarters
Bridge
Martiniere
RIVER GOOMTEE
DIL KOOSHA
Bibiapoor Ho
Bibiapoor
To Jellalabad
W. & A. K. Johnston, Edinburgh & London

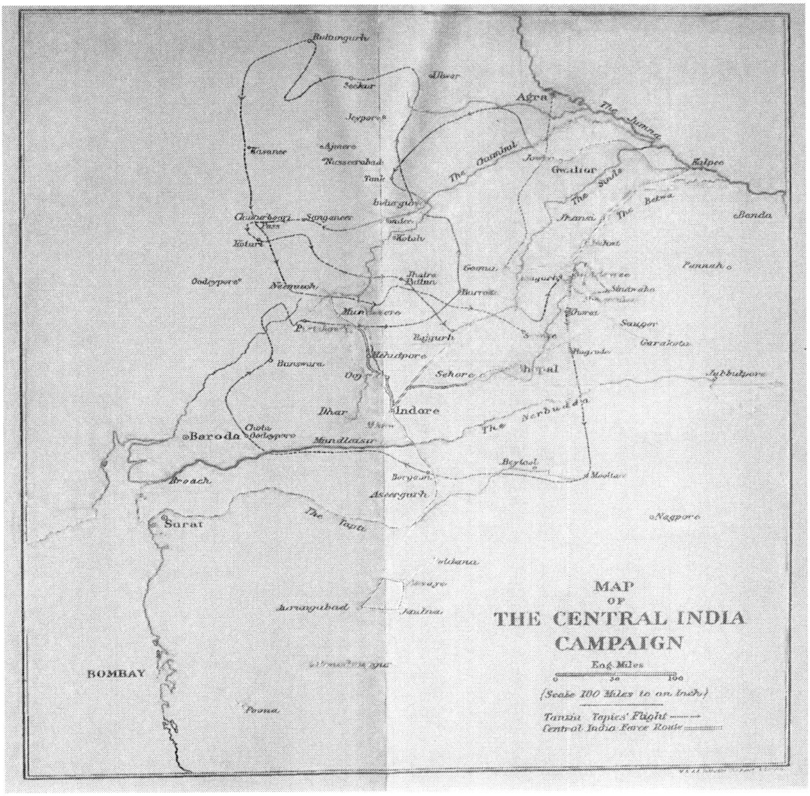
MAP
OF
THE CENTRAL INDIA
CAMPAIGN
Eng. Miles
0
50
100
(Scale 100 Miles to an Inch)
Tantia Topies' Flight
Central India Force Route
Agra
The Jumna
Kalpee
Banda
Gwalior
The Chumbul
The Sinde
The Betwa
Jhansi
Punnah
Saugor
Garakota
Jubbulpore
Bhopal
Sehore
Indore
Dhar
Mhow
Mehidpore
Oojein
Mundesore
Neemuch
Kotah
Jhalra Pattan
Seekur
Jeypore
Ajmere
Nusseerabad
Tonk
Sanganeer
Oodeypore
Banswara
Baroda
Chota Oodeypore
Mundlesir
The Nerbudda
Broach
Surat
The Taptee
Asseergarh
Nagpore
Aurungabad
BOMBAY
Poona

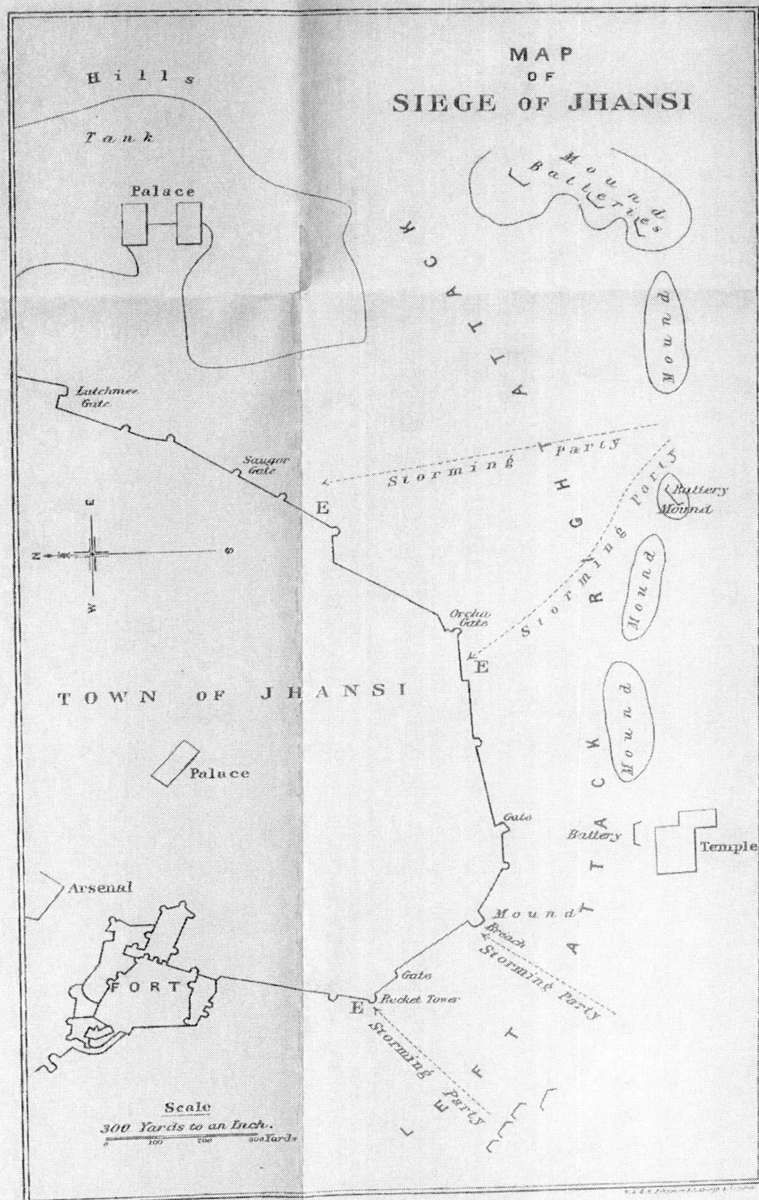

MAP OF SIEGE OF JHANSI
Hills
Tank
Palace
Mounds
Batteries
Mound
ATTACK
Latchmee Gate
Saugor Gate
Storming Party
E
Battery Mound
RIGHT
Storming Party
Orcha Gate
Storming Party
Mound
Mound
TOWN OF JHANSI
Palace
Gate
Battery
Temple
ATTACK
Arsenal
Mound
Breach
Storming Party
FORT
Gate
Rocket Tower
Storming Party
LEFT
Scale
300 Yards to an Inch.
0 100 200 300 Yards

INDEX.

INDEX.

A

L

M

N

O

P

Q

R

S

COLUMNS AND FORCES.

TROOPS.